The Pumpkin Patch

A Single Woman's
International Adoption Journey

Margaret L. Schwartz

CHICAGO SPECTRUM PRESS
LOUISVILLE, KENTUCKY 40207

CHICAGO SPECTRUM PRESS
4824 BROWNSBORO CENTER
LOUISVILLE, KENTUCKY 40207
502-899-1919

Printed in the U.S.A.

10 9 8 7 6 5 4 3 2 1

ISBN: 1-58374-118-6

Special thanks and tributes to:

Cathy Harris
Donna Arroyo
Meg and Michael Elmore
Patricia Mary Tinkelman
John Chomeau
The PAX Community
Jack Trovato
Tammy Ammon

This book is dedicated to my mother, Norma Jean Schwartz. May your light of love continue to shine down upon us all.

Contents

Forward

I have always enjoyed writing down my thoughts and feelings, so it was natural for me to start a journal when I made the decision to adopt. It was akin to having a secret friend who never tired of listening to me ramble on about the day's events. During the editing of my entries, I tried to balance the need to respect the privacy of people I dealt with and my desire to retain the raw emotion I felt while living the story. I have no wish to harm anyone about whom I have written, so in some cases I changed the names of individuals to mask their identity. I am grateful to all the people with whom I communicated on topics as broad ranging as Ukrainian Christmas traditions to head banging. I am especially thankful to those people who allowed me to include their adoption stories.

While my journal entries detail my personal adoption experience, the broader focus of this book is to expose the reader to the vulnerability of orphaned and abandoned children around the world. I believe that all human beings are connected at a spiritual level, and we must never allow ourselves to forget the impact one person can have on another. I may never see the day when all the orphaned children around the world are adopted. But I do hope that we, as a society, can join together to provide these children with access to decent health care, adequate education and, most importantly, a solid belief structure that includes the ability to love and care for both themselves and others in their lives.

The idea for the title of my book came to me one day as I was driving down a country road, reliving the events of the previous year. Most people have been to a pumpkin patch at one time or another—it's a ritual during the fall to travel to a farm in the countryside to find the perfect pumpkin for Halloween festivities. As you walk up and down the rows of pumpkins, you notice some are small and scarred, while others are large and lopsided.

Everyone wants to bring home the perfectly shaped, brightly colored pumpkin, but in reality it doesn't exist. What you end up with is a slightly misshaped squash with a few small scars on one side. It's hard to say what made you pick that pumpkin over the hundreds that were lying in the fields. At some point you accept the fact that your pumpkin has a few defects, but you are content in the knowledge that if you turn it a little bit to the left, you can't see that it leans to the right. And what happens to the ones that aren't picked? They are plowed back into the land to enrich the soil.

I know for a fact that when I walked into the orphanage that fateful Friday morning to find my children, I had visions of healthy, happy children who could seamlessly assimilate into my language and culture. Why did I pick children who had medical problems and developmental delays? I guess I knew deep down in my heart that, just like the pumpkins in the field, there is no perfect child. But unlike the remaining pumpkins in the field, the children I didn't bring home won't be forgotten.

I have tried to repay the kindness of those who helped in my journey by sharing my adoption experience in this journal. I pray every night that all the orphaned and abandoned children in Ukraine and around the world find happiness in their lives. If I can make that happen for just one child as a result of writing this book, then I have accomplished my goal.

Blessings,

Margaret

Part I

PLANTING THE SEEDS

Monday, October 28

My darling little ones: I have officially started the process to find you and bring you home. There are many tasks I will need to accomplish before my journey is complete. Part of the process will be to meet with a social worker so she can evaluate me and my lifestyle to make sure I will be a good mother to you—I hope I pass! I'm sure there will be many obstacles that I must overcome, but in my heart I know that it will all be worthwhile once I hold you in my arms for the first time.

You have probably been born and may be living in an orphanage. I woke this morning and prayed that your caregivers shower you with love and affection, keep your tiny bodies warm, and fill you with plenty of good food and nourishment. I am looking forward to the day I can give you all of that and more.

I have waited a long time before deciding to become a mother. I wanted to be sure I was willing to make the commitment to bring children into my life. I am ready now. I am 44 years old and single, although I came close to getting married several times. But there are some things I will wait until you are older to share.

For now the only thing that is important is finding you so we can become a family. What a wonderful word—family. I have a big family with lots of sisters, a brother, many nieces, nephews, cousins and dear friends. One day I will take you to visit your relatives. I will watch you play, and I will laugh at your antics. I will take pictures and put them in a family album. We will have so much fun. We will be a family.

Til later,

Mama

CHECKLIST

♣ Call social worker to discuss home study. Plan to meet first week of December at her office.

♣ Fill out INS form 1600 A (fee $510) and attach copy of my birth and baptism certificates.

♣ Request four notarized copies of my birth certificate from New York Department of Health, Vital Records (fee $60).

Thursday, November 14

Dear Journal: Well, the word has hit the street, and my whole family knows my plans. I was a little hesitant to tell them. What if things don't go as planned? What if I change my mind? When you have a big family, it's hard to keep a secret. I thought about pursuing a domestic adoption, but after looking at the available children on the Internet and talking to people about their experiences, I decided against it. Most of the children are older, and many of them are struggling with behavioral and emotional issues. As a single person who wants two children, I am not prepared to deal with such issues. I know it sounds cruel, but I be-lieve that I have to be honest about my feelings and understand what my limits are as a prospective parent.

Knowing that I wanted to adopt children who were Caucasian, I looked primarily at Eastern European countries and evaluated their processes and costs. I have settled on Ukraine for three reasons. First, the children are Caucasian. I am fair skinned with hazel eyes and dark blond hair, and I want my children to look like me. Second, I want to be the one to decide what children I bring home. Many countries, including Russia, pre-select children for adoptive parents. It is illegal in Ukraine to do this; instead people go directly to the orphanage and select the child they want. Lastly, I wanted a program that was financially reasonable. The U.S. government has a generous tax credit of $10,000 per adopted child, but I know that with agency fees, a single adoption can cost $30,000 to $40,000. Ukraine is the only country I am aware of that allows people to adopt independently—without the use of an agency.

So, after much research and soul seeking, I have decided to travel to Ukraine to find my forever children. I want two children because I can't bear the idea of raising an only child after growing up in a large family with five sisters and one brother. I don't want infants, which is a good thing because there are no infants available for adoption in Ukraine. I would be quite happy with two girls, or a boy and a girl, under the age of four.

I have decided to do this without an agency but with the help of Cathy Harris, a wonderful woman from Florida who runs the Web site *www.ukrainianangels.org* and helps people adopt independently from Ukraine. Cathy has been doing this for a number of years and has a solid network of contacts in Ukraine to help people like me navigate their way through the process.

I spoke with my sister Donna this evening about my decision. She has three children, one teenage son and two older girls. She studied early childhood development in school and operated a day care center in her home for several years. She's agreed to travel with me and help me take care of the children while we're in Ukraine. We have always gotten along well together (Donna is only a year younger than I am) and she will be a great help to me.

Thursday, November 28

Dear Journal: Happy Thanksgiving! I am on vacation in the Caribbean with my family and we're having a wonderful time. I'm sitting here on the beach, thinking about the many countries I have traveled to over the past 20 years. I have always had a great yearning to explore and learn about different cultures. Although I still love adventures, I am content in the knowledge that once I bring children into my life, my adventures will be of a different sort—watching them learn about seashells and seeing them make their first dive into the pool. I'm smiling right now because I know that any of the freedoms I lose when I become a mother will be more than compensated for as I watch my children grow and start to explore the world around them. Once they are older, I want to take them on trips to far-away places where we will have grand adventures.

I felt so blessed as we sat down to dinner this evening. I have my health, I have been enjoying a wonderful week in a beautiful location, and I am sharing the day with my family and loved ones. I wonder if my children went to bed hungry today because there was not enough food at the orphanage to fill their bellies. Do they have siblings? Are they getting lots of hugs and kisses from their caretakers? I hope so. I am doing everything I can to bring them home. I promise they will never be cold or hungry. I promise never to withhold my love no matter how they behave. I promise to be thankful every day that they have found their way into my life.

Tuesday, December 3

Dear Journal: I have had many dreams the past six months. Last night I did my meditation and asked for help in finding the direction to follow in my life. I have worked very hard this year to center myself—to find inner peace and a sense of calm. I am about to enter a whole new chapter in my life and I know I will need great inner strength to deal with all the challenges that come with becoming a parent. I do feel that my spirit has made a connection to the universe and it knows what I want. Now I need the courage and strength of my convictions to take the necessary actions to make my dreams a reality.

Wednesday, December 4

Dear Little Ones: Today I visited the local Immigration and Naturalization Service Center (INS) to be finger-printed. I know it sounds silly, but this is just one of the many hurdles I will need to overcome before I can travel to Ukraine to bring you home.

I sat in a large waiting area with the TV blaring. There were many different-looking faces in the room—a mixture of cultures and experiences. Everyone sat patiently waiting for his or her number to be called. How ironic that we were all in this one place—a true melting pot of people who have come to this country for many different reasons.

Part of me wanted to say, "I'm not really supposed to be here. I'm already a citizen and I shouldn't have to wait with everyone else. The only reason I'm here is to satisfy a requirement to adopt my children." But then I got to thinking about you. Will you be glad that I took you from your homeland and brought you here to this country? Most of these people are in this room because they wanted a better life for themselves and their families. Many of them don't speak English.

You will come to this country not knowing English either. I would like to find a way for you to retain as much of your native heritage as possible. Perhaps I can find people who speak Ukrainian near where we will live. The other day I received a note from one of the people in my adoption e-mail newsgroup with a Ukrainian Christmas story about a spider. I've saved it and I want to put it in a little book for you.

I wonder whether you will feel that my family is your family. I have read much about the collective unconscious and how we all retain memories that are passed down from our parents. Although the love that I have to share with you will be very strong, I don't want to erase who you are or the heritage that you bring with you from Ukraine. I was fascinated when my father showed me a family tree that a cousin of his had created. She listed all the descendents from when the first Schwartz arrived in this country over 150 years ago. I want to share all of this with you.

Sunday, December 8

Dear Journal: Everyone I've shared my news with has been so supportive. All my friends are full of encouragement, and they all seem to know someone who has recently adopted a child. I have found several on-line newsgroups made up entirely of prospective parents looking to adopt in Ukraine and people who have already done so. I've accumulated a gold mine of information ranging from what to pack to Web sites describing traits of fetal alcohol syndrome—a condition that unfortunately plagues many children in Eastern European countries.

Last week I sent a note to the newsgroup asking if there were any single women who were interested in forming an on-line support group. I received an e-mail from a woman named Judy who has just completed her home study to adopt a young girl from Ukraine. We have already developed a rapport and it's nice to have someone to chat with who is going through the same ordeal.

I've also been in constant contact with Cathy Harris. Her selflessness in helping hapless souls such as myself traverse the slippery slopes of filling out forms and dealing with government regulations is truly a blessing.

Monday, December 9

Dear Journal: I started checking with local adoption agencies several weeks ago to decide who I would use for my home study. I first called a local agency that came highly recommended. I could tell that the woman who answered the phone didn't seem terribly interested in answering my questions, and I got the impression that this was just a job to her. My next call was to Catholic Charities. Well, not only were they more expensive, but they made their home study recommendations by committee. I really didn't like the idea of having strangers decide whether I was fit to become a parent. They say three times is the charm, and, on my last call, I found a woman who worked in a small agency whose services were reasonably priced.

Enter my social worker—I'll call her Carol. When I spoke with her on the phone I sensed a level of understanding and compassion that had been missing with the people I had spoken to at the other agencies. Another plus is that she has handled adoptions from several Eastern European countries, including Ukraine.

I had my first appointment with Carol today at lunchtime to begin the home study process. After we exchanged formalities, I gave Carol some background information on myself, and I told her that I had been thinking of adopting for over a year. We talked about the adoption process in Ukraine, and I mentioned that I was going to be working with Cathy Harris. Carol was familiar with Cathy and said I would be in good hands with her. We discussed at length how many children I wanted, the scarcity of girls and the fact that I might not find healthy children in the age bracket I was seeking. I was surprised to hear that girls rather than boys were more likely to be adopted by Ukrainians. It has something to do with their notion that women are more hardworking than men.

As we started talking about paperwork, Carol brought out a folder full of forms—forms to prove that I could support the children financially and that I could get health insurance for them, guardian forms, medical forms, an addendum to my will and the list goes on—all to be notarized, of course. As we went over one of the forms to confirm that I didn't have a criminal record and wasn't on the "Sex Offender and Crimes Against Minors Registry," I thought to myself, "I didn't even know these lists existed." I was at the same time relieved that these checks were in place and frustrated that I had to spend the time and money to exonerate myself to satisfy a government requirement.

Then I spent another hour listening to the sins of corporal punishment and how it can scar a child for life. If you adopt in Virginia, you have to sign a form stating that you will not hit, spank, kick, throw, shake or inflict pain on your adoptive children. The last topic of our conversation had to do with attachment disorder and how it is often misdiagnosed. I started to zone out a little bit here. Not ever having had children, and being six to eight months away from finding a child to adopt, I was beginning to wonder how much of this information I was going to retain.

Finally, we were finished. After handing over a check and making plans to meet again after the holidays, I quickly departed. I had a lot of work ahead of me.

LIST OF FORMS REQUIRED
FOR MY HOME STUDY

1. Completed application
2. References from three unrelated people
3. Medical form indicating I am in good health and free of any addictions or diseases
4. Letter stating I have medical insurance for my children
6. Addendum to my will guaranteeing care of my children in the event of my death
7. A criminal background check from state police
8. A child abuse clearance
9. A budget detailing my ability to care for children
10. Net financial worth statement
11. Letter detailing my income
12. Tax returns from the past three years
13. Statement of acceptance of financial responsibility for six months should I relinquish custody of the adopted children for any reason
14. Agreement not to use corporal punishment
15. My birth certificate
16. Agreement to cooperate with post-placement supervision and reporting requirements in accordance with state and federal law as well as those of the adopted child's country of origin

---

CHECKLIST

- ⚜ Make initial payment to social worker (Fee $400).
- ⚜ Complete Name Search Request form for criminal history record and Sex Offender and Crimes Against Minors (Fee $20).

Monday, December 16

Dear Journal: The other day I received an e-mail from my Dad asking me to reconsider my decision to adopt. I know he loves me deeply and we have become especially close in the past 25 years since my mother died of liver cancer. I know his concern about my decision to adopt is based in love. He is worried that the children in Ukraine are not healthy (Cherynobyl, fetal alcohol syndrome, you name it), but I still feel sad that he could ask me not to proceed with the adoption.

But he is not the only one of my relatives to express concern about my decision. Last month I sent a letter to my godmother asking her to write a letter of reference for me (part of the requirements for a home study). She wrote back, telling me she could not do that in good conscience because she didn't approve of what I was doing—single mom, financial burdens, and so forth. I was really hurt that she didn't think I would be a good mom. But after thinking about it, I realized that's not why she wrote her letter. I have to remember that she, like my Dad, is from a different generation, and that does impact how you look at the world.

I know they both have my best interest at heart. It's still hard to know that some of the people closest to me don't approve of the decision I have made. I sent my father an e-mail tonight explaining to him how I felt. In my message I asked him, "What would your life be like if you had never married or had children?" I don't know if he will change his mind. I hope he will at least accept the idea even if he doesn't agree with what I am doing. I have always respected him, and it has been a long-standing point of pride when I tell my friends that my father has never chastised me or made me feel bad about any of the decisions I have made.

Only time will tell if I have made the right decision. One thing I know for sure—there is no one on this planet who can deter me from doing this. I refuse to accept defeat and will persevere, doing whatever it takes to bring my children home.

Sunday, December 22

Dear Journal: I heard from Judy again today. We have been writing to each other fairly regularly, and her messages have been a lifeline for me these past few weeks. When we first started corresponding, she was already finishing up her home study, getting ready to start work on her dossier, which is the set of documents required by the Ukrainian government. She decided that there have been too many changes in Ukraine, so she found an agency that works in Romania and has accepted a referral for a two-year-old girl whom she has named Olivia. Another reason she chose Romania is that she won't have to spend much time over there, and, since her leave from work is limited, this will allow her more time at home with her new daughter.

I wonder how many people think about adopting from Ukraine, but, when they learn about all the quirks and pitfalls associated with the process, choose another country. I have no doubt that many of the former Soviet Union countries have similar health issues regarding adopted children. I continue to pray that I have made the right decision in selecting Ukraine. I truly could not bear the thought of returning home without my children. I have invested too much energy in this venture to accept any other outcome but that my two children are waiting for me to find them and bring them home.

Saturday, January 4

Dear Journal: Happy New Year! Today is when we make resolutions for the coming year. Most people want to lose weight, fix up the house or find the perfect mate. I would like to focus on opening my heart to embrace a new chapter in my life. Looking back on some of the choices I have made, I realize that I never listened to my heart—I was always too busy telling myself what I wanted to do instead of asking myself what I should be doing.

I have been putting off making decisions for the past several years while I waited to see what would happen in my last relationship. I wasn't sure where I was going to be living or whether I was going to get married. Then, last year I realized that life was passing me by, and I really didn't have any more time to waste. So, I bought a sailboat and got my diving certification—two things I had wanted to do for a long time. As far as adoption was concerned, it was something I had to build up to—it's quite a different matter from buying a sailboat. Yet something in the back of my mind told me that part of my purpose in life lay with the children I will adopt. Perhaps it is to prepare them for some grand accomplishment or simply to give them a happy life. Perhaps it is to give me the opportunity to channel my energies in a direction that is different from what I am doing now. I can feel the positive energy building inside of me as I move forward with the adoption effort. The challenge now is to focus on myself with meditation, spiritual renewal and growth. I must spend time thinking about what is happening in my life and looking for the signs that will help me find my path in life.

So my resolution this year is to remember what the gifts are that I brought with me into this life and how I am to use them.

Monday, January 13

Dear Journal: I had my second home study meeting today and it went much better than the first. Carol and I talked about my family background and the fond memories I had of spending time with my grandparents. My father's parents had a summer cottage on Lake Erie, and we would spend many a summer weekend with them. Carol asked me all kinds of questions about my parents. How did they meet? How old were they when they got married? What type of relationship did they have? Our session lasted about two hours, and then we made arrangements for her to visit my apartment the following Monday.

CHECKLIST

❖ Make second payment to social worker (Fee: $400).

Monday, January 20

Dear Little Ones: I did it! I passed inspection and should have my final home study by next week. Carol and I spent about two hours talking about the next steps—places where I can take you to play, local resources for children's activities and more.

We also discussed some of the recent changes in the personnel at the National Adoption Center (NAC) in Kiev. This is the government agency (part of the Ministry of Education) in Ukraine that oversees the selection of children for adoption. The new director has made a number of statements about how it will be harder for single applicants to adopt, especially those wanting younger children. She said she would favor giving younger children to traditional families—those with two parents. The director also said that anyone wanting two children would have to accept an older child as well.

Carol told me that her agency used to have a Ukrainian adoption program until last year when two couples she was working with were told to give a certain official $5,000, or they would not be shown any children. Fortunately, they were able to find a child without paying the official by using a different facilitator. It appears that corruption is a way of life over there. I asked her why would people in Ukraine make it so hard to find good homes for these children, especially since one of the couples was seeking a child with a missing limb. She told me there were two reasons. First of all, some Ukrainians figured out that they could make a lot of money by charging big fees, and second, there is little incentive to place all the children as that would mean closing down some of their orphanages, and the people in charge would lose their jobs. It is heartbreaking to think of all the roadblocks put up for people around the world, not just Americans, who want to open their homes to these children, removing them from places so poor that they don't even give you the clothes the children are wearing when you decide to adopt them. That's right. You have to buy new clothes to dress the children when you leave the orphanage because their clothes stay there.

We discussed my options. As I told Carol, I was looking for two children, ages two to four. She told me I should indicate in my home study that I was willing to take a child as old as six, and that I should make sure my facilitator in Ukraine understood my preferences. She also said that she wouldn't advise waiting too long as I will turn 45 next month, and many countries don't let you adopt very young children when the age difference is more that 45 years.

Don't worry little ones. I will come for you soon. My heart has an empty spot in it that only you can fill. I have no doubt that you are waiting for me to come and bring you home. Know that I am thinking of you every day.

CHECKLIST

❧ Make final home study payment: (Fee: $400).

Monday, February 10

Dear Journal: My heart skips a beat every time I check my e-mail and read the messages from the adoption e-mail groups. Yesterday, I learned that two of the former officials at the NAC were being investigated on charges that basically amounted to baby selling. It's hard to believe that anyone would consider doing such a thing, yet I also know that the people in Ukraine are in a survival mode and may use any method they can to get money.

There have been many changes in the last six months in Ukraine. When I first started looking into adoption, the NAC would allow prospective parents to see any number of children at an orphanage. Now, you have permission to visit only one child, and if you reject that child for any reason, you have to return to the NAC to select another child.

I spoke with Carol on Friday and confirmed that my home study is now approved. A month ago it was such a huge hurdle; now I can see that there will be many such challenges before I get on a plane to Ukraine later this year. The next step is to send my home study to the Immigration Naturalization Service (INS). They have the power to accept or reject Carol's recommendation that I be approved to adopt two orphaned children from Ukraine. INS approval should come within two to three weeks. Then it will be time to finalize my dossier, which is what will be sent to Ukraine for translation and submission to the NAC. Once the dossier is accepted, I will be put on a waiting list for appointments. I have sent an e-mail to Cathy Harris asking her to verify all the documents I need to finalize my dossier. If everything goes as planned, I will travel to Ukraine in August with Donna.

I had a conversation with Terrie, a co-worker, on Friday about my adoption plans. She told me she was adopted as a young child, and now she wants to find her birth mother. She has received court approval to submit her request to the agency director that handled her adoption to investigate whether he can locate Terrie's birth mother and find out if she is interested in meeting with Terrie. She is very excited about it, but she hasn't told her adoptive parents. I guess she doesn't want them to feel that she is abandoning them or doesn't appreciate everything they have done for her. I wonder, when my children are grown will they want to return to Ukraine and find their birth parents? I can't imagine how I would feel about it. I hope I would understand and support them.

Last week I sent a request to the e-mail group asking if anyone had a medical checklist I could use. One person sent a five-page list of all the questions I should be asking. I wonder what questions the Ukrainians will ask me?

Wednesday, February 26

Dear Journal: It seems that governments everywhere seem to do everything in their power to make it difficult and expensive for people to adopt children from other countries. On Monday I learned that the NAC has issued a new requirement for adoptive parents. I must now compile two separate dossiers if I want to adopt two unrelated children in Ukraine. The documents will be exact duplicates, except that they all have to be originals that have been notarized and stamped. I don't know if the children I will be adopting will be related so I'll have to spend several hundred dollars more to get the extra ten documents authenticated.

I am reading a book by Robert Collier entitled *The Law of the Higher Potential*. One of the passages speaks about desire and faith and states "....obstacles are merely negative conditions that will disappear as darkness disappears when you turn on the light. It is the prize that they kept their eyes upon. And it was the prize that they reached out and plucked." These are the thoughts I must keep in my mind as I work through this process.

Another section in the book talks about making a treasure map to help you create that which you desire in life.

So last week I cut out pictures of two small children from a parenting magazine that I found at my hair stylist's shop. Then I pasted them onto a sheet of paper and wrote the affirmation, "I will adopt two young children from Ukraine this year."

I am spending five minutes each day praying and focusing on the images and the statement. I imagine what my life will be like with two young children. I want so much for them. I want to give them the opportunity to challenge their imagination, to explore the beauty of the world around us. I want to have fun with them. Go sailing. Have indoor picnics on rainy days. Explore museums. Make puppets out of socks and have puppet shows.

I have been thinking about where I will make my home with my two children. Part of me wants to move back home to be closer to my parents, but that would require a huge upheaval in my life (not that adopting two children won't have the same effect). I certainly can't stay where I am now—a one bedroom apartment in a huge condominium complex. But strangely enough I'm not worried about it. I have complete faith that the right house will turn up, whether it's in Virginia or in Buffalo.

I got an e-mail from Judy today, and she sent me pictures of the room she has decorated for Olivia. It looks like the perfect room for a young girl, with lots of stuffed animals and a frilly bedspread. It is a source of great encouragement and consolation to know that we are both going through a tremendous struggle to bring our forever children home to us.

I am anxious for the day when I bring my two children home with me and start my journal entry with the words, "Now the real fun begins."

Tuesday, March 25

Dear Journal: It has been over a month since my home study was submitted to the INS for approval, and I am still waiting for a response. The bad news is that I can't do anything more with my dossier until I have their approval. Carol has called her contact at INS several times but has not received any response. I have heard that the delay is due in part to the department's restructuring to ensure terrorists are not allowed into this country.

I spend each day reading all the messages from the adoption e-mail newsgroups. I now have a small treasure trove of printouts detailing every step of the process, including medical information to evaluate the children's health. I am constantly amazed at the fortitude of the people who are willing to put their faith in God's hands that they will find the right child to bring home. I have read so many stories in which people say that they knew they had found their son or daughter the instant they set eyes on the child.

I feel that I am in limbo. I can't do anything to move the adoption process forward. I keep telling myself that there is a reason things are not moving as quickly as I had expected. Maybe the universe is waiting for me to find a place to live before I travel to Ukraine. In that case it's time to pull out the paper and start looking at the real estate section.

Wednesday, April 23

Dear Journal: This evening I gave a speech entitled "The Forgotten Children" at my local Toastmaster's Club. It highlighted the need for foster care and adoptive parents. I shared handouts from the Casey Organization that showed what people could do to promote May as National Foster Care Month. The depth of response I received from the audience after I finished my speech surprised me. Several of the members approached me afterwards and told me how deeply touched they were and asked for copies of the material to share at their offices. I continue to be amazed at how my passion for this topic has evolved. I've never been an activist, but somehow the plight of abandoned children brings out the fighter in me. I want to mobilize people and work to provide care and support for these children whom I have never even seen.

Monday, April 28

Dear Journal: It's here! My INS approval from the Bureau of Citizenship and Immigration Services finally arrived in the mail. It came in an ordinary envelope, but inside, it held the key to my future. There, in black and white, it read "It has been determined that you are able to furnish proper care to an orphan or orphans as defined by Section 1010 (b) (1) (F) of the Immigration and Nationality Act." I am in heaven. I can now complete the rest my dossier, which in itself will be no small task. All of the documents must be valid at the time of my visit to the NAC, which could be any time this year. I must also ensure that the notary's commission for each document doesn't expire before the end of the year.

LIST OF DOSSIER DOCUMENTS

1. Home Study
2. Social worker's letter of employment and license along with adoption agency license
3. Medical form
4. Copy of my passport
5. Power of attorney (for my Ukrainian facilitator)
6. Approval letter from INS (I-171H)
7. Statement of employment
8. Petition to adopt
9. Letter of Obligation
10. Criminal clearance

Monday, May 12

Dear Journal: Everyone tells me how different my life will be once I have my children. I tell them I can't wait for it to change. My daily schedule now is to get up, meditate and do some simple yoga stretches, eat breakfast and then go to work. I spend 30 to 40 minutes driving to an office where I sit in front of a computer all day, attending conference calls and sending e-mails. I don't see the sky or feel the sunshine on my face unless I get up and walk to a window. I don't get to see many people unless I make plans to have lunch with one of my co-workers. After dinner, I check my e-mail, take a walk, or read a book.

I guess I'll have more laundry and cooking to do. I'll probably learn where all the local playgrounds and kids' clothing stores are located. I'm really looking forward to getting (and giving) hugs and kisses every day. Smiles will be plentiful and sounds of laughter will fill the air around me. I even look forward to answering all their questions such as, "Why is the sky blue?" "Where did I come from?" and "Is there really a Santa Claus?"

I want to record their every move. I will have a camcorder and a camera and keep a journal about their experiences and accomplishments. I don't want to have kids and then put them right into day care. I have waited too long for this to happen to not experience every moment of it. I want to be there when they wake up and put them to bed at night. I want to teach them to be kind to all living things and to have confidence in everything they do.

I want to be their mom, the one person in the world they can trust with anything, whether it is a scratched knee or broken toy. Wow! What a tremendous responsibility. I can't wait for my life to change.

Wednesday, May 21

Dear Journal: I found the perfect home. It's a California-style bungalow nestled in a small town in the suburbs of Washington, D.C. It's sorely in need of a new kitchen and bathroom, but there are beautiful hardwood floors, an upstairs loft that would be a perfect playroom for the children and a great yard with lots of shade. It hasn't been lived in for some time, and the neglect is evident in the leaky roof and trampled yard, but the architecture is stunning. I know it will be a wonderful home for my children and me.

I was talking with Steven, a co-worker, today about my adoption plans, and he had some of his own plans to share with me. He and his wife adopted a young girl several years ago in a private adoption, and they now want to grow their family by adding a son. They recently traveled to Austin, Texas, to witness the birth of a boy they had hoped to adopt. The birth mother had agreed to give up the child and had selected Steven and his wife as the parents. However, once the boy was born, his biological father refused to sign the papers, so Steven and his wife returned home empty-handed. His story was sad, but they haven't given up and are determined to find their son. I have such admiration for people like Steven. For me, I refuse to believe that I will return home from Ukraine without my children.

Friday, May 30

Dear Journal: The reality of what I'm doing is slowly sinking in. I received a packet of documents today from the U.S. Embassy in Poland stating that they have received confirmation of the approval of my application for Advance Processing of Orphan Petition (I-600A) from the INS. My petition to adopt two children is valid for 18 months from the INS approval date of April 24. More paperwork. The U.S. Embassy in Poland is the regional center for processing immigrant visas for children adopted in Belarus, Latvia, Lithuania, Poland and Ukraine. This means that, once I have completed the adoption of my children in Ukraine, Donna and I must travel with them to Warsaw to get their U.S. visas. I would travel anywhere to bring them home with me. It really doesn't matter now what I have to do, I will do it. There is no turning back.

I heard from Judy today. She has given up on the idea of adopting Olivia from Romania and has contracted with an agency to adopt a baby girl from Guatemala. I can't imagine how she must feel about abandoning the young girl she thought was going to be her daughter. Romania has by all accounts, closed its doors to international adoptions. From what I hear, part of the reason is to curtail the corrupt practices that amount to baby selling. What a sad, sad situation. To know that there are hundreds of infants and older children desperate for a home, yet their government is not capable of handling the process to help them find their forever families.

Monday, June 9

Dear Journal: Depression. Elation. Back to depression. Every day I read about the problems other applicants are having with the adoption process. I have spent the last three weeks getting my health letter re-signed by my doctor because it wasn't on letterhead. Then I had to get a new copy of Carol's license because it expires the end of June. What if she had decided to stop being a social worker and didn't renew her license? There is so much bureaucracy it makes my head spin.

Now, finally, I have all my documents. On Friday I sent a copy of them to my translator, Victor, in Ukraine, for review. I will pick up a copy of Carol's new social worker's license after work on Wednesday. I will send the documents to Richmond tomorrow to get my dossier documents stamped by the Virginia Secretary of State's office; then I will go into Washington, D.C., on Friday morning to get the documents stamped at the U.S. Department of State.

It is official now that the NAC is being reorganized and it will be closed in July and August. I have read bad things about the new director and one couple just sent a heart-wrenching e-mail about being stuck in Kiev for almost three weeks while the NAC jerked them around. They finally decided to come home empty-handed. How depressing. Cathy Harris is traveling over there in a few days to meet with the new director and other Ukrainian officials. She is taking a big book full of annual reports of adopted children. I hope things get better.

I am anxious to send my dossiers to Ukraine so I can get an appointment sometime this fall. I talked to Donna last week, and she isn't sure she can come with me now that I won't be traveling this summer. She is applying for several jobs at local schools and doesn't know if she can get the time off once the school year has started. I don't want to think about having to make this trip by myself, but I will do it if that's what it takes to bring my children home. I did speak with the folks on my team at work and told them about my plans. At the very least, I want to spend several months at home with my children before returning to work.

CHECKLIST

♣ Send dossier copies to Victor in Ukraine (Fee: $72).

Tuesday, June 10

Dear Journal: I read an e-mail from a couple in Ukraine about adopting their child and reminded myself why I am doing this:

Hello, List mates!

We had a two-part court hearing, Monday afternoon and Tuesday morning, due to the fact that we were missing one piece of paperwork from the NAC that was in transit Monday night from Kiev. We concluded our court hearing this morning and had the 30-day wait waived (which we understand is very unusual these days in all regions). We are very grateful to currently be in transit back to Kiev to finish up there and hopefully return to the States over the weekend. Our new nine-year-old son Vitaly is with us and enjoying being reunited with his biological sister and new brother (also adopted from Ukraine in 2001). To those of you in process now, everything you're going through will be worth it when you reach this moment of having your new child with you.

CHECKLIST

❖ Pay Virginia Department of State for validating notary seals (Fee: $240).

Wednesday, June 18

Dear Journal: I read an e-mail today from another couple who have just returned from Ukraine. Due to their work situation, they needed to ask the judge to waive the 30-day waiting period so they can return home. The waiting period was originally intended to allow Ukrainians the opportunity to adopt the child, thus keeping the child in the country. It has morphed into a process that allows judges and other officials to accept fees to waive this waiting period. The judge told this couple he wanted $1,000.

The woman said he simply wrote the figure on a piece of paper, and they agreed to pay him. For them it was worth it. This amount of money in Ukraine is comparable to $10,000 or more in the U.S. I don't know how much of this I will encounter on my trip. It all seems so matter of fact. I guess these payments are a part of life over there, but it seems so unfair to profit from the misery of children.

Monday, June 23

Dear Journal: Right now I have a stack of papers sitting on my lap. They all have the great seal of Virginia and the U.S. Department of State. What a paper shuffle these past two weeks have been! One of my documents got lost in Richmond, and I didn't realize it until I had all of my documents authenticated at the Department of State. Fortunately, the lost paper was the only document of which I had a spare original. Then I realized I hadn't bundled the papers correctly, so, unless I go back to the Department of State and fix it, I will have to spend another $240 in fees at the Ukraine Embassy. Therefore, tomorrow I go back to the Department of State and then send my precious packet of papers to the Ukraine Consulate. The next step is to sit and wait for nine days until my papers are stamped yet again. I feel as if I am fighting an invincible force that is giving me every opportunity to give up and admit failure.

I have been reading more e-mails from the newsgroup about expediting fees. These fees are commonplace in Ukraine, and part of the role of the facilitator is to negotiate them with the judges and other officials. From what I have heard, Americans are being treated very poorly—worse than other foreigners. The reason being given is the lack of support and involvement from the U.S. Embassy, which is where we all have to go to complete the adoption paperwork. I don't know if this is true or not. It is so easy to get caught up in the e-mail postings, and it becomes hard to separate fact from fiction.

This morning I thought to myself, "I shouldn't have told anyone about my adoption plans. Now when I see them they all want to know how things are progressing." What would they say if I decided to give up? I know they are just being nice, but it's so hard to talk about it. What if I get the children and then decide it was all a mistake? How will I make a living? How will I find my soul mate? Sometimes the idea of becoming responsible for two young lives is the most frightening thought I have ever had. The only living beings I have ever been responsible for are my plants and two cats.

I have tried to be good about saying my prayers every day—thanking God for helping me find my forever children. I do believe that the power of the universe can be used to help us achieve our goals, but we must tell the universe what it is we want—and believe that it will happen.

Monday, July 7

Dear Journal: Today I received the e-mail that I have been looking forward to for six months. My translator, Victor, has received my completed dossier and will begin translating the documents for submission to the NAC. Words cannot describe my happiness at this moment. All the days of frustration have melted away, and I am now anxiously awaiting news of my appointment so I can make my travel arrangements. Once the NAC has reviewed and approved the dossier, they will give me a travel date. This could take weeks, but I am content to wait for a while.

I forwarded an e-mail to Donna today that contained the story of one of the families who had just returned from Ukraine with their newly-adopted daughter. It is rife with all their emotional highs and lows, long train journeys, countless hours of waiting to get stamps and signatures, all rolled into a 26 day, once in a lifetime trip. I want my sister to know what she has signed up for since she has never traveled outside the U.S. except for Mexico and Canada. Donna is a real trooper and is very excited about the trip. She has already started sending me questions about the trip along with ideas and catalogs on activities for kids.

This week is the 25th anniversary of my mother's death. There isn't a week that goes by that I don't think of her. If I miss her now, I can only imagine how much I will miss her when I finally have my children. What woman doesn't beam with pride when she shows her children to her mother for the first time? I will make sure that my children know what a wonderful woman she was, and I will continue to use her as my role model. She was always there for us, though how she raised seven children as a stay-at-home-mom I will never know.

I am only three years younger than my mother was when she died. It's hard to believe that she was so young, yet she had done so much. I know she regretted that she never went to college. She wanted all of us to achieve our goals in life—whatever they may be. She was always looking out for us first and put her needs last. It has taken me a long time to be in a position where I can consider someone else's needs before my own. Perhaps that's one reason why I chose not to have children before now. There is a time and a season for everything or so the saying goes. "A time to be born and a time to die….a time to love and a time to hate." This is my time and I will not let it slip by me. I will seize the moment, and I will find my children. I know it.

Wednesday, July 9

Dear Journal: Meryl, one of the women I work with, gave me an update today on Alison, a friend of hers, who decided to become a mother through adoption. Alison is single and lives on the west coast in a beautiful home. She is in her forties, and like me, isn't prepared to wait for Mr. Right to come along to start her family. Alison decided on a domestic adoption and, through her attorney, found a 32-year old woman from Philadelphia (I'll call her Mary as I don't know her real name) who was pregnant but did not want to keep the baby. Although Alison wanted a girl, the tests on the unborn child showed it would be a boy.

I often wonder about women who decide to surrender a child for adoption. I guess that when you haven't been able to get pregnant yourself, it's hard to imagine giving up something so precious. Then again, until you walk in someone's shoes, it isn't fair to judge them. Mary has already given birth to six children and is not currently married. The unborn child's father is an alcoholic, and Mary is in a methadone drug treatment program to help wean her from her heroin addiction.

From what I understood, Alison planned to cover Mary's living and medical expenses during the pregnancy. Mary has one of her children, a son, living with her. The others are either living with relatives or in foster care. Since Alison had never met Mary, she paid to fly her and her son out to the west coast several weeks ago. Alison described Mary as being heavily tattooed and a smoker, as well as physically very beautiful, with dark hair and olive skin.

Well, the news was not good. Alison had never seen Mary's medical records and had been trying to get them for several months. She finally saw them, and they contained a big surprise. Mary had lied on the health forms she had given to the attorney. She was HIV positive and had Hepatitis B. Apparently, it is not a forgone conclusion that the unborn child will be HIV positive, but there is a two percent to a 25 percent chance that he will be, depending upon the medical treatment of the mother during pregnancy. It was all too much for Alison. She terminated the adoption process and is now searching for a new candidate.

After Meryl finished telling me this, I couldn't help feeling sorry for the unborn child and wonder about his future. We both agreed that if Mary's son was born without the HIV virus, someone would adopt him. But what if he does have the virus? It was clear that his mother didn't want him even if he were born healthy.

Tuesday, July 22

Dear Journal: Still no news from Ukraine. I got flustered the other evening when I realized I never made copies of my dossiers before I handed them to the courier to be sent to the Ukrainian Consulate. I thought I would get duplicates of everything when the dossiers were completed. Instead all I got were copies of the Ukrainian Consulate stamps on the back of the Department of State letters. In a panic, I sent an e-mail to my translator, Victor, letting him know that the set I mailed to him was the only copy. How could I have been so stupid?

Thursday, July 24

Dear Journal: Yesterday I was on the phone with Cindy, a co-worker. I don't know how the subject of adoption came up, but it seems to creep into every conversation I have these days. One thing led to another, and she ended up sharing with me the story of how she adopted an infant girl from the 15-year old daughter of a co-worker. She started the process in the mid-nineties using word-of-mouth to let people know of her intention to adopt. Finally, in late 1996, she found out about this girl who, after speaking with Cindy, agreed to let her adopt her unborn child. Cindy had just moved to Texas from California where the co-worker and her family lived, but she did not let the distance between them deter her.

I could hear the emotion in her voice as she described the challenges she faced, not with paperwork and bureaucrats, but with a large cadre of the girl's family members, all of whom had different opinions on the girl's decision to give up her child, including the stepfather, who did not believe in adoption. When I heard that, it made me think of the plight of a single man who had recently shared his Ukrainian adoption story. The judge did not believe the child would have a better life with a single man than he would living in an orphanage and she did everything possible to prevent the adoption. I am amazed at the impact cultural beliefs have on adoption.

Cindy and I talked about how our own families responded to our initial decision to adopt. She said that, at first, some of her family wanted nothing to do with it. Fortunately, her husband's parents, who live in California, were very supportive. In fact, she stayed with them right after the little girl was born. Five days after the birth, Cindy was told by her agency that the girl had decided to keep her child. Cindy said that it was too much to bear. She cried herself to sleep that night as her bewildered in-laws looked on at this strong woman who had finally reached her breaking point. I can only imagine the anguish she must have felt. Cindy was there at the birth and had cut the umbilical cord. Now she was being asked to walk away from this baby girl whose mother was still a child herself. Fortunately, the girl changed her mind, and three days later, just as Cindy and her husband returned to Texas, she signed the release papers. Cindy told me that reliving this moment still brings tears to her eyes.

Cindy kept telling me how wonderful it was to have a child in her life, and I believed her. She mentioned that soon after bringing her daughter home, she and her husband attended a family gathering. There was a lot of clucking going on about their new arrival when, suddenly, one of her husband's aunts announced that she had given up a child for adoption when she was very young. No one in the family had known about this. Cindy then said the most wonderful thing, "It was like the closing of a circle—to bring an adopted child back into the family."

It's amazing how many adoption stories are out there. Perhaps those of us who become parents by adopting share a special bond, just as those women do who make the decision to give up a child. I feel as if I'm about to enter a secret society of motherhood. In the past few months I have sensed a bonding that never existed before with my sisters and co-workers. Now when the conversation includes a discussion on potty training or whether children should sleep in their parents' bed at night, I feel connected instead of bored. I keep hearing "Your life will change so much." For once, I can't wait to find out just how true that will be.

Thursday, July 31

Dear Little Ones: Tomorrow I will close on my house—your future home. It is in a wonderful neighborhood in a small town, but all you will care about is that you can run around on the lawn and climb the trees. I have already met several of my neighbors and they are very nice. There is a couple with a four-year-old son moving in next door to us, and there are two young girls who live down the street.

The house has a big front porch that is begging for some comfortable chairs that I can sit in to enjoy the cool evening breezes. I have picked out your bedroom in the middle of the house so it will be nice and warm even on the coldest day. Your windows look out onto trees and grass. I'm even thinking of putting a swing and a sandbox out back. I can't wait to move in and start organizing your bedroom. There is a spare bedroom that I am going to make into a play-room so you can spread out all your toys and games. I want everything to be ready for you when I bring you both home—to your new home.

Tuesday, August 12

Dear Journal: Rumors abound on the e-mail newsgroups. Today I read about the Ukrainian Mafia. Well, every other country has them, why not Ukraine? One woman wrote about her encounter with a couple who did not go through the normal adoption process. She described her conversation with them during a potluck dinner that was organized for folks who had adopted children from Ukraine. This couple had stayed in Ukraine only three days—just long enough to pick up a healthy baby girl to bring back to the States. They paid their U.S. adoption agency over $50,000 in fees rather than the normal $14,000 to $18,000. When she asked them about their visit to the NAC, which everyone has to do, they ended the conversation and left the party shortly afterwards.

Another e-mail described how the Mafia held back children in certain regions to sell to couples. This was done with the knowledge of local officials, including the orphanage director. Birth certificates would be created using the names of children who had died, something you read about in spy novels or see in the movies. If the children got too old or no one wanted to adopt them, the director was allowed to put the children's' names on the official list of adoptable children.

Do I believe this? I don't know. Apparently many of the Eastern European countries have a shadow economy where organized crime groups run drug rings, smuggle guns, sell women into sexual slavery and control the distribution of certain luxury items. But baby selling? Is it such a great leap to believe that this can still go on? Why not, when we continue to read how little value human lives have in certain countries.

I know it sounds crazy. But after hearing an amazing story from Mary Ellen, one of my co-workers who adopted a girl from Romania thirteen years ago, there's nothing I wouldn't believe. She told me she would have brought two children home with her instead of one, but the mother of the second girl, who lived in a mud hut and had no knowledge of the outside world, truly believed that Mary Ellen wanted to take her daughter back to the States to use her as body parts—and to eat her. This sounds absurd, but this was the situation she faced. In addition, one of the government officials told her that the daughter she did bring home should not be adopted because she was from a family of gypsies; therefore, she would grow up to steal and would be incapable of learning to read or write. I have met Mary Ellen's daughter, and nothing could be further from the truth; she is a beautiful, intelligent young lady.

But there is also a great deal of dignity among the Romanians. The father of the girl Mary Ellen adopted re-

fused to take money from another couple who also wanted
to adopt the girl. As poor as he was, he said that he had
made a promise to Mary Ellen, and he would not go back
on his word. Mary Ellen had not pledged any money to
this man in order to adopt his daughter. How many of us
would have refused the money knowing it was the only
way to feed and clothe our other children?

Thursday, August 14

Dear Journal: The e-mails in the adoption newsgroups
from the last few days have been full of messages from
people who have recently submitted their dossiers and are
waiting for an appointment. One couple, who are also using Victor as their translator, wrote that he told them that
there were no NAC appointments left in October. I refuse
to believe this. I worked so hard to get all that paper work
done, and now it is just sitting in a pile on some official's
desk. I have read that the NAC was in total disarray and
that delays in getting appointments were to be expected.

No one who sent his or her dossier in later than I did
has received an approval letter. I don't want them to get
theirs until I get mine. Isn't that selfish? Yes, it is, but that
is how I feel. It's like standing in line at the store or bank
with ten people behind you. Then, a teller opens a new
checkout, and suddenly the person who was last in line is
now first in the new queue. "Not fair," we all say. I, however, refuse to drag myself down with negative thoughts.
My approval will come soon. I will get an October appointment, and my children will be waiting for me in the NAC
adoption books. I cannot accept any other outcome.

Monday, August 18

Dear Journal: It was waiting for me in my in-box when I opened my e-mail today. I printed it off as soon as I read it. I had to hold the message telling me I have been registered as a prospective adoptive parent at the NAC in my hand. Yes! My dossier has been accepted. Victor will soon receive a document from the NAC regarding my registration. Then I need to fax a request for a travel date.

I know deep in my heart that my children are now ready for me. This is a sign telling me to start preparing for motherhood. I spent the weekend at the beach with some of my siblings, including my brother John, his wife, Renae, and their two young sons, ages four and two. The boys are so dependent on their parents for everything. It was fun being with them, but it was exhausting as well. I know there are many life-style changes in store for me.

Tuesday, August 19

Dear Journal: One of my co-workers, Sue, stopped by my workstation today. She noticed the boxes next to my desk and asked if I was moving. Well, one thing led to another and I ended up telling her about my adoption plans. It turns out Sue and her husband, both of whom are Filipino, adopted a one-year-old girl last year from the Philippines. Sue went through Catholic Charities and had to spend only four days there to pick up their child. When I asked her what the cost was, she told me it was about $13,000. Being an employee of a Fortune 500 company, Sue was able to get time off with pay upon her return. Since I am a consultant, I don't get any company benefits. This is one time in my life when I miss having them.

They were a childless couple, and Sue was unable to have children. She told me that in her culture it is not uncommon for a man to leave his wife if she can't bear children. I guess adoption is not well thought of either. She spoke about her fear that her husband might leave her if she went through with the adoption. Sue told me about the criticism she incurred from her siblings and parents when they were told about her decision to adopt. She said that they couldn't understand why she and her husband wanted children when they had such a nice life-style. They could travel and do anything they wanted, but for some of us there's a empty spot in our lives that only a child can fill.

I saw her face light up when she spoke about her little girl, Ruth Ann. It was obvious that this child was truly loved. I asked Sue if her husband enjoyed having a daughter. "Oh yes!" she said with enthusiasm.

Sue told me that she is now thinking about adopting a little boy from the Philippines. We were commiserating about how much paper work there was to do—as well as the expense involved. I have read many e-mails from people who are returning to Ukraine to adopt a second or third child. I continue to be amazed at the number of people who, even with three or more biological children, still have the desire and the resources to travel throughout the world to bring home another child. God bless them.

Monday, August 25

Dear Journal: I got another e-mail from Victor today. I needed to send a request to the NAC formally requesting an appointment. I went to the local copy store tonight to send the fax, but it wouldn't go through, so I finally scanned the letter into a file and e-mailed it. What a tiring way to spend the evening.

Tuesday, August 26

Dear Journal: I got an e-mail from a friend, Nancy, who wrote to me about friend of hers, Jan, who is considering adoption. Jan is my age and has tried to get pregnant for the past two years, fertility drugs included, to no avail. She is married, but Nancy's e-mail indicated that her marriage might not last. Nancy asked if I would talk to Jan about my experience, and I told her I would.

Nancy is in her early forties and had a miscarriage last year. She was considering taking fertility drugs to help her get pregnant again and then she and her husband decided against it. I can't believe how many women in my age group are going through the same angst as Nancy and I are in deciding whether to bring children into our lives. I've often wondered about the desire to procreate. It's easier for animals—they do it instinctively, but we humans have a choice. When I was younger I used birth control pills to avoid getting pregnant. Now I feel I am too old to get pregnant and would rather embrace a child who is already born and needs a loving family.

For some women, the decision is not to have children, either by birth or adoption. I say, more power to them. It's a gift from God to be able to decide whether to bring a child into this world. I would have been a terrible mother had I gotten pregnant in my thirties. I was too selfish and very focused on my career. Now I am ready and I thank God that some woman, half way around the world, had the courage to surrender her child so that he or she might have a better life. I will honor her memory and teach my children to appreciate the sacrifice she made for them.

Monday, September 8

Dear Journal: I sent an e-mail to Victor on Friday asking if he had any more information on when I could expect to get my appointment date. This evening I logged on and saw his response. Big disappointment. He never got the e-mail I sent him two weeks ago with my signature requesting an appointment at the NAC. So, I made a trip to the Fed Ex store to send a hard copy as I can't deal with another technical glitch. Worst of all, I am now reading about people who expect to get January appointments. Please, please let my date be sooner.

The only problem with people knowing that you are adopting is that they are always asking the same question. "So when are you going to travel?" It's like being out of a job. Everyone is very sympathetic and understanding, yet you just want to yell out, "Don't you think I'd tell you if I knew when I was traveling?" These setbacks are so frustrating. I feel as if I have reached the top of the ladder only to find out that another ladder, taller than the last one, is in front of me.

Tuesday, September 30

Dear Journal: Nothing new to report. I'm still waiting for a response from Victor about the status of my request for an appointment. Time is ticking away.

Now I am reading about all the people who have appointments at the NAC who were approved after my documents were accepted. How frustrating. I know, everyone says that things happen in their own time, but is it so selfish of me to want to know what my date is so I can decide if I'll be able to go on vacation this fall? I haven't had any time off since last November, and I really need to relax. It probably sounds like I am whining and I guess I am.

I sent a fax to the Ukraine Embassy on Monday to ask if they could intervene on my behalf. I haven't received a response from them. I suppose it's naïve to think that they could do anything, but right now I'll try anything that might help.

Wednesday, October 8

Dear Journal: I received a care package in the mail today from my brother John and his wife, Renae. They sent several tapes of children's songs for my upcoming trip. They know how to entertain little children because of the long plane trips they have taken with their children from Salt Lake City to Buffalo and back.

I have also received offers of clothes and other useful items from friends and co-workers. I feel so blessed to have such a strong support group in my life.

Monday, October 13

Dear Journal: There was an e-mail in the newsgroup today that created quite a ruckus. A woman wrote about a letter to the editor that had appeared in her local paper in response to an article about a family who had just completed an international adoption. The gist of the letter was that American children are languishing in foster homes, so why don't we, as prospective adoptive parents, take care of our own before flying off to the far corners of the world to rescue some third world child? What an outcry that provoked!

Many of these people have been foster parents and have tried to adopt their charges, only to see these vulnerable children thrust back into the care of parents who are on their third or fourth attempt at drug or alcohol rehabilitation. Other qualifications are equally unjust, from deciding at what age a person is too old to become an adoptive parent, to requiring that you be married for five years before your relationship is judged to be stable enough to adopt a child.

One woman wrote about how she and her husband had tried to adopt a two-year-old who was in foster care. The judge kept giving the mother, a drug addict, another chance to rehabilitate herself. The child is now 15 and is still in the foster care system because her mother couldn't stay off drugs. It is a very tragic story.

I admit I feel guilty telling people that I am adopting from Ukraine. I have seen the faces of children waiting to be adopted in this country. They are cute, clever, and desperate for a loving family. They also get excellent medical and mental health treatment, a family that clothes and feeds them, and access to the best schools in the world. Compare that to children in Ukraine or other third world countries that survive on pennies a day for their food and clothing allowance. Education is minimal and their future in a society that blames them for their parents' indiscretions is bleak at best. Yet economics is only part of the decision-making process. Deciding whether to pursue a domestic or foreign adoption is a difficult and personal choice. Much depends on one's circumstances and the health, age and gender of the child one wants to adopt.

For myself, I'd rather focus the attention on how we can improve the lives of all orphaned and abandoned children instead of pointing fingers and making accusations. The bottom line is that no child deserves to be left behind, regardless of where he or she lives.

Friday, October 17

Dear Journal: Last night was a first for me—I attended a support group meeting for adoptive moms. A few months ago, Mary Ellen had given me information about an adoption magazine and a local support group. She told me about the many close friends she now has as a result of her support group, and I started thinking how nice it would be to have some female friends who could relate to what I was going through. I recently joined Families for Russian and Ukrainian Adoption (FRUA) and saw an e-mail invitation to one of their "Mom's Night Out" which was being held right down the street from me in a nice restaurant. There was no reason not to go.

There were six of us at the table. Two of the women had recently adopted from Russia, and the other three were in the early stages of their paper work to adopt from Russia, where children are pre-identified and there are fewer risks involved. We chatted for several hours about all the trials and tribulations of bringing adopted children into your life. It was really nice to talk with other women face-to-face and hear their stories.

Monday, October 20

Dear Journal: Kate and Meryl, whom I work for at my consulting assignment, have been very supportive and flexible in working with me on my departure date. I haven't spent much time thinking about how I will handle going back to work once my children are here. In my fantasy life I have developed a real estate empire and have enough cash flow from my investments so I don't have to go back to the office—ever. I feel that I will have scaled Mt. Everest by the time I return from Ukraine, and the idea of going back to my old life does not sound appealing at all.

Alas, there is still no date for me. I have sent yet another e-mail to Victor, but, like all my e-mails sent since the beginning of September, his response is silence. My documents will soon expire, and, based upon what I have heard, I will have to start preparing them all over again.

Wednesday, October 22

Dear Journal: It finally happened. This morning I opened up my e-mail and there it was—my appointment date with the NAC has been set for November 26, the day before Thanksgiving. WOW! I walked into Meryl's office at work and told her the good news. Then I started to cry. She got up from her desk and gave me a big hug. It was a very emotional moment for me. I felt light-headed and giddy. The next few hours were a blur. I couldn't tell many people because I was in back-to-back meetings, but I did manage a call to Donna to tell her to start packing. Now I need to start making a list of everything I must do between now and when I leave—visas, banking, packing, and collecting baby items. Kate, who has two young boys, has offered to supply a number of items and clothes that her children no longer need. I feel very grateful to be connected to all my friends at a time like this.

My heart is beating a million miles a minute right now. Just the thought of traveling to Kiev to find my two children is so exciting.

Thursday, October 23

Dear Journal: All sorts of emotions have been running through my head these past 24 hours. Excitement, fear, exhaustion. I feel that the past year has simply been a fire drill for the real thing. Now I'm ready to use the information I have been collecting, including how much money to bring ($20,000 in crisp new $100 bills) and what clothes to pack (it was 37 degrees today in Kiev).

This morning I went to a local medical clinic that serves immigrants and travelers like myself going to the far flung corners of the world. I started the inoculation process for Hepatitis A and B. I also got a tetanus shot. Many of the people on the e-mail newsgroup recommended doing this. Donna has already started the process.

My sister Pat Mary uses a pediatrician who participates in my health care plan, and, according to his staff, he has worked with adoptive children. She has been very happy with him, and I plan to use him when I return with my children. I am trying to determine if he is willing to be on call for me while I am in Ukraine. I have read time and time again that the medical diagnosis of the children in Ukraine is either incomplete or incorrect. In addition to having a physician available for a medical consultation via phone or e-mail in the U.S., I want to have a physician to travel with us to the orphanage to examine the children before I make my final decision on whether or not to adopt them. I ordered a booklet from FRUA that lists common ailments of orphaned children in Ukraine and Russia. All prospective parents are encouraged to make a list of maladies they are willing to accept before traveling to Ukraine. I still haven't done this. Somehow the idea of a written list of exclusions is too sad to contemplate.

Right now I have more pressing things to do, including applying for visas for Donna and me. Along with sending the visa applications to the Ukraine Embassy, I must express mail a letter with my signature to the NAC stating that I have accepted my appointment date. Why I have to keep sending these letters is beyond me.

CHECKLIST

✣ Visit medical clinic for vaccines (Fee: $225).

✣ Send double entry visa application (Fee: $110 x 2).

✣ Send letter to NAC in Ukraine (Fee: $73).

Monday, October 27

Dear Journal: Last week my yoga class instructor, Frances, said, "You need patience for your poses just as you need patience in your life." That really struck home to me. Now that I have shared my good news with my friends and family, everyone is asking me the same questions. "What will happen when you get there?", "How old will the children be?", and "How long will you be gone?" Of course they are all interested in my trip, but I must have answered the same questions at least two dozen times in the past week.

I am truly overwhelmed by the outpouring of good wishes from everyone. Several people have offered to host a shower for me upon my return. After having attended dozens of wedding and baby showers throughout the years, I finally get to have one for me. I know that sounds silly, but it really does make me feel good that I have friends who care enough about me to do something like this.

I am now working on my travel arrangements. The only open issues are what I will be charged if I need to change my return flight from Warsaw, and how much I will be charged for one-way tickets for the children. It sounds so strange to be thinking of *my* children. It is still a fairly abᴊᴛᴜᴄᴛ ᴄᴏɴᴄᴇᴘt in my brain that I will suddenly assume responsibility for two living beings. My only prior experience was owning two cats, and, as all pet lovers know, you never really own a cat. It's a symbiotic relationship whereby you give them shelter, food, and loving care, and, in return, they give you hair balls, furry clothes and an occasional purr. I guess you could say almost the same thing about children, so maybe I will be okay after all!

Thursday, October 30

Dear Journal: Three weeks and counting. The reality of what I am doing is beginning to sink in. Last night I sent our proposed travel itinerary to Donna along with a recommended packing list. I'd like to spend a few days in London to visit Jan, a friend of mine, before we continue on to Kiev. It's going to be bloody cold in Ukraine, but at least Donna and I know how to dress having lived up north for the first two decades of our lives. I scheduled our return flight for December 23. I'm being optimistic, hoping Donna can catch a plane on December 24 to celebrate Christmas with her family.

Saturday, November 1

Dear Journal: The weather was absolutely gorgeous today, so, instead of working on my house which is where I should have been, I took off to the marina in Maryland where my sailboat has sat patiently waiting for me to come and put it to bed for the winter.

A friend and I spent the day tackling some minor repairs and generally puttering around the boat. It's now out of the water, but I still get a kick from being on it. There was only the slightest hint of a breeze, giving me a small level of compensation for the fact that the sailing season is over.

When I tell my friends that I'll have my two little ones on the boat with me next spring, they all laugh—especially the ones who already have kids. "You think you're going sailing with a one and a three year old?" they say with smiles on their face. "Sure you will...." Well, I don't see why not. There are plenty of people who live on their boats, and they have small children aboard. I don't mind giving up some things in my life, but I see no reason why this has to be one of them. I want my children to be exposed to the water early on in life so they can enjoy all the pleasures boating has to offer them.

The past week has been especially hard for me. I need to make sure I am eating right as well as getting enough rest. The physical toll is not as bad as the emotional stress. I'm working on the house in the evening after spending a full day at the office, and it all adds up after awhile. Knowing that I will be leaving my work assignment and taking several months off has added to my concerns. I have a deep inner belief that I will always have enough money to support myself. It's just that I want to do so much with the gifts I have been given from God.

Sunday, November 2

Dear Journal: Although I was raised a Catholic, I haven't been a regular churchgoer for a number of years. I did register at a local church last year when I knew I was going to adopt, but I did that more for the children. I wanted to belong to a parish in order to have them baptized. Now that I'm getting my children, I feel a renewed desire to join a spiritual group that will embrace the children and give them a sense of belonging.

A month or so ago one of my sailing friends, John, told me about a small Catholic community called Pilgrims After Christ (PAX). The group formed over 30 years ago and uses the meeting hall at a local church. It sounded interesting, so I decided to give it a try. The atmosphere is very informal and everyone knows each other. A few visits were all it took to convince me to join the congregation. There are a number of children in the group, and everyone made me feel very welcome.

Today, John and his wife Maria invited me over to their home for brunch after Mass. John is retired from the U.S. Navy and speaks fluent Russian. He has been to Ukraine several times and still has friends over there. Before I left their apartment, John told me that if I needed help in order to get my house ready for the children I should make up a list and he would let the PAX community know what needed to be done. I told him I wasn't used to asking for help, but he was adamant in letting me know help is there if I need it. As a parting gift, he gave me a pocket sized Russian/English dictionary.

I thanked John and Maria for both their hospitality and their generous offer of help. I guess I didn't convince John that I could do it on my own; he called me later in the day and offered to come over to the house next weekend and help me make a list of what needed to be done.

Later in the afternoon, I stopped by Meg and Michael's house next door to me. They are two of the nicest people I have ever met, and we have already become good friends. They made a similar offer of help. Meg even offered to help my sister Pat Mary unpack the boxes I have stored at a friend's house so my kitchen would be usable upon my return.

I must admit, I feel guilty asking for help. Thinking about it, part of my reason for hesitating is that I don't want people to think I'm using them or that I am incapable of taking care of things myself. It sounds pretty silly, but I'm so used to doing things by myself, including hard, physical labor, that I'm just not used to admitting I need help. Call it pride or stubbornness—either description probably works just as well.

Monday, November 3

Dear Journal: Ka-ching! That's the sound of a cash register. Okay, so it's really a credit card authorization machine, approving yet another financial transaction that will get me one step closer to my goal of adopting my children. This morning I had my second inoculation for hepatitis at a local clinic.

When you are adopting, you get to a point where you really don't care about the money. In a sense, there's nothing you can do about it—if you want to adopt, you have to pay the price. Sure you can cut corners, but you have to weigh the risks. I've never had shots for any of the countries I've visited—Egypt, Israel, Peru, Russia, Mexico. I don't know if I'm doing this now since I'm older, and supposedly wiser, or if I'm worried what would happen to my little ones if I got sick and couldn't take care of them. Probably a little of both.

I circled November 20 in red on my calendar at work. I will be leaving in two and a half weeks. It seems as if everything needs to be done at once and I feel that I am drowning in quicksand and can't move a muscle. I'm sure it will all happen the way it is supposed to, but I am really ready to just relax somewhere with no phones, no computers and, most of all, no e-mail. I keep telling myself,

"Once you are back from Ukraine you can take a real vacation, somewhere warm and relaxing." That is one promise I will try very hard to keep.

CHECKLIST

❖ Visit medical clinic for hepatitis A and B shots (Fee: $90).

Wednesday, November 5

Dear Journal: I took a quick trip to the local mall tonight and bought two money belts—one for Donna and one for me. I only hope the bills don't stick out too much under our clothing. I also went to the local hair salon for a haircut. Then I started thinking. How many times am I going to be able to run out to the mall after dinner for a few hours? Will I have to lug my kids with me or beg a neighbor to baby-sit? I guess when you're pregnant, you get used to having another being inside of you, growing larger each month. When you adopt, it's a pretty radical transition. One day you're single and can go anywhere you want and the next day you have these two little children who can't even go to the bathroom without your help. Yikes! What have I gotten myself into?

Thursday, November 6

Dear Journal: Two weeks to go. I've booked our airline tickets and made reservations at a small hotel in London, England, for two nights. The city will be cold but very pretty with the stores full of their holiday decorations. I told Donna that it wasn't fair for me to drag her all the way to Ukraine on her first overseas trip without some small semblance of a grand tour, even if it is only one city.

Last night I met with John and we took an inventory of what needed to be done at my house. It took about 45 minutes to go through every room and make all the notes. John has already sent out an e-mail earmarking Saturday, December 13, as the date when all the volunteers will assemble at my house. I feel so fortunate that people I barely know are willing to help me. I hope I remember their generosity when I am asked to help others.

I was thinking of my cyber friend, Judy, today. She is still waiting to get her little girl from Guatemala. I feel a little guilty writing her about my good news as she actually started her process before I did. I've never met her but I feel as if I know her. I feel closer to her than I do some of my friends because of what we have both been going through these past nine months. I pray every day that her little girl comes home to her soon.

I bought a large folder to hold all my forms and documents and started a separate pile for all the papers that I will need to make copies of as well as things to pack, such as extra film and batteries. My bedroom looks like a war zone, and I haven't even started looking for my cold weather clothing.

CHECKLIST

♣ Purchase plane tickets to Ukraine; return
via Warsaw ($680 x 2).

Monday, November 10

Dear Journal: The days are just flying by now. I went to the bank on Friday during my lunch break and withdrew $20,000. I couldn't believe how thin the two envelopes were that I carried out of the bank. I had never seen $20,000 in cash before, and somehow I imagined the pile to be much thicker. I will give half the money to Donna to carry in her money belt, and I will keep the other half.

I spent the weekend working on the house and made some good progress. The walls and most of the ceilings are painted, but there is much more to be done. I brought my work clothes with me today so I could do more painting after work, but it was 9 p.m. when I finished running some errands, and I just couldn't convince myself to drive back to the house and do any painting.

I now have a big satchel in my closet into which I am tossing anything that I will need to take with me—extra batteries, shower shoes, and a CD player. Donna sent an e-mail today asking questions about the trip. She had a list of items that she had read were good to take with us, such as a portable alarm clock. Of course I have one, I told her, I just don't know where it is. I will never be ready. I'm already starting to have a nightmare that I'm on the plane to London, and all I can think about is what I didn't do. I know I am trying to do too much, but I can't stop the momentum now.

Only ten days left before I leave. My throat is feeling a little sore; I hope my health holds out. I had some hot tea after dinner tonight and am going to bed early.

Friday, November 14

Dear Journal: Less than a week before I leave and there is still so much to be done. Last night I wrote out all my bills and the dates they were due. I feel that I am in the eye of the storm with papers, lists and dirty clothes all swirling around me.

I've spent the past week with Sandra, a marketing consultant, who will take my place at work while I am gone. It has been a pretty intense week at the office. Every day I look at the calendar and see November 20 circled in red. I can't believe it's been three weeks since I got my travel date. I forwarded my itinerary to Victor today and asked him if I should bring any gifts with me. I've heard that many of the adoptive parents bring clothing and other hard-to-find items with them to Ukraine.

Everyone is asking me if I am excited about my trip. I must admit I really don't know how I feel right now. Part of me is terrified that I will freak out when I come home and realize I am responsible for two children, that I can't just go outside and putter around the house without getting the kids dressed and making sure they don't wander away. Then I think about my conversation with Sandra, the new consultant. She is 42, single and independent— very much like me. She loves to travel and has a wonderful life planned for herself. Why couldn't I be happy with my life the way it is? I hope I don't have any regrets.

Having spent all of my life responsible only for myself, I sometimes wonder what insane reasoning compelled me to adopt two children? I have no parenting skills to speak of, although, after being a manager for many years, I have definitely learned how to negotiate squabbles between people.

Saturday, November 15

Dear Journal: I went to one of my favorite sailing Web sites today. There is a section for boat owners seeking crew. Most of the ads are from men who are looking for a female companion to sail away with them into the sunset. I used to fantasize about sailing around the Caribbean with a handsome sailor. Every once in awhile one of the ads catches my attention and I think to myself, "I wonder if he likes children?" I don't know what my life will be like once I return from Ukraine. I'd like to think that one day I'll have my own boat, big enough to sail with my two little ones, and go anywhere in the world we choose to visit.

I've read about people having second thoughts right before a wedding. Perhaps this is my version of getting cold feet right before the trip. Maybe I shouldn't be writing in my journal at 11 p.m. after a tough week of work and two glasses of wine with dinner. It's getting late and I should get ready for bed. I haven't slept past 7 a.m. for the past few weeks, and I don't need my alarm to wake up. I guess my mind is so active it can't wait to start the day. I already have a long list of errands for tomorrow.

Sunday, November 16

Dear Journal: The PAX congregation gave me a special blessing for a safe and successful journey at Mass this morning. After the service, a number of the members came up to me to wish me well. It's a wonderful feeling to have so many people praying for you. I don't know if I would have been so bold as to ask people for their prayers if I hadn't tried it earlier this year. I had minor outpatient surgery in January, and, for the first time in my life, I sent out an e-mail asking friends and family to pray for my recovery. I firmly believe that one of the reasons the procedure was so successful was the positive energy that was sent my way. I have to believe it will work for me again.

I attended my first baby shower this evening at a friend's home. There were four couples plus my friend Jack and me. I was both surprised and deeply touched that they wanted to do this for me. We had a lovely dinner and afterwards came the gifts. I received several gift cards to local stores and a certificate from a store where you can take your children to make their own teddy bear.

I was really touched by the card and gift from Charlie, Jack's closest friend, and Charlie's girlfriend, Linda. She is in her 50s and has no children. Her work demands most of her energy, and what she has left goes to Charlie, but she has a wonderful mothering instinct about her, and I'm thrilled that she has taken such an interest in my upcoming journey. Linda had picked out two of her favorite books, *Twas the Night Before Christmas* and *Storybook Tales,* as gifts for my new children. The card that she gave me was so very appropriate it almost brought me to tears. It spoke to the love that one feels for new children when they enter your life.

Monday, November 17

Dear Journal: It was a busy day at the office as I continued to transition my work to Sandra. I headed to the house after work and spent a few hours painting and getting things ready for my friends from church to work on my house. I spoke with my Dad tonight and he told me that he supported me and would keep me in his prayers. I seem to cry at the drop of a hat these days. I guess all the emotions I have been harboring these past few months are now surfacing.

Tuesday, November 18

Dear Journal: I drove to the airport to meet Donna this evening after I finished my yoga class. We stayed up until 12:30 a.m. talking about the trip and discussing what we still needed to buy. It's only 48 hours until we leave and I'm starting to get butterflies in my stomach.

Wednesday, November 19

Dear Journal: Packing is in full swing, and the apartment is full of plastic baggies, cameras, clothes and paper work. I'm scrambling through all of the documents I've accumulated over the past year, deciding what I need to take with me on the trip. I sent a final e-mail to the adoption newsgroup to let them know I am leaving tomorrow and to tell them how grateful I am for all the information and support I have received from them.

Thursday, November 20

Dear Journal: I logged on to my e-mail early this morning, and I saw a reply to the e-mail I had sent last night. It was from Karen, a local woman who had traveled to Ukraine by herself last year and returned with two children, a seven-year-old boy and a five-year-old girl. The content of her message was chilling, and, after I spoke with her on the phone, my nerves were completely shot.

In our conversation, Karen told me about her children's behavioral problems that eventually caused her to quit a high-paying job. There were physical ailments she had to deal with as well; her son Alex had crossed eyes, and her daughter Tanya had a cleft palate. The kicker was that several weeks ago both children were diagnosed with Fetal Alcohol Syndrome (FAS). Karen went on to tell me about her experience in Ukraine. At one point, she met a couple whose facilitator told Karen that she could get two healthy children for $10,000. Karen was willing to pay the money, but her connection fell through, and she didn't find her children until the third visit to the NAC.

As we were conversing on the phone, my stomach was slowly beginning to churn. I couldn't believe I was hearing this on the day I was to leave on my trip. At the end of our conversation, Karen invited me to come to her house to collect some of the research she had accumulated about FAS and other medical related material. I gratefully accepted her kind offer.

I was totally overwhelmed between getting ready for the trip and having the phone conversation. I took a long, hot shower and calmed down enough to finish packing. By 5 p.m. my sister and I were in Jack's car and on our way. We arrived at Karen's and were greeted by her two adorable children. They were very friendly and spoke excellent English.

Karen, who had married earlier this year, is now a stay-at-home mom. She had good medical information to share with me, and I have to admit I felt embarrassed as she asked me question after question. "Do you have a growth chart?" "Do you have this or that?" And I said no to every one of them. I couldn't believe this woman who had recently received such devastating news about her children had the courage and kindness to contact me and give me all this information. I don't know what it was that led her to respond to my e-mail. Perhaps it reminded her of all the struggles she had endured.

Karen gave me a whole bag full of medicines, translation books and medical information. She also gave me her contact information and offered to help me find a doctor in Ukraine whom I could trust to give the children a thorough neurological exam before I committed to adopting them. Part of me was tremendously grateful she had shared this information with me, but there was another part of me that just wanted to ignore it, believing that it would never happen to me. I have to trust that the forces of the universe were at work here and that, if I heeded her advice, everything would turn out all right.

We made it to the airport with plenty of time to spare. For the first time in months I found myself sitting quietly, content in the knowledge that, finally, there was nothing more for me to do except to sit back and enjoy the ride.

Part II

TENDING THE GARDEN

Friday, November 21

Dear Journal: Our overnight flight to London was blissfully uneventful. It was so comforting to have Donna sitting next to me on the plane. We went over every detail of the trip again and again, making lists of things to remember once we arrived in Kiev. Now we were ready to play tourists in London for a few days.

Neither of us slept much on the plane and we had two meals in six hours. We were two weary but well-fed tourists as we traveled through the underground subway until we reached our hotel. It was 10:30 a.m. by the time we arrived at our room, but neither of us could fall asleep, so we opted to pack a day bag and explore the city.

We spent the day sight-seeing, taking in all the highlights—Hyde Park, Buckingham Palace, the Tower of London and a river boat cruise on the Thames. We ended up at Harrods and after half an hour of browsing, we finished the day with a nice meal at one of the local pubs. Once back at the hotel, we quickly settled in for the night.

Saturday, November 22

Dear Journal: We awoke to the sound of rain which remained constant throughout the day. Undeterred, we enjoyed a relaxing breakfast and set off to see more of London. We spent several hours trekking through the streets, admiring the statues and learning little tidbits of history, all despite a steady downpour.

By early afternoon we headed off to Kings Cross Train Station to catch the train to visit with my friend Jan. The train was clean and warm, something I can only hope for on the trains in Ukraine. We soon met up with Jan and headed off to Bourne where she lives with her four children—Samantha, Ellie, Nick, and Bethan. We spent the rest of the day and evening chatting and looking through family photos. By 9:30 p.m. we were both struggling to keep our eyes open, so we headed upstairs for the night.

Sunday, November 23

Dear Journal: We didn't get up until 9 a.m. this morning—a sure sign that we were catching up on our sleep. Donna and I caught an early afternoon train back to London and arrived at Westminster Abbey with just enough time to light a prayer candle and leave before they locked the gates behind us for evening service. We had talked about going to the Ritz for high tea, but, with dusk approaching and the rain still falling, we opted for a quick meal of fish and chips at a small shop near our hotel.

We spent several hours repacking our luggage and went to bed early so we would be well-rested for our 5 a.m. wake-up. It is now 9 p.m. and neither of us can sleep. I'm not sure if the fried fish and chips are to blame for my insomnia or the fact that tomorrow I will be getting on a plane that will take me on the trip of a lifetime. I feel caught up tidal wave that is sweeping me forward, and, even if I tried, I couldn't stop the momentum. I am both excited and very frightened. I have no idea what will happen to me in the next few days. I keep telling myself to offer up all my fears and worries to God, putting my faith in Him that everything will work out all right.

Monday, November 24

Dear Journal: Five a.m. came awfully early. I had asked for a wake-up call (never got it), set the alarm in the room (never went off) and as an extra precaution used my tiny travel alarm clock (worked perfectly). Donna and I took the Heathrow Express back to the airport, and, with three large suitcases on wheels, two carry ons, two backpacks and our winter coats, we literally had our hands full every minute of the journey.

The plane held a mixture of English and Russian-speaking passengers. What really surprised me on the two and a half hour flight was that red wine was the beverage of choice for breakfast, and cognac was the preferred after meal drink. I couldn't believe it when I heard the beverage requests, but the stewardess didn't blink an eye as she handed out the bottles. I know alcoholism is a major problem in some Eastern European countries, but this was a bit much.

Today I was reminded that there is a big difference between sitting in front of your computer talking about adopting two children and actually doing it. The term "armchair traveler" came to mind as Donna and I were rolling our luggage through Boryspil airport. We had no trouble going through immigration, but hit a bit of a snag at customs. I had heard it was a good idea to find a female agent, someone who might be sympathetic to the idea that I was coming to adopt orphans and who would let us pass without questioning us about the amount of money we were bringing with us. We found a female agent and she was anything but sympathetic. We were hustled into a separate room where we had to show her all the money we were carrying. We each had $10,000 in our money belts, and I had a few hundred extra dollars in my fanny pack. For a moment I started to panic as I wasn't sure I had written down on the customs form the exact amount of money I had in my fanny pack. After the agent was convinced we weren't smugglers, she used sign language to indicate that we had to show her everything else we were carrying, including prescription drugs, before she would let us pass through.

We spilled into a large waiting room full of aggressive taxi drivers and hapless emissaries holding small white placards with the names of their passengers. Donna and I finally met up with Victor after waiting over an hour in the crowded room. He was a medium-built man in his late 50s or early 60s with thick glasses, and he looked as if he hadn't shaved for a few days. His clothing was clean but rumpled, and he wore a cap on his head, as did most of the men in the airport.

We left the airport and piled into his rusty, 30 year old Russian-built car. I began peppering him with questions as he sped down the road. I was disappointed when he told me that Svitlana, who was to have been my facilitator, was still working with another American woman. A man by the name of Yuri would replace her. I asked Victor how long Yuri had been working with adoptions and he replied three years.

The tourist hotel that we checked into was nice and clean. Victor escorted us to our room and then sat down in one of the chairs. He told me that I was not to discuss financial terms with anyone except him, nor was I to mention his name at the NAC or other government agencies. Victor explained that he was responsible for many adoptions, and sometimes it was thought that he represented too many people. I thought it was a strange request, but it didn't matter too much either way. Then Victor said, "Now it is time for you to pay." All I could think about was one of those cold war spy movies where bundles of money were exchanged for state secrets in a dingy hotel room somewhere in Eastern Europe. In this case the money was being used to pay for the adoption of two children. I carefully counted out $4,500 in crisp, new $100 bills from my money belt—$4000 for Victor and $500 as an orphanage donation to be managed by Cathy Harris.

I feel as if I am here on a business trip with my paperwork and schedule of meetings. I have done that dozens of times, but the stakes have never been quite this high. The lives of two little children are hanging in the balance, as well as my own future. I keep thinking about Karen and the tone in her voice as she shared with me the challenges she faces every day—for the rest of her life. I re-read the material she gave to me, and I plan to take it with me to the NAC on Wednesday.

After unpacking, we spent an hour in the Internet room located in the hotel lobby to let our friends and family know we had arrived safely. The rest of the day was spent exploring the local markets and relaxing. It's now 8:30 p.m. and I can barely keep my eyes open. I continue to pray that I receive the proper guidance in my selection of children. Second visits to the NAC for those who choose not to adopt their first selected child can take up to two weeks to schedule. At that rate, it could be the end of January before we return home since the NAC is closed between December 19 and January 12. For now I will settle for a good night's sleep.

Tuesday, November 25

Dear Journal: This was the first morning since we left on our trip that we could relax. We had nowhere to go and no one to please but ourselves until 11 a.m. when we were scheduled to meet Yuri, my facilitator. He turned out to be pleasant-looking, tall, in his 40s, with dark hair and warm, engaging eyes. After we introduced ourselves, he offered to act as our tour guide as soon as we had finished our business for the day, and I gladly accepted his offer. Donna wasn't feeling well and almost didn't join us, but I convinced her that some fresh air would help her and she relented.

It took us only a few minutes to walk from the hotel to the metro going into the city center. The subway cars are very crowded—it costs only ten cents to ride the train. People were selling goods as they walked through the cars: household items, small toys as well as beautiful calendars with brightly colored religious paintings depicting the Russian Orthodox saints. I bought several calendars for less than a dollar each.

Our first stop was at the notary office so I could sign a document giving Yuri power of attorney for the adoption process. I had already done this for Svitlana as part of my dossier documents. Since she was no longer involved in my adoption, this had to be redone. It felt odd signing a document that was totally in Russian. Yuri, as my facilitator, will guide me through the adoption process and stay with me until all the paperwork is complete and I am ready to travel back home.

Donna, Yuri and I spent the next two hours sightseeing at St. Mary's Church and the surrounding complex of buildings and caves. The compound is located high on a hill overlooking Kiev and the Dnipro River that runs north and south, cutting the city in half. We decided to join a tour to view the caves where the monks had lived and were buried. It was very interesting although we didn't learn much from the guide as she spoke only Russian and Yuri's translation was minimal.

There is a marked difference in the way people dress here. The old people, especially the women, walk with a cane and have stooped shoulders. Most of them wear a head scarf, short boots and cloth coats with fur collars. Women in their thirties and forties have fur hats and long fur or leather coats. These women wear more makeup and have carefully groomed hair. Younger women in their twenties tend to wear stylish caps and short leather coats and jackets with small bits of fur trim. Older men wear fur hats, and all the men, regardless of age, are dressed in black leather jackets. Yuri said that most people in Ukraine are terrified of retirement because the old-age pensions are so small. Ukraine has been independent for only 13 years and it is still learning how to deliver social services in a country where very few people pay taxes on what they really earn.

Once we finished our tour, we decided to take the local bus back to the downtown area. We stopped off to see the Parliament building and the Presidential Palace. It was nice to walk around and get some fresh air. The weather was not too bad—the temperature hovered in the 40s and the sky was overcast. I continued to ask Yuri about the Ukrainian Mafia, the NAC, his prior adoptions and what the remainder of the trip would be like. My first impression was that I could trust him, which was important considering we would be totally dependent upon him for the next several weeks.

It was very disturbing to hear him talk about people who were willing to trade their children to the Mafia for drugs or alcohol, but it was also very reassuring to hear him say that this would not happen at the orphanages.

I've been in this country for only 24 hours, and I already feel as if I'm a million miles away from home.

We stopped at a large cafeteria in downtown Kiev around 3 p.m. to eat. After we finished our meal, Yuri suggested that we buy some perfume as a gift for the female psychologist at the NAC. He said they would prefer we give them cash, but they were afraid to accept it for fear of getting caught. According to Yuri, these so-called psychologists are very rude and are unhappy with their jobs. Only ten appointments are granted each day, and I will have only an hour or two to look through all the children's files.

It was almost 4:30 p.m. when we finished up and headed back to the hotel. Yuri will be staying there tonight in a room down the hall. Before we went back to the hotel, we went across the street to the little market shop and bought some bottled water, juice and a bottle of wine. The street markets were full of delicious and exotic looking food, clothing, kitchen gadgets and everything else you can imagine.

Back at the hotel, we invited Yuri to come to our room later in the evening to share the wine with us. By this time the night had already settled upon the city and the sky was dark. We decided it was time to empty out the laundry bag and wash out some undergarments and shirts. I had a feeling we would be doing a lot of hand washing on this trip. I felt relatively calm. I had prepared as much as possible for my meeting at the NAC. Every once in a while a shadow of doubt entered my mind and I tried to chase it from my thoughts as quickly as possible. One of hardest things to reconcile about this process is knowing that everyone's experience is so different. While we were at the notary this morning we ran into George, another one of Victor's facilitators. He was all smiles and full of positive stories about the people he had helped to adopt children. And then Karen's situation came flooding back into my consciousness.

They say God never gives you more than you are capable of handling with His help, and I pray that is true. I want to believe that whatever problems my adoptive children have, they will never cause me to stop loving them. I have to put my faith in God that I will select the right children tomorrow.

Yuri came to our room around 9:30 p.m., and I talked about what ailments I could deal with such as crossed eyes, clef palates and missing limbs. Then we talked more about the adoption process, and what life in Ukraine was like for most people. Yuri showed us pictures of his family, including his wife and daughter. I was surprised when he told us that he and his wife had adopted an infant girl. She's eight years old now, and they haven't told her that she is adopted. The adoption process he went through sounded very simple compared to what I have to do before I can return home with my children.

Yuri's full time job is working for a women's rights organization that focuses on abolishing white slavery. Living in the U.S., I find it very hard to believe that this disgraceful practice still exists. According to Yuri, young women are lured abroad with the incentive of a good job. Their passports are then taken from them, and they are forced into prostitution in a foreign country where they have no money and can't speak the language. I asked Yuri what happens to the ringleaders when they are arrested. He told me it is very difficult to prosecute them because there are no laws against what they are doing.

Yuri also told us about the history of Ukraine and how the country has changed since the collapse of the Soviet Union. He said Ukraine was torn between working closely with the U.S. and its European allies or Russia. Many people believe the Russian Mafia has infiltrated the entire country and has members in parliament and in most large businesses. These "new Russians," as they are called, drive

Mercedes and wear custom tailored suits. He told us about a former Ukrainian president who is in prison in the U.S. for extorting millions of dollars during his term. It was a very plausible story given the lack of government controls. The sad thing is that thousands of children in this country are pawns in this game and often end up the losers.

Wednesday, November 26

Dear Journal: The morning began just like any other morning, even though in many ways it will be the most special day of my life. After breakfast, it was time to get ready for my 11: 30 a.m. appointment at the NAC. Donna and I put on our best clothes and makeup, and I carefully reviewed all the documents in my file for the umpteenth time. I was very nervous but was trying hard to stay calm. One of the hardest things for me to deal with here is the lack of people who speak English. I have traveled to many foreign countries, but this is one of the few times I truly feel totally dependent upon someone else to take me around the city. How was I going to make myself understood at the NAC?

Donna, Yuri and I took the metro again and walked a short way to the Ministry of Education where the NAC is located. It is a very unobtrusive looking gray building. We turned into a small alley, and, as we approached the entrance, Yuri went inside to a small window to register me for my appointment. Later on, he told me that he wrote my name on line number 13, and it made him very nervous, wondering if this was a bad omen. I'm glad he didn't tell me about this until after our visit was over.

We walked up four flights of stairs to a small hallway and sat down. The only other people in the small waiting room were an Italian couple. After a ten-minute wait, the longest ten minutes I have ever waited, Donna, Yuri, the Italian couple and I were all ushered into the office. We all walked down a long hallway in silence and were told to go into the last room on the left at the end of the corridor.

The room was empty except for three small, old desks with several chairs around each desk. The Italian couple sat down with a female psychologist, and we sat at the middle table with Vlad, the male psychologist. He was an older gentleman with graying hair, and his right hand shook uncontrollably at times. He greeted Yuri while totally ignoring Donna and me. Yuri sat in the center chair, and Donna and I were on either side of him. Vlad didn't speak to us or even look at us to acknowledge our presence. I thought we were in for a bad ride.

The Italian couple were already looking at pictures in a red binder, but Vlad held on to the binder at our desk. He made comments to Yuri as he leafed through the pages. The first thing he told Yuri was that it would be impossible for me to adopt two children since I was unmarried. I remembered the advice I had been given by folks in the adoption e-mail newsgroup to be firm but polite. So I immediately whispered to Yuri to tell Vlad that the NAC had accepted my two dossiers, and that allowed me to adopt two unrelated children. Yuri had warned me that many people know more English than they admit to, so I should be careful what I say. Then Vlad said that it would be impossible to adopt two young, healthy children. I figured he was testing me to see how I would react. I simply asked Yuri to request the binder from Vlad so we could view the files.

Yuri took possession of the binder, and we started looking at the files of all the children ages one to three. All of children had some type of disorder; Hepatitis C, AIDS and mental illness. Many of them were also diagnosed with heart disease or a disease of the central nervous system, whatever that means. Every time Yuri turned the page, it broke my heart to know that I was leaving that child behind.

Suddenly a young American couple burst into the room carrying a young, healthy, looking girl. They had brought flowers for the female psychologist as a thank you for helping them find their child. I saw Vlad smile at this exchange, and I hoped I could use this opportunity to break the ice with him. I asked several times if there were any new children (children that had just become available for adoption), but Vlad kept saying that these were all of the available children. He never offered to show me the binder of siblings, which I knew existed as I had read many accounts of it from other adoptive parents.

Yesterday, I had asked Yuri how many children were orphaned in Ukraine. He said there were thousands of children, but the majority of children were too ill to be considered for adoption. The truth is that no one knows exactly how many children are in orphanages and, of those, how many are truly available for adoption. Some parents leave their children at the orphanage because they are too poor to raise them, but they retain parental custody. They are required to visit the child at least once every six months, or the child will be put on the list for adoption, but I have heard stories of parents not visiting their children for several years. These children languish for years with no hope of having a permanent family life.

All the photos in the red binder were very small—less than passport size. They were taken when the child was brought to the orphanage, so most of them were grossly out of date. Vlad told Yuri that many of the children in these binders had been looked at by other people and had been rejected. A child must be at least 14 months old before foreigners can adopt him unless he has a severe medical condition. The idea behind this is to allow Ukrainians the opportunity to adopt the child and keep him in the country.

As I leafed through the pages, I saw a picture of the sweetest looking boy. He had strawberry blond hair and blue-gray eyes. He was mute and the file indicated that his mother had been diagnosed as being mentally ill. Yuri asked Vlad some questions about the boy, but he was very negative in his response. He said that the boy was also mentally ill, and that was why he was mute. I didn't believe him. But I also knew that if I picked this child and then decided not to adopt him, it would set me back at least one week, possibly two, running the risk that I might not complete the process before the holidays.

I felt very shallow and guilty about rejecting him. There was something in his eyes that just drew me to him. Perhaps it was because he looked like my brother John when he was very young. Yet I knew that as a single parent, I had limits to what I could do, especially as I wanted to adopt two children. So I let Yuri turn the page, forever closing the door on this innocent little boy, but the image of his face remained in my mind for the rest of the day. Multiply this experience by a hundred and you will come close to understanding how I felt.

One of the reasons I decided to adopt from Ukraine was so I could select my children instead of having them pre-selected for me; however, I wasn't prepared for the guilt I felt as I decided to pass up child after child. An hour later we had looked through three binders with no success. Then I noticed Vlad had two individual sheets of paper under his hand. I asked Yuri if we could look at them and Vlad handed them over. One sheet described an 18-month old boy in the Kiev region, which has very high expediting fees. The other sheet had an 18-month old girl in the Lugansk region near the Russian border. Both children had become available for adoption yesterday. This was a big decision. Adopting two children from different regions is very expensive and time consuming, and I really didn't want to do it. Then Vlad told Yuri that I couldn't get a referral to see both children. He said I would have to chose one, and then I could return if I wanted to adopt the other child as well. Vlad said that I would be allowed to see other children at the girl's orphanage. There were over 100 children there, and at least five of them were available for adoption. I asked Yuri if he believed Vlad was telling the truth and Yuri said yes. Vlad said that the little girl was very healthy although she had been born two months prematurely. The picture of her was very small. She appeared to have a small rash on her forehead, but Donna and I couldn't see if she displayed any FAS symptoms.

It was now 1 p.m. and the Italian couple was long gone although the woman psychologist who had worked with them was still in the room. Afterwards, Yuri explained that it was she who insisted that he would need to return to the NAC if I found a second child in Lugansk instead of sending a faxed request. I decided to select the girl, Tamara, since other children were available at her orphanage. I had to believe that my forever children were waiting for me there. Towards the end of the meeting, the female psychologist got up and put several of the red binders in a small locked drawer before leaving the room. Was that where the binder with all the healthy children was located? I doubted I would ever find out.

As we left the room, I took Vlad's hand and shook it, telling him thank you in Russian. Yuri offered to give Vlad $100 as we left the office, but he declined the offer. Yuri said he thought it was because Vlad was afraid of getting fired if he were caught by his superiors accepting a gift.

It was 1:15 p.m. by the time we left the building. The only emotion I can remember having was a sense of gratitude that the meeting was over, and that I had found a child who appeared healthy. We had some free time before Yuri had to return to the NAC to make copies of my dossier, so we went across the street to visit St. Vladamir Church. It was stunningly beautiful inside—every square inch was painted with images of the Madonna and Christ. Donna and I bought candles and placed them in front of the Madonna and Child portrait. I said a prayer of thanks that my meeting had gone well and I had found a child.

Donna and I then headed back to our hotel via the metro on our first solo outing since arriving in Kiev on Monday. She was nervous about finding our way back, but I knew we would find the hotel without any trouble. I saw several men walking in the street with open bottles of beer. Yuri's wife, who is a teacher, had told him that many children in her school drink alcohol and take drugs. What a sad thing to hear. I reminded myself of how fortunate I was to live in a country that has a social structure where men and women have the opportunity to lead productive and fulfilling lives. Even though we have issues with alcoholism and drugs, we have many resources in place to minimize the impact of these problems upon the lives of children.

Once Donna and I arrived in our hotel room, we dumped our coats and backpacks and headed back to the Internet room. I wanted to share the good news with all of my friends and family that I was on my way to finding my forever children. I felt as if I were in a dream. It was all happening so matter of factly that I had to pinch myself. Was it really going to be this easy?

We then returned to our room to wait for Yuri who was going to meet us for a late lunch. By the time he arrived, Donna was not feeling well again, so Yuri and I went downstairs to the cafeteria for a quick bite to eat. Yuri is a very nice man, and I am glad he is our facilitator. He is taking good care of us, even walking with me to the market across the street to buy some bottled water and bread for my sister. He isn't obligated to spend any time with us other than for official adoption functions, but he seems to bond quickly with the families he works with to adopt children. Last night he came over to our room wearing a Michigan Wolverine shirt and sweat pants. He has been invited to the States by many of the couples he has helped, and I believe they would welcome him with open arms. He appears to be very honest and forthright in his dealings with me, and I admire him for that.

Later, Donna was feeling well enough to snack on some bread, cheese and fruit we had bought at the market. Food is extremely cheap and plentiful in Kiev. I bought four bananas and four apples in the open market for just over one dollar. Tonight I am being lazy, reading one of the novels we brought and snacking on chocolate. This has been a very big day for me, and I know many hurdles are still ahead. Still, a big part of me is relieved that I have found a child and can start the adoption process soon.

Yuri needed our passports to buy the train tickets for our travel tomorrow. When I asked him why they were needed since it was a domestic trip, he simply turned to me as he was walking out the door, threw up his arms and said, "It's Ukraine!" That said it all. Later he called to say that there were no train tickets available. He was told to return to the station early tomorrow when tickets might be available. I have a feeling these tickets will come with a surcharge attached.

Thursday, November 27

Dear Journal: Happy Thanksgiving from Kiev! Donna and I spent the morning eating breakfast, repacking our bags and e-mailing friends and family about our news. I still don't feel any emotion when I think about Tamara. I've read many stories about people who look at a child and know right away whether that child is meant to be theirs. I hope that is what I feel when I see her tomorrow. I pray I will know if she will become my daughter.

Yuri came by around 1 p.m. and we decided to go downtown to have something to eat. He got our train tickets although each one cost an extra $2. It seems that there is an expediting fee connected to everything in this country. We found a favorite spot of his and sat down for a hearty meal. Afterwards, he went back to the NAC to get my referral letter, and Donna and I navigated the streets on our own as we made our way back to the hotel.

Victor picked us up at 4 p.m. sharp to go to the train station. It seemed to take us forever as we crept along with the busy street traffic. I kept looking at my watch to make sure we arrived in plenty of time to board our overnight train to Lugansk. The train was fairly clean, but it did not have a dining car. We had stocked up on supplies earlier in the day so we would have enough food and water to carry us through tomorrow morning. The train toilets had been the subject of many e-mails in the adoption newsgroup, especially among the woman. The description was pretty accurate—dirty, cold, and smelly. The train was stifling warm and loud music was playing from the corridor speakers.

We passed the time talking and finishing off the rest of the wine from the previous night. Our compartment had four long benches, two on each side with an upper and lower bunk. We had to pay separately for sheets and blankets, but it was worth the extra two dollars. Yuri made up all of our beds, and then he waited outside while we changed into our sweats for the night. I really don't know what to expect when we arrive at the orphanage tomorrow. Will I bond with Tamara? Will I feel any emotional connection to her at all?

Friday, November 28

Dear Journal: We arrived in Lugansk around 8:30 a.m. It was a chilly, gray morning, and I was tired, hungry and cold. We unloaded the luggage onto the train platform, and Yuri negotiated with one of the taxi drivers to take us on our errands. It would have been nice to sit down and relax in a café with a hot breakfast, but we had too much to do.

Donna and I had worn our jeans and sneakers yesterday so we would be comfortable on the train. I didn't realize that we wouldn't have time to change clothes for our meeting at the orphanage. So in addition to wearing yesterday's clothing with no chance of a morning bath, we rode in a taxi that smelled of some type of solvent. We ended up keeping the windows open so the cold air could eliminate the fumes. It was a miserable, long ride.

We drove over 30 miles to a small town called Slavyanoserbsk where we needed to get a signature from the Inspector of the Department of Education of the District Administration. This is the government agency in charge of the orphanages. Sonia, the inspector, was not available so her secretary signed the letter giving us permission to visit the orphanage. It was 11:30 a.m. before we headed off to the orphanage. I felt like I was being hijacked. Yuri was in complete control and I was totally dependent on him. How would I be able to decide if Tamara was the right child? I had to keep telling myself that it would all work out the way it was supposed to.

After driving miles and miles through open fields, we arrived at the orphanage in Lotikovo. The houses in this tiny town were small, well kept and close together. We drove into a large compound of bleak, gray buildings and stopped in the courtyard where we saw a playground with swings. The driver parked the car and I looked at Donna. I had never been so nervous. This was the moment I had been waiting for all these months. I grabbed my binder full of the medical information from Karen and we went inside.

Natalie, the orphanage doctor, and Oxana, the orphanage director, greeted us at the door. Both women looked quite young—mid to late 20s. Natalie was petite with short blond hair and heavy eye make-up. Oxana was taller with short dark hair. It was nice and warm inside as we made our way to Natalie's office. I had stopped off to go to the bathroom, and, when I entered the office, Donna was holding Tamara. She was a sweet looking girl, very small for an 18-month old and still unable to walk on her own. She had wispy blond hair and was wearing a sleeper outfit. She had a cold but didn't fuss at all. I have to admit that my heart sank as soon as I saw her. Natalie insisted that she was healthy and that there was no record that her mother was an alcoholic, yet when I looked at Tamara I saw several of the facial characteristics of FAS. I pulled out the papers Karen had given to me. She had a very low bridge on her nose and didn't have the two vertical lines between her nose and mouth. She had a very thin upper lip, and I couldn't get her to focus her eyes on me. Her eyes were slightly droopy, but that could have been because of her cold. I looked at Donna and asked her what she thought. She tried to be positive but she agreed that Tamara had many of the symptoms described in Karen's material.

It was time to make a decision. All I could think about was the conversation with Karen and her words of warning. I didn't have the luxury to wait for a doctor to examine Tamara, and I didn't want to wait a week to ponder my decision. I told Yuri that I would not accept her. I felt as if I were looking at a fabric sample and had to decide if I wanted to buy the whole bolt without seeing what was under all the folds. There was a big knot in my stomach when I looked at Tamara, and I knew I couldn't take the chance she had FAS. I heard Natalie say something about Americans to Yuri but I was resolved in my mind with my decision. The whole meeting lasted about 30 minutes, long enough for me to decide that Tamara and I would never see each other again. I felt very sad for her. I wished with all my heart that I had a home and the resources to care for her regardless of her disability, but that is not the case. So I took a deep breath and handed Tamara back to Natalie.

Part of the reason I accepted this referral was that other children were available for adoption at the orphanage. I asked if there were any other girls and Natalie said, "Nyet, only boys." I didn't believe her but there wasn't much I could do about it. Ukraine is very different from the U.S. Here you must accept what you are told, and it is not possible to argue with officials. Everything is so decentralized, and there is no customer service representative or local congressman to handle your complaints.

We walked into another section of the building and entered the small hallway. I could hear children playing in the next room. They told me there were three boys available, rather than the five children that Vlad, the NAC psychologist, had said I would find there. Two of the boys were relatively healthy, and the third child needed surgery on his feet. The first boy they brought in for me to meet was named Sergei. He was a handsome looking boy, two-and-a-half-years-old, with blond hair and blue eyes. His parents had given him up for adoption when he was two months old because he had hydrocephalus, a condition that causes fluid to build up in the brain. He was operated on a year and a half ago and a shunt was inserted into the back of his head to drain the fluid to his stomach. According to Natalie, his health had improved greatly since the surgery. I could feel the shunt when I ran my hand over the back of his head.

Sergei was rather shy but he came and sat on my knee. I was sitting cross-legged on the floor so I could have good eye contact with him. Donna and I played with him for about 30 minutes, checking his motor skills and asking questions about his health. I tickled him and he laughed. I have to admit there was not an instant "wow," but I did feel comfortable with him. He didn't speak at all and only grunted or made gestures to communicate.

I asked if we could see the second boy, Nikita, who had a problem with his left eye. In contrast to Sergei, Nikita had dark brown hair and brown eyes. He was two months older than Tamara and he was very active. His vision appeared to be fine, but it was evident that his left eye did not track properly. He was very serious looking, but when I gave him one of the toys to play with, he walked over and sat on my lap and smiled. He didn't speak either, and I assumed both boys were developmentally delayed due to the lack of nurturing at the orphanage.

Nikita had good eye contact and good eye-to-hand coordination. Another couple had seen him last month but decided not to adopt him because of his eye problem, but I felt that even if he ended up blind in one eye, that would be okay with me. For me, a physical disability was not a problem at all. I would have taken him even if he were blind in both eyes. Both of the boys were very cute and pleasant. I really wanted a little girl, but I knew that would not be possible unless I was willing to return to Kiev and wait for another appointment at the NAC. I had to believe that fate was handing me two very sweet boys who needed a home. I knew I could always adopt a little girl later on if I really wanted to have a daughter.

Yuri was asking me again "Will you adopt these two boys?"

I looked at Donna and took a deep breath. I looked back at Yuri and simply said, "Yes." We left the boys and went directly to Oxana's office where she gave us more information about the boys. It felt strange leaving them, but I don't think it had really sunk in yet that these two boys were going to become my children. I learned that Nikita's mother was 27 when he was born. I assume she was unmarried, but I don't know for sure. Sergei was the first child born to his mother, but they didn't know her age. I assume she was fairly young. His parents were married, and he had been a wanted child. I can only guess as to why he was given up for adoption. Perhaps his parents couldn't afford the medical treatment, knowing that he might need surgery.

Yuri asked me again if I was sure I wanted to adopt the boys. At this point I had spent about 30 minutes with each child, and now I started to ask more questions. "Were they potty trained?" and "Could they eat by themselves?" The answer to both questions was yes. Oxana said they were eating lunch now and agreed to let me see them one last time before I made my final decision. We peeked into the playroom, and the children were sitting at the little table wearing huge plastic, orange bibs that were tucked under their food. Each child had a huge soup spoon and was eating a thick soup with onions and perhaps some other vegetables.

I walked back to the office and told Yuri I was ready to adopt both boys. So it was done. Very businesslike but also very unreal. Then it was time for us to leave. There were other people waiting to meet with Oxana, and we still needed to get the inspector's signature and find a place to stay for the next few weeks. We had to pile back into the same stinky taxi and drive another 30 minutes back to the first town we had visited.

The impact of what I had just done did not register in my mind for several hours. It didn't seem possible that it had happened so quickly. There were no questions from

Oxana about my background or ability to care for the children. To her, I was just another foreigner looking for children to adopt; for me, it was one of the most important decisions I will ever make.

Yuri was able to make arrangements with Ina, the inspector's secretary, for us to stay with her at her flat in town. I guess it was not unusual for Ukrainians to make their flats available to foreigners, especially those who were there to adopt children. There were no hotels in Slavyanoserbsk, and Lugansk was too far away as we would be traveling to the orphanage each day.

Ina is in her mid-fifties, slightly plump, with bleached blond hair. She lives by herself. Her flat is on the third floor of a seven-story concrete apartment building that has as much style as a brown shipping box. She has two bedrooms (Donna and I will share one, and Yuri will use the second room). Ina will sleep on the coach in the living room. Her cat, Maxine (Max for short), has been dislodged from his favorite lounging spot on our bed, a fact I'm sure he's not likely to let us forget during our stay.

It was early afternoon before we got settled into the apartment and realized how hungry we were. We walked down the street to the local market shop. It was a large open room with shelves all along the wall behind the counters. Only the basics were available—eggs, juice, fruit, sausage, cheese, milk and bread. We bought enough food for lunch and breakfast and then headed back to the flat. Once we returned, Yuri started making calls to the inspector's office. He was very upset to learn that she would not sign the letter we needed to take to the NAC until Tuesday. It would take two more days for them to process the petition for me to adopt the boys. That meant we couldn't ask for a court date until next Friday at the earliest.

We spent the rest of the afternoon unpacking and relaxing. The weight of my decision to adopt the boys grew heavier throughout the day. Was I making the right decision? Was I sure neither boy had any FAS symptoms? I still felt that I was sleepwalking and that I would soon wake up in my own bed and marvel at the strange dream I had had.

Yuri told us that Ina wanted $35 per day for lodging, and we would have to buy and prepare all our own meals. He thought that was too much. I asked him what would be a reasonable fee and he said $15 to $20 per day. Later, when she returned from work, Yuri was able to negotiate her down to $30 per day, but that was still very expensive in a country where the average salary is $50 per month.

Yuri had scoped out the two cafes in town—the miserable one (as he called it) and the less miserable one where we ended up eating dinner. The café was very tiny with four tables in an enclosed patio and three tables inside. It was very basic fare, but good tasting and cheap. We started with a salad of beetroot with mayonnaise. Our entrée was pork steak dipped in egg batter and fried, along with mashed potatoes and shredded carrots. We washed it all down with some good Ukrainian beer called Taller. The total for four beers and three meals was $7.

I had read adoption stories in which the orphanage director allowed children to leave the orphanage before the court hearing, but I did not think this would be the case with us. Yuri planned to call Oxana tomorrow to get permission for us to visit the boys over the weekend. Part of me still hoped for a girl, but I knew there was a grand plan in place for my two boys and me. It's a strange feeling to suddenly be responsible for two young children. I kept telling Donna how glad I was that she was with me, since this would have been an even tougher day without her help.

As I look back on today's events, I feel lost in a fog. Everything at the orphanage today seemed so matter-of-fact. I'm relieved, not elated, that I have found my children. I'm still nervous about the boys' medical conditions. I have to believe that everything will work out the way it is supposed to happen.

Saturday, November 29

Dear Journal: I didn't sleep well at all last night. I went to our room around 9 p.m. to do some reading. When I finally turned out the light, my mind started whirling, and I couldn't stop thinking what-ifs about the boys' health. I decided to read some more and finally drifted off to sleep early in the morning.

Yuri had already cooked our breakfast by the time we were dressed. I swear if he weren't married I would bring him home to the States with me. It was another cold, gray day, and all I could think about was escaping to a tropical beach to rest under an umbrella. I know that sounds strange, but the enormity of what I have done is very scary and part of me desperately wants to retreat to a safe haven.

We arrived at the orphanage and greeted the boys while Yuri left to make phone calls. Sergei seemed to recognize us, but Nicki was just happy to play and have some attention. An Italian couple was there with their new son, who looked to be about three-years-old. The boys seemed very happy; I kept looking at Nicki to make sure I didn't see any symptoms of FAS. I am starting to look at them differently now, not as orphans, but as my children. I'm still very nervous about my decision to adopt the boys. What will happen if it turns out Nicki has FAS? I will already have adopted him by then. Sergei, on the other hand, is so sweet and quiet. He will sit on my lap and play with a toy for the longest time. Soon afterwards, Yuri came back into the room and said he had made an appointment for us to meet Sonia, the inspector, at noon. He needed to have her write the letter in which I will state that I am rejecting Tamara for adoption. He told me he may be able to get it signed this weekend but it would cost $200.

We met Sonia at her office, which was very small and sparsely furnished. Sonia is in her mid-to-late 30s with short blond hair. She and Yuri spoke a while before she turned on her computer, typed up a letter and printed it. Yuri then asked me to handwrite a letter stating that I didn't want to adopt Tamara. I wrote that I believed she had FAS. He then translated the letter into Russian and told us to go downstairs and wait for him. Yuri said afterwards that Sonia acted surprised when he handed her the $200, although she quickly took it from him and put it in her purse. He also said that Sonia would try to get the administrator to sign the letter tomorrow so he could travel back to the NAC in Kiev. Such bureaucracy.

We went to several shops to buy more food after our meeting with Sonia. Yuri had promised to make borsht for us, so we went from market to market, buying all the ingredients: pork, carrots, garlic and beets. The only thing we couldn't find was sour cream. I couldn't believe how barren the shop shelves were in this town. The clerks in the shop used an abacus, something I haven't seen in years, to calculate the total cost of our groceries.

Ina's daughter and her husband were at the flat when we returned. I was not in the mood to chat, so I picked up my book and went into the bedroom. I really wanted to be alone and collect my thoughts. This whole process seems so surreal. I still can't believe I'm going to be the mother of two little boys. I have no idea what Sergei and Nicki are really like. All I know is what I've gathered in the few hours from seeing them in the orphanage.

The TV was on all day, and it was hard to escape the loud noise. The Russian game and variety shows are the worst. Donna suggested we play cards, so the three of us cracked open a new deck and we played gin rummy. Then Yuri decided that he couldn't make the borsht without the sour cream, so we decided to return to the little café in the town square for dinner.

Back at Ina's, I tried to stay interested in the TV shows but couldn't deal with it, so I went back to our bedroom to read my book. I was grateful we had something to read. I needed something to keep my mind off the day's events. I kept thinking about all the adoption stories I had read where people immediately say, "This is my child" moments after meeting him or her for the first time. I am still waiting to feel that bond and am starting to second-guess myself. I pray I am doing the right thing.

Yuri told us about an Amish couple he had worked with who first agreed to adopt a six-year-old girl and her two-and-a-half-year-old brother. Then they changed their minds and opted for a seven-year-old boy. They changed their minds again without explaining why. Victor was able to convince the couple to adopt the seven-year-old. Yuri said he had written several letters to that couple but never received any response. I don't want to change my mind. I hope I will feel better about the boys after a good night's sleep.

Sunday, November 30

Dear Journal: Another night of not sleeping well. I tried several relaxation techniques and finally went to sleep around 1 a.m. Yuri was already up and cooking in the kitchen when we awoke. He had gotten up at 7:30 a.m. to go out and buy fresh cow's milk for breakfast. I have to admit I felt as if I were transported back 100 years when I heard that. He was cooking kashi, a traditional meal of milk, rice, vanilla and raisins. It tasted like rice pudding to me, but he definitely enjoyed eating it.

Yuri had already spoken with Sonia and told us she was trying to get the letter signed by the administrator for us today. After breakfast, he said he had to go buy some coffee and chocolates for the person who had to stamp the letter that was being signed. I have given up trying to figure out the process. It is so unpredictable and confusing.

Yuri has worked very hard to get us this far. Still, as I sat in the taxi on our 30-minute drive to the orphanage, a huge knot gathered in my stomach, and I knew it wasn't from eating the kashi. I kept wondering if I was doing the right thing. Thank goodness I had my sister with me. In additional to being a great traveling companion, she has helped me evaluate the boys' skill level and general well-being. I couldn't imagine traveling to Ukraine to do this by myself.

I keep thinking about all the life lessons I have learned this year. I am trying very hard to listen to my inner self and trust my instincts. As independent as I am, one of the biggest lessons I have learned is to be open and to accept help from others. The support and guidance I received from the people in the adoption news groups have been invaluable to me. I have to believe these lessons were necessary for me to learn before I went on this trip.

We pulled into the compound at the orphanage and went straight to the children's room. It would have been nice to see the whole complex, but we weren't invited to wander around. I don't know if they are preventing us from doing this for a specific reason, but I would think Oxana would want to show us the rest of the children and their facilities. Perhaps it doesn't matter to them if I am impressed at how well the children are cared for at the orphanage. I have to admit I was curious to see the other children. Was it really possible that there were only three children available for adoption—and no girls?

The boys were already eating lunch, so we tried to stay clear of the glass doors that led to the playroom so as to not distract them. As soon as the children finished their meal of soup and bread, they were ushered into the next room and made to sit on the toilet until they did something. In the meantime, the caretakers played a cartoon on the TV for the children to watch. Sergei soon appeared and came out to greet us. He had seen me during lunch; as soon as he walked in to the room he opened up his arms to me. I picked him up and just cradled him on my shoulder. He was very quiet, so Donna suggested I sing him some lullabies. I could feel him breathing as he gripped my arms with his hands. He laid his little head on my shoulders, perfectly content to be rocked and stroked. I kissed his cheek and whispered, "I love you." I must confess though, that my words sounded hollow. How could I say to this boy that I loved him when I didn't even know him? I guess I said it to convince myself that I could be his mother and take care of him.

Meanwhile Nicki had entered the room ready to be entertained. Donna kept him busy as he played with the Italian couple's little boy, Paolo. I could see the look in the Italian couple's eyes as I rubbed Sergei's back. I think they would have liked it if Paolo were more cuddly, but he is very active, just like Nicki. Meanwhile, Yuri left to see if he could buy a train ticket to Kiev tonight. He was gone about 30 minutes, and, when he returned, he said there were no tickets available.

When it was time for us to leave, Sergei started to cry. I'm not sure if he cried because he couldn't play with the toys anymore or because we were getting ready to depart. It was very obvious to me that the orphanage caretakers have a genuine interest in the children. As I watched the women interact with the children, I could see it in their eyes and the tone of their voices. Still, I doubt the boys get many hugs and kisses with all those children in the play group. I wonder what my life will be like with them. I can't wait until I hear them call me mama for the first time.

Donna has been sharing mothering tips with me throughout the trip. I am feeling very frustrated to be so ignorant about child rearing. I am normally very much in control of a situation and if I don't know something, I find someone who has the answer. Learning to become a mother is not so simple. I don't know how I will learn it all before they grow up.

Yuri suggested we drive to Lugansk to see if he could buy a train ticket there. Alex, our driver, who had been with us since the morning, knew exactly where to go. Driving through the city, we saw remnants of the old Soviet régime. The red star and hammer and sickle were emblazoned on bridge railings and building facades throughout the city. Dozens of larger-than-life statues depicting strong, Aryan-looking men and women were scattered in various squares. Their physique was superhuman and any sports club would have been proud to use them as a model. Most of them carried guns or a hammer in their hands. While we were in Kiev, we watched the Russian elections and were surprised that the Communist party made such a strong showing. Yuri said that even though people are glad there is no more Soviet Union, they remember that time as being very stable, when prices were low and everyone had a job. Change is hard, I thought to myself, feeling grateful that I was staying in this country for only a few weeks.

No luck getting tickets at the train station, so we drove to the bus depot. Yuri was able to buy a ticket to Kharkiv, a small city about a third of the way back to Kiev. It would take him eight hours to get there, and then he would try to catch a train to go the rest of the way to Kiev. Everything in Ukraine seems to take so long—even a simple train trip is not so simple. We decided to grab a quick bite to eat before returning to the bus station. During lunch, Yuri suggested I give a gift to Vlad, the psychologist at the NAC who had been very helpful in moving the process along. I gave Yuri $100 and asked him to find a way to give it to Vlad that wouldn't arouse any suspicion. I didn't mind giving gifts to people here who had been helpful, but it is harder to hand over money when people demand a certain amount in order to get something done.

I asked Yuri if I paid more fees since I was an American, but he said all foreigners pay the same fees. Yuri explained that some people get such low wages that they need to supplement their income by charging a small fee. Alex drove us back to the bus depot after we finished lunch and we said our good-byes. We shall see Yuri again on Tuesday morning.

Our next stop in Lugansk was the Internet café. It was very small and cramped, full of pre-pubescent boys playing violent video games. There was only one computer available in the dimly lit room, so Donna and I had to share it. I got an update from our sister Pat Mary on the work being done on the house. I feel as if I am on Mars—thousands of miles away from everything. Since Alex was waiting for us, we spent only 30 minutes in the café. It was very cheap—less than one dollar to use the computer. It was then time to return to Slavyanoserbsk, the little town that was our home away from home. I gave Alex 160 hryvnia, the equivalent of $40 for his services.

Ukraine is so different from other countries I have visited. Where else do you have problems buying a simple train ticket to the capital city? It is such a struggle to do anything here, and our journey has just begun. I know I have to have patience, but all I want to do right now is take the boys home and start my new life with them.

It was nearly 3 p.m. when we returned to the flat. Donna and I had talked about going for a walk before it got dark, but Ina had made a big pot of soup and was pointing in her English/Russian dictionary to the word eat. Donna and I quickly agreed that eating a home-cooked meal was a better way to spend the afternoon, especially since the sun, which had barely been visible today, would be gone in 30 minutes. Ina was baking bread in hollowed out tin cans, something I had never seen before, but it appeared to work very well for her. We opened the wine we had bought yesterday to enjoy with our meal. After tasting it Donna, who lives in California, told me that there's no worry that Ukrainian wine will soon take over the U.S. market.

I had been fighting a sore throat and cold symptoms, so I took my vitamins to help fight off the germs. I really craved some quiet time, and, fortunately, there was blessed silence in the flat for the rest of the afternoon. No blaring TV show or radio crowded the airwaves in the apartment. Ina read a book in the living room while Donna and I caught up on our journal writing. Then around 5:30 p.m., the TV came back on—time to go wash my hair and do laundry.

My mind keeps going back to our visit at the orphanage today. I did feel a sense of bonding with the boys—especially Sergei. Neither of the boys has any language skills, so it's very difficult to communicate with them. Nicki is definitely more challenging than Sergei. He has to be entertained, or he'll wander back to the doors of his playroom. I hate to admit it but I'd rather spend time with Sergei and let Donna play with Nicki. She seems to know what to do and how to keep him focused on an activity or a toy.

Tomorrow is another big day for us. We will travel to the orphanage, pick up the children and Natalie and travel to Lugansk to have the boys examined at the regional children's hospital. I hope to get some answers about Nicki's left eye, which doesn't track the same as his right eye. Most people call it a lazy eye although the medical term for it is *strabismus*. He may have one of several eye conditions, but Natalie has no clue what happened to cause this problem. She said they first noticed it in September. According to the FRUA medical booklet, it is easy to cure with glasses, eye drops, or a patch. As for Sergei, I am concerned about the shunt that was inserted to prevent pressure buildup on his brain.

This evening, Donna and I worked up a list of questions to ask the doctors. I am beginning to feel much better about my decision to adopt the boys.

Monday, December 1

Dear Journal: I finally got a good night's sleep last night. We set the alarm for 7 a.m. so we would have enough time to get ready before Alex arrived to transport us to the orphanage in his private taxi. All the vehicles here are small and old, and most of them are very clean inside. I'm sure that owning a car here is very expensive, and most people probably keep them until they are ready to be sold for scrap.

The caretakers at the orphanage bundled the boys in layers of clothes from head to toe as we got ready to leave for the hospital. Sergei had boots on that were at least three sizes too big, and Nicki had so many clothes on that he looked like a stuffed toy. Both children stared in amazement as we drove away in the car with Natalie in the front seat. I had Sergei on my lap, and Donna held Nicki since there are no such things as car seats or seat belts in Ukraine. Both children quickly fell asleep as the car sped towards Lugansk. The sun had finally broken through the dense gray clouds to give us our first peek at the sun in ten days.

This region is known for rich farmland, coal mining and steel manufacturing. Except for a few large factories and buildings, all we saw from the car window were miles upon miles of rich black soil in the plowed fields. The main road between the towns isn't bad, but the local streets look like mine-fields with huge potholes. Overall, the landscape is dreary and bleak. Even Yuri called this area miserable and longs to be back home in warm, sunny Crimea.

The Children's Hospital in Lugansk looks like any other large complex of buildings. We met up with Violette, one of Natalie's friends, outside in the parking lot. She had agreed to act as my translator with the doctors since Yuri was in Kiev. Violette told me our first visit was with a neurologist to have Sergei's head and shunt examined. We went inside the building and took the stairs up one flight since no one was using the elevators. We walked past a crowded hallway into a small room where two older female doctors were sitting across from each other at small desks. This was the examining room. The doctor checked Sergei's arm and leg reflexes with a little hammer. Then she moved a pencil back and forth to see if his eyes moved from side to side while looking at the pencil. She didn't get up from her chair or undress him. She did measure Sergei's head and I managed to get a few questions answered, but many more were left unanswered. I asked if the doctor would also examine Nicki, and she agreed. I told Violette to ask the doctor what she knew about FAS. The doctor replied, "I'm not that kind of doctor."

People in Ukraine either don't want to know about FAS or don't understand the impact of having this condition. One of Karen's comments to me before I left was that they dump all of their sick kids on foreigners who are so desperate for children that they don't worry about the child's health. In a country where alcoholism is rampant, I can't believe the doctors and government officials don't know the ramifications of pregnant women imbibing large quantities of alcohol. If I could give one piece of advice to people coming to Ukraine to adopt, it would be not to believe anyone when it comes to the health of these children unless you are dealing with a doctor who is trained to handle FAS.

Then it was time for Nicki to visit the eye specialist. We walked up another flight of stairs, past another crowded hallway. The walls and floors were bare concrete; it was not like any hospital I had ever visited. The doctor used a small hand instrument and a magnifying glass to examine Nicki's left eye. She didn't put any eye drops in the eye to dilate his pupil, and there was no equipment in the office. All she said was that I should take him to an eye specialist as soon as we returned to the States. What a waste of time. I really don't understand why we had to do this since we got very little information that we didn't already know. I paid Violette $10 for her services, and we headed back to the orphanage.

I held Nicki on my lap on the way back, and he was in a very playful mood. We had given both boys little teddy bears that had been presents from my friend Jan. Nicki played with his for a while, and then he started playing with my watch. He is so curious. We spent the whole trip playing and laughing. Nicki is a very sweet boy with long eyelashes and short, dark hair. He has only four teeth; his two top and bottom front teeth. I asked Natalie why he didn't have more teeth, and she said perhaps it was because he didn't get enough vitamins. I have noticed that he sometimes rocks himself back and forth, especially when he is sitting down. I understand that this is a common practice among children who have been institutionalized. Every time I notice this behavior I pick him up and hug him. I want Nicki to know that there is someone who will love him.

Once we arrived back at the orphanage, the boys were eager to return to their caretakers and the familiarity of their playroom. I wish we could spend more time with them each day. It seems that we barely arrive, and then it's time for them to return to the playroom for lunch. Slowly, each day they reveal another layer of their personalities. It was fun playing with Nicki in the car today. It gave me a chance to interact with him without any distractions. And now, after today's visit to the hospital, I'm beginning to feel more responsible for the boys' general health and well-being.

As we drove back to the flat, I was thrilled to see the sun still shining over the open landscape. There were a number of people walking or riding bikes in the small towns we drove through, and everyone was bundled up in warm leather coats and jackets. I paid Alex $32 for his driving services when we arrived back at the flat. He doesn't speak any English, so we have been communicating using the Russian phrase book my friend John gave to me.

Ina, her daughter and son-in-law were at the flat when we returned from the orphanage. Ina had cooked a large pot of borsht for lunch and invited us to join them for a meal. The soup was delicious and we quickly devoured it. Our plan was to have a quick lunch and then do some sightseeing before the sunset.

After everyone had left to return to work, I grabbed my video camera, and Donna and I filmed a tour of Ina's flat to show the folks back home. According to Yuri, Ina's flat is a typical home in Ukraine. The kitchen is quite tiny with a small sink and no hot water faucet. There is a small drain board that holds all the dishes, a mixture of delicate china plates and cups. At the other end of the room is a small gas stove. The table is big enough to seat four people, five if you pull it out from the wall and there are four stools that fit under the table. Next to the kitchen is an enclosed, unheated porch that Ina uses to store food that doesn't fit into her small refrigerator. From the kitchen you walk into the living room, which is nicely decorated with a couch and several chairs. Ina has a large cabinet against one wall with pretty china plates and crystal glasses. The commode is in a very small, unventilated room and next to it is a separate room where the bathtub and sink are located. Although Ina's flat is a cozy place for one or two people, it makes me appreciate all the space I will have in my new house even more than I did before.

Once we were finished filming, we bundled up and headed outside. We had noticed a huge abandoned church on the way into town, so we planned our route to pass by it. It is the closest thing to a tourist attraction we were going to find in this town. We met three schoolchildren as we were walking down the street, and they were very taken with us. They trailed us all the way to the church, trying to converse with us. They didn't speak any English, but they were very charming and we had fun trying to communicate with them. We stopped at one of the markets to buy instant coffee, wine and eggs before we returned to the flat. There is no such thing as packaged eggs on the shelves. I presume the shopkeepers raise their own chickens and sell the brown colored eggs to folks like Ina who live in apartments.

We had a light snack once we returned to the flat and then curled up with our books as the sun set past the other gray buildings. I would liked to have traveled in Ukraine in the summertime, but the decision as to when I traveled was totally out of my hands. Yuri tells us how beautiful the flowers are in the springtime in Crimea. Perhaps one day I will return to Ukraine to adopt an older girl—who knows?

Yuri called this afternoon to tell me he had the new referral letter for the boys and that he would be returning by train to Lugansk tomorrow morning. The rest of the week will be pretty routine—visiting the orphanage in the morning and returning to the flat in the early afternoon. We may need to return to Lugansk tomorrow as Yuri mentioned something about needing photos of the boys.

This adoption process seems to have no end to it. I am beginning to feel like a bag of money that is filled up each morning only to be emptied out by the end of the day. Perhaps it's because I'm not used to paying for everything in cash. Back home I use my credit card for everything—food, gas, clothes. I had hoped to know more about each of the boy's medical conditions today, but I do not feel their medical problems are insurmountable. I am beginning to feel that they are my children now and that their future welfare will be my top priority. Of course, it would have been nice to find children that were perfectly healthy in every way, but I do believe that I was led to these children for a reason. They both need a loving home and someone to care for them. I have so much love to give and will do all that is possible to ensure they have the best medical care possible.

After we came back from dinner at the local café, we were feeling very silly and decided to make a list of the top ten things any prospective adoptive parent should be willing to deal with while they are in Ukraine. I guess it was a way for us to express how homesick we were feeling in this foreign land.

So, you think you're ready to spend a month in Ukraine?

1. Don't call or talk to any friends or relatives. Send e-mails using a dial-up Internet connection that works only every other day.

2. Don't use any paper products except paper towels from a public bathroom and packs of tiny travel tissues.

3. Wear a hearing aid that scrambles everyone's voices so you can't understand them. Then hire a total stranger to handle the most important transaction of your life.

4. Don't read the newspaper or any of your favorite periodicals. Read only romantic novels such as you find at a beach house on your summer vacation.

5. Move in with a strange woman and her cat and share a bedroom (and bed) with your sister.

6. Do without any of your favorite foods. Shop every day at multiple markets and bring your own packing bags. Go to the butcher where the workers don't use gloves, and the scale is also used for passing change back and forth.

7. Carry a money belt with more cash than you've ever seen in your entire life on your body for 24 hours a day.

8. Wear the same two outfits for several weeks and do laundry by hand in the bathroom.

9. Put your car keys away and walk everywhere you need to go. Take a public bus or hire a driver for longer distances.

10. Meet two children for the first time and make a snap decision to take responsibility for them for the rest of their lives.

Tuesday, December 2

Dear Journal: Donna and I waited in bed this morning until we heard Ina leave for work. It's a tiny apartment, especially when there are three of us trying to use the bathroom and kitchen, so we decided it was nicer to wait and have the flat all to ourselves. Yuri was scheduled to return from Kiev this morning, so we puttered around and had a leisurely breakfast. He arrived on time, tired and hungry, but he quickly cleaned up and went out again. He met with Sonia to get the new referral letter signed and to arrange for the letter granting me permission to adopt the boys. Those two pieces of paper will cost me $100—$50 for the administrator and $50 for the typist. That's a month's salary someone just made in less than an hour.

Yuri told us about his trip to the NAC in Kiev. He had arrived there at 5 a.m. yesterday and was told that the director was not in the office. Fortunately, the woman who was in charge agreed to give him the new referral letter so he could return on the afternoon train. It is so hard for me to understand why all these things have to be done in person.

Yuri told me that when he went to the NAC with Tamara's rejection letter, the female psychologist who had been in the room with us last Thursday gave him a lot of grief about my decision. She also told him she didn't believe him when he told her about the boys' health problems. It's hard to understand their system over here. Most of these people do not appear to have the skills to make decisions about the lives of these children. I try to remind myself that I am in no position to judge others, but my heart keeps going out to the children. They continue to languish in these orphanages made out of brick and mortar when what they really need is a home made out of love and compassion.

I told Yuri about our experience at the hospital with the boys. He told me that some doctors buy their medical degrees from universities. He also said that students must pay their professors to get good grades as well as for the privilege of taking the class exams. University professors take bribes, judges take bribes, government officials take bribes—everyone knows this is happening, yet no one does anything to change it. Why? Because that's the way it has always been done.

After Yuri returned from Sonia's office, we drove to the orphanage. We went to the boy's playroom but it was empty. All the radiators were being replaced, so the children were relocated to another room. We went with Yuri to Oxana's office to give her the new referral letter, and to find out where the boys were located. She had some papers to give me, including a baby picture for each of the boys. I also learned the boys' birthdays; Nicki's is March 14, and Sergei's is May 5.

I took the baby pictures from Yuri and showed them to Donna. I then gingerly placed them in my wallet. I felt so proud of my little boys. It was then Oxana dropped a bombshell on us. She said Nicki has some water in his right testicle that would need to be surgically drained. Vitaly told me that this was a common ailment among young boys, but Donna said she had never heard of such a thing.

Oxana said the problem could be treated here, or I could have it done when I return to the States. She said Nicki would have to remain in the hospital overnight even though it was a minor procedure. I didn't know what to do. I really didn't want to deal with this once I returned to the States, knowing I would be on my own with the two boys. I also knew the hospitals here are not as sophisticated as those in the States.

Since it was a minor procedure, I decided to have it done before I took the boys from the orphanage. I asked Oxana how soon it could be arranged, and she shrugged her head, saying that perhaps it could be done tomorrow.

Donna and I wondered if anyone would stay with him at the hospital. I then asked Yuri to confirm that there were no other health related issues that we hadn't been told about, and Oxana assured us there were none.

Before we left, we gave Oxana the toothbrushes and toothpaste that had been donated by my dentist, Dr. Lee. Yuri scoffed at us when we told him what we were doing. He said they wouldn't use them at the orphanage, but I didn't care what he said. These children deserve as much support and attention as we can give them, and I have to believe that these toothbrushes will be used by the children.

Next, we were off to Lugansk to have the petition for adoption requests notarized: one for the NAC director, one for the judge, one for Oxana and one for Sonia. We arrived at the notary's office around 12:30 p.m., and when we were told to return later, we decided to get lunch. Alex drove us to a local café that was as upscale as anything we had seen so far in Ukraine. It was very cosmopolitan and had a hip decor and menu. Believe it or not, there were government stamps on the menu. I swear you can't do anything in Ukraine without getting it stamped by someone.

Donna and I were anxious to return to the Internet café, so we hopped back into the car after lunch and Alex whisked us away. We had about 30 minutes to read and send out a few messages. It was good to share the news about the boys with everyone back home. The Internet connection was painfully slow, but this was our only link with our friends and family, and, right now, that meant a lot to us.

On the way back to the notary's office, Yuri told us that being a notary is a very prestigious profession in Ukraine, and one has to go to University to complete the requirements. Yuri was amazed when I told him that virtually anyone in the U.S. could become a notary and that most banks will notarize documents for you at no charge if you have a banking account with them. All documents of any significance in Ukraine require either a signature or stamp, preferably both, and most likely they will have multiple stamps.

Today I signed the petition papers, written in Russian, that Yuri will need to give to the officials who will then give me permission to move forward with the court hearing to formally adopt the two boys. As I was signing the papers I felt as if I were caught up in a huge wave that was carrying me in one direction, and I was powerless to stop it. It's not that I don't want to adopt the boys; it's just that I don't feel that I really know them. In a perfect world, I would have the opportunity to spend several full days with the children before making up my mind. Unfortunately, Ukraine is the last place on earth I would call a perfect world.

Our last stop of the day was at the post office to buy postcards—each with a beautiful Christmas greeting—and stamps to send them to our family. The cards and stamps cost $7, which was as much as I spent on our three meals at the little café in Slavyanoserbsk. It was mid-afternoon when we finished our errands. The sun had turned into a large red ball touching the far horizon, while the cloudless sky was a brilliant, deep blue. It reminded me that some things are the same regardless of where you are in the world.

After returning to our flat, we made up some snacks and relaxed after a busy day. The apartment was warm, cozy—and empty. Yuri told us that he had to go see Sonia again and oh, by the way, he needed two $50 bills. He wanted to thank the head of administration and the office typist for drafting the permission documents so quickly.

Wednesday, December 3

Dear Journal: The gray skies have returned to our little corner of the world, and a thick frost has covered the barren landscape. Yuri left the flat after breakfast to retrieve a letter from Sonia, the omnipotent inspector. He also needed $20 to help him secure the passport applications.

When Yuri returned, we piled into the car and drove to the passport office in town. He then called Oxana to make sure she would be available because she had to sign and stamp the applications as well as the notarized adoption petition papers. On our way to the orphanage, he asked me to give him the boys' new names.

Donna and I had been discussing this at great length. I had names for two girls or a boy and a girl but not two boys. I decided that I would change Sergei's name to Rupert, my mother's maiden name (Ruppert), and I would change Nikita's name to Nickolas and give him my paternal grandfather's name as a middle name. Their full names would be Rupert Sergei Schwartz and Nickolas Rudolph Schwartz—such big names for my little boys. It was very important to me that I give them names that bonded them to my family. They may be the only children I have, and I want to give them part of my heritage so they will grow up knowing that they belong to a family with whom they will be forever entwined.

A light snow began to fall, and Donna and I serenaded Yuri and Alex with Christmas songs. Even though I was a long way from home, the snow conjured up memories of Christmas traditions from my childhood. One of my favorite memories is the lighting of candles on the holiday wreath every evening during Advent, after which my Mother would pass around all the Christmas cards that had arrived that day. Then we would each pick a song, and the whole family would sing it together. I hope my boys have the same warm memories from their childhood.

By the time we arrived at the orphanage, the road was covered with snow. We quickly made our way to Oxana's office where she signed all the papers. We then went to visit the children, while Yuri negotiated the amount of the donation to the orphanage that is expected from adoptive parents. Many people refuse to give cash and, instead, purchase clothing, food or needed equipment. I'm not sure that makes a difference after hearing about how shipments of donated supplies that are sent to orphanages never make it to the children.

I know the orphanages have many needs, and I don't begrudge them the money although it would be nice if it weren't expected. In the end I got off pretty easy; Oxana asked Yuri for $500 and I agreed to pay it. I know others have paid up to $1,500 for one child in different regions in Ukraine. I went into the bathroom, opened my money belt and said a prayer over the money that it would buy the needed supplies for the children we would be leaving behind. Then I returned to the room and gave the money to Yuri to pass on to Oxana.

The boys were all smiles as they walked into the small playroom. Sergei, or Rupert as I now call him, let me hold him in my arms again. I peeked into the small mirror hanging on the wall and I could see a big smile on his face. Donna told me he now knows I'm his mama. It was a wonderful feeling. Nicki was his usual happy self, full of energy and smiles.

We asked Yuri to speak with Natalie for permission to undress the boys and inspect their bodies. I had expected the doctor to examine them more thoroughly at the hospital, and in light of what Oxana had told us about Nicki's testicle, I wanted to know if they had any skin problems or other issues. As a matter of fact, Natalie had told us that Oxana was wrong about Nicki's testicle needing treatment, so no surgery was needed.

I held on to Rupert while Yuri helped Donna to undress Nicki. He had on an undershirt, a long shirt with a sweatshirt on top, knit tights and thin pajama pants. The soles on his shoes were so thin they had holes in them. I couldn't believe how skinny his arms and legs were—it wasn't hard to believe that he only weighed 17 pounds. He has a small round scar on his left shoulder, probably the result of one of his vaccination shots. However, the most shocking discovery was the six small, red sores on his lower back. We asked Yuri what had caused the sores, and he said he had no idea. He didn't seem to be in any pain, but I will check him every day to make sure these lesions are healing.

One of the information sheets I had brought with me was a chart that showed the standard range for head circumference as well as weight and height by age for boys and girls from birth to 36 months. I wanted to measure Nicki since one of the symptoms of FAS is a small head. His head measured 18½" putting him in the 15th percentile for his age. The fact that he was on the chart at all for his head size was reassuring, especially since he didn't register on the other chart due to his low weight and height.

Rupert was next. He, too, was wearing three shirts, two pairs of pants and paper-thin shoes. There was a small scar above his belly button. I assume that was where the doctors inserted the tube to drain the fluid from his brain into his stomach. I'll have to wait until I return to the States to get answers to why he developed this problem and what action will be needed to monitor the shunt. Rupert's head measured 21" which is half an inch over the 95th percentile for his age, but that is to be expected because of the fluid build-up in his head. Rupert's back looked fine, but when we saw his buttocks, we both gasped in horror. His little cheeks looked like someone had taken a green marker and checkered his behind. Yuri assured us that this green substance was a medicinal cure for diaper rash. This country's medical practice scares the heck out me. I can only pray that neither my sister nor I get sick enough to need hospitalization while we are in Ukraine.

The Italian couple that we had seen before was visiting with Paolo, their little boy. He was Rupert's size—perhaps a little bigger. This child was a little whirlwind. He would not stop moving and seemed to get more agitated if you engaged him in any physical activity such as swinging him in your arms or playing peek-a-boo. At one point he looked as if he was going to hit Rupert with a toy before his father stopped him. I did not know if this boy has any behavioral problems, but I thought he would need a lot of love and attention from his new parents. He was a pleasant looking boy with wavy brown hair but there was something in his eyes that gave him a faraway look. There are so many children in this country that need a caring and loving home. I pray that with enough love and guidance this little boy has a healthy and joyous life with his new family.

Our time at the orphanage passed quickly and then, suddenly, it was time for the boys to eat their lunch. They obediently followed their caretakers into the playroom. I may be their new mama, but when food is available I take a back seat. I can't wait to get them home and start putting some meat on their bones—especially Nicki who never had the luxury of drinking his mother's milk. Donna and I didn't bring any cookies today. We decided it would be better to buy bananas and begin introducing new foods to the boys.

We were on the road again to Lugansk by late morning. Our first stop was the train station, where Yuri was able to buy a train ticket back to Kiev for his second visit to the NAC. The court administrator will not accept the adoption petition until it has been signed and stamped by the NAC Director. Since it could take Yuri up to three days for the NAC to give this permission we may not see him again until Tuesday morning. It's hard to describe the relationship I have with Yuri to someone who has never been in this situation. I am totally dependent on this man for everything, and when he is gone I feel very frustrated at not being able to communicate with anyone at the orphanage.

After leaving the train station, we headed back to the notary's office to get the passport application copies notarized. More documents, more signatures. We decided to go to a cafeteria for lunch today. It wasn't as good as the food we had in Kiev, but we were all very hungry. I went to use the toilet at the cafeteria and was stopped by a little old lady sitting at a small table outside the washroom. There was a sign on the door, and I surmised I needed to pay 50 kopecks (about ten cents) to use the facilities. After I handed her the coins she carefully counted them, then entered the amount and time of day in a ledger she kept on her desk. She then gave me two small sheets of toilet paper. I wondered to myself if this woman had spent her entire life at this job, carefully counting out two sheets of paper to every customer.

On the way to the Internet café, Alex got pulled over by a cop who was standing on the side of the main street. He got out and went to talk to the officer who was standing behind the car. I saw Alex put a ten hryvnia note inside his passport papers before he handed them to the policeman. We couldn't figure out what he had done to get pulled over, but my suspicion is that one runs the risk of getting pulled over just by driving down the street in this country.

There were two computers available for us today at the Internet café, and it was the first time since we left Kiev that we didn't feel rushed. It was nice to spend some time reading messages from everyone, including Karen who asked about the boys' health. She has been unable to find a Ukrainian doctor that specializes in FAS for me to contact about Nicki. Her main concern was that certain types of eye problems can be symptoms of FAS. Donna and I have had many conversations about Nicki's behavior, and neither of us thinks he has this condition, although we are certainly not experts in this matter. I keep praying that Nicki's mother loved him enough to stay sober during her pregnancy. One of the pieces of literature I received from Karen on FAS said that 12,000 children were born each year with this preventable condition. My guess is that you could double or even triple that number if you included all the Eastern European countries.

Nicki has an contagious laugh and loves to play. The plastic bag that held the building block toys that the Italian couple brought for Paolo fascinated him. He kept taking one of the blocks and putting it in the bag, then turning the bag upside down to dump it out and put it back again. It's hard to look at a child objectively and consider whether you would still adopt him if you learned he had a behavioral disability.

Many people who come to Ukraine and Russia to adopt are willing to accept children with all types of problems, but I am not one of them. It's hard to explain why I feel this way. I look at my life and know how much I enjoy being active—sailing, traveling, entertaining. I guess I'm prepared to make only certain changes in my life and don't feel that I would be comfortable dealing with a behavioral disability, especially as a single parent. I continue to pray every night for guidance in making the right decision about adopting Nicki.

After leaving the Internet café we drove to the Department of Justice. Yuri wanted to speak with his contact about the procedure to have the boys' birth certificates reissued with their new names. Then it was back to the train station to drop off Yuri for his ride back to Kiev. Donna gave him a set of earplugs to help him sleep through all the noise in his compartment, as he will share it with three other people. We also gave him some of our snacks, since he always seems to forget to eat.

The sun had already disappeared from the sky as we sat in Alex's car heading back towards Ina's. We had made a shopping list to replenish our meager food supplies, so we grabbed some empty shopping bags at the flat and headed towards the market. The first shop we visited faced the small town square. We chatted as best we could with the store clerk, telling her that we were from America, and I was here to adopt two children. We showed her some of the pictures Donna had taken at the orphanage, and I found myself feeling so proud of my new sons.

My life this past week has been a strange mixture of everyday routines such as eating and reading, as well as making life-altering decisions. And it seems to happen so casually—and quickly. A week ago I didn't even know these boys existed, and now they are the main focus of my life. Is that what having children does to you? The impact they will have on me is slowly developing in my mind. There will be doctor visits, playrooms to set up, new foods to prepare—all for two little boys who have no idea what will happen to them in a few short weeks.

I think constantly about all the prayers that have been offered up by my friends and family. This is the biggest undertaking I have ever attempted, and it warms my heart to know that I can reach out for help and guidance from Donna as I move through this process. I pray to God that I am making the right decision to adopt these two boys without knowing the full history of their health.

Thursday, December 4

Dear Journal: We are slowly slipping into a dull, daily routine. Get up, bathe, eat and dress by 9 a.m., drive to the orphanage, spend some time with the boys, leave by 11:30 a.m., return to the flat, eat, go food shopping, read, eat and read again. It's too cold to spend much time outside, and there really isn't much to see anyway. It's a good thing we both like to read since there isn't anything else to do in this one-horse town, especially since it gets dark by 4 p.m. even on a sunny day.

There was another heavy frost this morning, and it covered every tree and blade of grass we passed as we careened through the countryside on our drive to the orphanage. It looked like a winter wonderland, full of silvery trees and glistening glass branches. All I could think about was the winter scene from Dr. Zhivago where Omar Shariff and Julie Christie have taken refuge in a country dacha that is encased in crystallized ice. Looking outside the window of the car I found it easy to believe that such a place could exist.

When we arrived at the orphanage the caretakers stuffed the boys into coats and hats since the small room in which we were to play with them was unheated and right next to an outside entrance. It was uncomfortably cold. The Italian couple was nowhere to be seen, and I kept wondering if they were in Lugansk working on their adoption process. There were no toys to play with in the room, so I popped into the main playroom and grabbed a few toys.

After we greeted the boys, we got out the banana we had bought at the market. I broke off two small pieces and gave them to the boys. Rupert quickly shoved the piece into his mouth and wanted more. Nicki didn't seem interested in eating it, so Rupert ended up consuming it all. Rupert spent the entire 90 minutes sitting quietly with a little workbench where he continued to hammer a small ball into a round hole, only to retrieve it and start all over again. Donna had brought the cassette tape player and was playing one of the pre-school song tapes that my brother John and his wife Renae had sent to me. Rupert seemed fascinated by the music on the tape and wasn't bothered by the headset. On the other hand, Nicki was very restless and kept walking back towards the room where all the other children were playing.

Donna told me that we didn't have enough toys to keep Nicki occupied and I agreed with her. When it was time for lunch, we walked the boys back into the playroom and left the building. I don't know why we can't spend more time with the children each day. It wouldn't take much to let us stay for lunch, but I guess the staff considers us a disruption in the children's schedule. I keep wondering what it will be like when I have them all day.

Both Donna and I had our postcards ready to mail, so we asked Alex to drop us off at the post office in town instead of the flat. We decided to walk home from there and stumbled upon an open market in the town square. Most of the vendors were selling clothing, but some had shoes, toys, and blankets as well as household items. We found a small set of three little cars that I bought for under a dollar. I also bought a musical keyboard that I will no doubt grow tired of hearing long before this trip is over. The last toy I found was a series of colorful stacked plastic rings that connected to each other. All told I spent $7 on the three toys. Goodness knows, it will probably be the cheapest outing for toys I will ever experience.

It was early afternoon when we finished eating lunch, so we decided to go for a walk—anything to avoid the big, white bag of dirty laundry that was lurking in our bedroom. We strolled down the street in a part of the town we hadn't seen yet. All the homes were made of brick or stone and most of them had a stucco finish with decorated wood trim painted in white, bright blue, or green. There were diamond shaped patterns under the windows and corners of the houses and most of the homes were well kept. In contrast, the sidewalks and grassy areas near the street looked like a disaster zone, full of trash and debris.

I was feeling a bit chilled when we returned to the flat, so I snuggled into bed with a new book, hoping to chase away the Thursday winter blahs. Donna cooked up some grilled cheese sandwiches that were delicious, and we kept each other in good cheer throughout the meal. I was washing up the dishes when the phone rang. It was Yuri who had promised to call us with news of his progress at the NAC. The connection was not good, but the news he had to share with me came through loud and clear. He would have the approval for the petition to adopt both boys on Friday and would be back in town by Saturday morning. Whoopee! That meant he could go to the court on Monday and file the papers to get the hearing scheduled for later in the week. It has been hard to keep track of all these processes, so Donna sketched out a calendar so we could track our progress. There is still much for us to do before the NAC closes in two weeks for the holidays, yet with a bit of luck we may still be home for Christmas.

After dinner, Donna dug out a small cloth sack she had brought along and we began to assemble all the little toys I had bought, along with some of the gifts from my brother and his wife. I took a shoelace from my sneaker and made a drawstring for the bag. I would never have thought to put this play bag together, much less buy the toys, if Donna hadn't suggested it. Ask me to host a business meeting for 20 executives, complete with graphic presentations, and I would know exactly what to do. But tell me to entertain two small boys for several hours, and I am at a total loss.

I feel as if I am on the verge of getting a cold—sneezing, minor congestion and an achy feeling all over. I'm trying hard to stay focused and healthy. My thoughts vacillate between worrying about the health of the boys, the ongoing adoption process and wondering what is happening back home with my house renovations. Pat Mary is planning to move all my furniture and boxes to my new home this weekend. I really wish I could be there to make sure everything is organized. I still don't know if the house will be ready for me to move into when I return—just one more thing to keep me awake as I lay in bed, trying to get a good night's sleep.

Friday, December 5

Dear Journal: We were excited to show the boys their new toys as we made our way to the orphanage this morning. As we walked into the building I noticed an old mini van with the red cross symbol on it parked outside. I mentioned to Donna that it looked like an ambulance, and all sorts of terrible thoughts ran through my mind. Had something happened to Rupert or Nicki? We went inside to find the boys being dressed in warm coats and hats. We were told they were going to Lugansk to have their photos taken for their Ukrainian passports and their U.S. visas.

The boys were gone within five minutes of our arrival. What a disappointment. We had driven all that way and missed spending time with my little ones. The only thing we could do was get back in the car with the toy bag in hand. We were back at the flat by 10:30 a.m. with nothing to do for the rest of the day. This is a charming little town, where nothing ever happens, and the only thing to do besides walking through the streets, stuffed into long underwear, hat and scarf to ward off frostbite, is to go to the local market and buy more water, eggs and butter.

Saturday, December 6

Dear Journal: It's Saturday here and the routine of our days stays the same. We had a very good visit with the boys this morning. They loved their new toys, and we had fun showing them how to stack the plastic rings. We brought a banana to share with the boys, but Nicki wasn't interested in eating it. Rupert ate the whole thing in three huge bites. We gave Nicki a small fruit bar that I had in my backpack, and he was very quick to gobble it up.

We arranged with the caretakers to let the boys eat with us when it was time for lunch. What a mess. The bibs that are worn by all the children are huge pieces of brown plastic that extend down to their waist. Each child automatically places the bib under his or her food—the better to catch all the spills. The boys each had two bowls of food, a piece of bread and a broth served in a large teacup. Rupert grabbed the cup and held it tightly against his face until not one drop was left. Then both boys started to gobble down their meal. The soup looked very hearty with small shreds of chicken and slices of onions and carrots. The other bowl contained a small dumpling with ground meat. Once they had finished eating, we took them by the hand and gave them back to their caretakers. It was potty time, so they went into the next room to sit until they had finished their business.

Yuri was waiting for us at Ina's when we returned from the orphanage. We were very happy to see him again. We knew he hadn't eaten yet, so I suggested we go to the café for lunch. While we were waiting for our food, I asked

Yuri how he got started helping people adopt children. Of course, I was also very curious to know how much of the money I had paid to Victor went to Yuri. I didn't ask him directly, but he intimated that he was not well compensated. People in Ukraine are so poor by our standards, it's easy to feel sorry for them, especially knowing how restrictive their lives were under the previous Soviet rule.

After we left the café, we did some grocery shopping on our way back to the flat. This has become a daily occurrence because of the size of Ina's refrigerator. Yuri insisted on carrying all the bags, and I teased him about how good his manners are with women. After we returned to the flat and put away the groceries, Yuri said he had a present for us. We had asked him to pick up some Christmas music, and he had returned with a CD of Ukrainian Christmas songs. The songs were sung in classic church style with an all male choir. The music was beautiful and I know I will enjoy playing it for the boys when we celebrate our first Christmas together.

We spent the rest of the day relaxing in the living room. Yuri tried to teach us a new card game called *Durck* which means fool in Russian. It could be described as a combination of bridge and hearts. We played about six practice hands but could never quite figure out all the rules. I don't know if it was for lack of trying or too much wine, but, either way, we quickly returned to our standard game of gin rummy.

Sunday, December. 7

Dear Journal: Part of the reason we went grocery shopping yesterday was so Yuri could make his long-promised borsht. He told us it would be ready by the time we returned from the orphanage, so we headed off to see the boys.

We had a good visit with them; I spent most of the time with Nicki, but it was hard to keep him entertained. He loves to be held, and he really loves to be rocked, cuddled and swung back and forth. He laughs when I swing him around or upside down. I can't wait to get him on a swing in the playground back home. I put the headphones on him for the first time, and he sat very still for 15 minutes, listening to the children's songs. His attention span is much shorter than Rupert's, and there isn't much to do in the small room. Every once in a while he will wander back to the doors that lead back to the playroom, and I have to carry him back to our area. I continue to vacillate between feeling excited that I have found my children and terror, knowing I will soon be solely responsible for their daily care.

Yuri was waiting for us at the flat, and the borsht was finally ready to eat. We each put a large dollop of sour cream in the soup just before eating it. It tasted different from the only other borsht I have ever eaten, which was ordered from the menu at The Russian Tea Room in New York City. Yuri told us that borsht is simply the Russian version of vegetable soup, and there are many different ways to make it. I had two big bowls of soup along with several slices of fresh brown bread.

Yuri's Recipe for Borsht

Ingredients:
1 carrot
2 beets
3 potatoes

2 onions

¼ of a small-sized cabbage

3 garlic cloves

tomato paste

vegetable oil

salt/sugar/dill to taste

¼ cup chopped parsley

²/3 pound of pork

4 chicken bouillon cubes

3 quarts of water

Shred the beets and the carrot, chop the onion, peel the potatoes and chop them into small cubes. Cut the meat into bite-sized cubes and boil it until soft. Sauté the onions in oil, add the shredded beets and carrot, cook until soft. Add sugar and tomato paste. When the meat is ready, add the cooked vegetables, potatoes, and chopped cabbage and cook for 15 minutes. Then add the garlic, dill, parsley, and bouillon cubes and cook another 15 minutes. Let soup sit for 30 minutes before serving with sour cream and brown bread.

The three of us, Donna, Yuri and I, are getting along together quite well. We haven't had any disagreements or awkward moments since we met Yuri over a week ago. We have had a lot of time to get to know each other. Yuri told us that his family was Catholic; however, the Soviet government did not condone any religious activity. As a result, many people, including his wife, were raised as atheists. He said he wants to learn more about his religious roots and would even like to get remarried in a church ceremony. It was very refreshing to hear a man talk about his beliefs and values in such an open manner. So far, Yuri has been extremely polite and trustworthy. I have to depend on him as he acts as my go-between to pay off all the officials. I guess it's possible that in his position he could tell me that a certain fee was required, and I would never know the difference, but I don't believe that's the case with Yuri. In any event, I have too many other things that occupy my thoughts. I think we would have been friends had we lived nearer to each together.

Yuri and I are very close in age, yet we have lived very different lives. He has never traveled abroad. He was required to spend time in the army and lives in a small apartment. I wondered to myself—what kind of life would my children have if they remained in this country? On one hand, this is a very exciting time as Ukraine develops its economy and social structure. On the other hand, poverty and lack of decent health care is rampant. Opportunities are definitely hard to come by, especially for children who have no family to support them.

The rest of the afternoon slipped quietly by—Yuri and Donna watched a movie on TV while I did some reading in our bedroom. Our return date of December 23 seems so far way. We have been in this tiny town for only nine days, but it seems like ninety. We will find out tomorrow how long we have to wait until we can take the boys from the orphanage and travel back to Kiev.

The evening was spent the same way the past five evenings have been spent—reading and playing cards. I can't remember when I have done so little each day. I try to do my daily yoga exercises even though it's hard to scope out an area that's large enough to stretch out. My neck and back feel so tense, and my mind is not at rest. It's hard to believe I can get so tired when I'm not doing much, so the mental stress must be affecting me. Donna and I decided that tomorrow we would take a long walk in the afternoon to shake off this hibernation funk of ours.

Monday, December 8

Dear Journal: Yuri made several phone calls early this morning, including a call to the local judge. The local prosecutor told him that I must be interviewed on Wednesday before they will hold the court hearing. Yuri countered with a proposal that would allow me to be interviewed today with the court hearing on Wednesday. Such posturing. Then Yuri spoke with Oxana about getting her signature on a document needed for the court hearing.

It was another chilly day with a cold wind blowing. We drove to the orphanage with no good reason to be in Ukraine except to bring my children home. Oxana was waiting for us in her office where she had placed a dozen large bags of clothing, including shoes and sweaters. She indicated that she had used my donation to buy the clothes for the children. In my mind, I had to believe that my money had been used to purchase these items although I will never know for sure. She and Yuri had a lively conversation, but he didn't share any of the details when I asked him what had transpired.

By the time we were finished, the boys were ready to eat lunch, so we returned to town without seeing them. We stopped at the courthouse to find out how much the judge would charge as an expediting fee to waive the 30-day waiting period. The waiting period was put in place to allow any Ukrainian who wanted to adopt a child time to submit a request with the court. Yuri told me that the judge was fairly new and was intimidated by the female prosecutor in his office. She was a wild card in this process, and I still couldn't figure out the role she played in the proceeding.

When Yuri returned to the car after meeting with the judge, he asked me if I had my money with me. I told him that I had it in my money belt around my waist. I have not taken it off except when I slept, and then I put it under my pillow. He told me that the judge, after vacillating back and forth, had asked for $800—a king's ransom in Ukraine. The alternative was not very pretty—to spend another 30 days in this country was out of the question, and it would cost more than that to go home and fly back. Neither option was acceptable, but I had to make a choice. I handed the money to Yuri, double counting it to make sure none of the new bills were sticking together. Yuri took the money and disappeared back in to the building. No receipt. Nothing.

It was past noon when we returned to the flat. The more questions I asked Yuri about his meeting with Oxana this morning the more frustrated I became. The issue had to do with getting a letter to validate the boys' urgent medical needs to guarantee that the 30 days' wait would be waived. Apparently Oxana had already requested a letter for Rupert, and she didn't want to do the same for Nicki, despite her pledge to do everything she could to assist me in the adoption process. Nicki is the one who really needs the urgent medical attention because of the problem with his left eye.

The process to get a letter is quite involved. Oxana has to ask the regional doctor at the children's hospital in Lugansk to write a letter stating that Nicki needs urgent medical treatment and should be allowed to leave the country as soon as possible. I was very upset with both Yuri and Oxana. Yuri said that the prosecutor could make a lot of trouble for me at the court hearing if I did not have a letter for Nicki. He's worried about her; he said this was the first time he'd ever had to deal with anyone other than a judge for an adoption hearing. I was very upset that he hadn't told me all of this while we were still at the orphanage.

I told Yuri that he had to find a way to get this letter for Nicki. He tried unsuccessfully for the next hour to reach Natalie at the orphanage. I decided I needed to meditate to release some of my anger and turn the problem over to God. I knew there was very little I could do on my own, and I wasn't prepared to leave this town without both of my children.

The mood was somber at dinner. The day's events still hung over us like a dark cloud as we tried to make light of things for our own sanity. The next two days would be decisive for me. I needed to make sure that I stayed involved in the conversations that Yuri has with Oxana and Natalie. I did not want to leave this country with only one child. I told Yuri that it was very hard for me to understand how these people could be so selfish at the expense of these children. Even if neither boy had a medical condition, they were certainly undernourished and desperately needed someone to take care of them. Is that not enough of a reason for any person to do everything in their power to grant a speedy removal from an institutional environment?

I went to sleep knowing there are many people who were keeping me in their prayers. I said my own prayer to God to watch over me and guide me through these daily challenges.

Tuesday, December 9

Dear Journal: There was a strange silence this morning as I lay in my bed. When we got up and greeted Yuri he didn't seem like his usual happy self. It turned out he has a nasty cold—perhaps he caught it from Ina who has been dispensing cold medicines to herself for the past several days.

Our plan was to leave the flat at nine and go straight to the orphanage. Donna and I tried to cheer ourselves up by singing Christmas carols in the car. Yuri was very quiet. I knew he was very worried about the prosecutor and the court hearing scheduled for tomorrow. He told us last week that he has a heart condition and an ulcer. This is the last profession I would ever recommend to someone with those types of health problems. I need to focus on keeping Yuri healthy and positive. He is my connection to everything over here, and I cannot afford for him to be less than 100 percent effective.

Once we arrived at the orphanage, we located Oxana and Natalie. Yuri started talking to them in a very lively manner; then Oxana looked at me, smiled and gave me the thumbs up sign. Yuri explained to me that Natalie would go with us to Lugansk to ask the eye doctor at the hospital to sign a form stating that Nicki needed urgent medical treatment. This was all a ruse, even though he does need treatment, to secure a speedy court decision and get the 30-day waiting period waived. It seems ironic that even relatively healthy children have to have a severe medical emergency to get the judge to waive the 30-day waiting period.

So the four of us piled in to our car and headed for Lugansk. Yuri sat in the back with Donna and me while Natalie sat in front. She looks so young to be responsible for 150 infants and young children. I have nothing against Natalie personally, but I don't trust anything she tells me about the boys. While we were in the car, Donna asked Yuri if he knew what had happened to the Italian couple we had met at the orphanage. He told us they had returned

home and would fly back to Lugansk after the 30-day waiting period had elapsed. I envy them their ability to avoid
the fees to the judge and prosecutor. I also pray that they
enjoy a happy life with their new son.

Once we arrived at the hospital, Yuri told me that he
would need some money for the doctor to sign the form.
He asked me how much I wanted to pay her. I took a deep
breath and asked him what the standard fee was to do this.
It really bothered me because this was the same woman
who last week looked at Nicki's eye and didn't know what
was wrong with him. Yuri told me the doctor normally
charged $50, but he would see if she would agree to do it
for less. I peeled five, new $10 bills from my wallet and
handed the money to him. Donna and I stayed in the car
while he went in with Natalie. We never saw him hand
money over to anyone. He would always go in alone with
the cash and return to the car when he was done. Yuri
strongly discouraged our presence when money was exchanged. Fifteen minutes later, Yuri returned and he was
smiling from ear to ear as he handed me the signed form. I
was thrilled.

Yuri was anxious to get the letter to the judge, so Alex,
our driver, took us back to town and dropped us off at the
courthouse. On the way back to town, Yuri told me that
Natalie had informed him that Tamara had been selected
for adoption by a Canadian couple. They had adopted a
sick child from Ukraine three years ago, and now that girl
is doing very well. He said they took Tamara to the Canadian Embassy in Kiev where she was examined and
declared healthy. I was floored that they had been allowed
to take her to Kiev to be examined, but I was even more
surprised that they believed she was healthy. FAS is a difficult condition to diagnose, but I am not a medical doctor,
so perhaps my assumptions were wrong. She is two months
younger than Nicki, but she was only three quarters his
size. She has two teeth compared to his four and still had

the look of an infant. Both Donna and I were thrilled that she had found a family that would love and care for her, and, as much as I wanted a girl, I knew I had made the right decision to adopt Rupert and Nicki. I had no regrets about my decision.

The rest of the day passed quickly. After a long afternoon walk, Donna and I returned to the flat to see Yuri and he was smiling. The combination of homemade chicken soup for lunch and good old American medicine that we gave him did the trick. He was feeling much better, and I told him it was payback for having taken such good care of us on this trip. He said he had something to give me and disappeared back into his room. He returned and handed me two small pictures. Natalie had given him an extra set of passport photos of the boys, and I immediately tucked them away in my wallet next to their baby pictures. Now I'm ready to go picture for picture the next time I'm talking to a proud parent.

After dinner, Donna brought out a booklet of Christmas songs to cheer us up. As we sat in the kitchen I wondered to myself if Ina, who was sitting in the next room, believed in God or if she had been brainwashed by the communists into rejecting any notion of a higher authority. At that moment I felt very sorry for all the people we had met since coming to Ukraine—sorry that they had been robbed of the ability to seek peace and healing from the one entity who was responsible for all of us being here on earth.

Wednesday, December 10

Dear Journal: This is the day I have waited for all these months when I will finally become a mother to my two little boys. I can't wait until this evening to record the day's events so I have decided to make my entries throughout the day.

8:10 a.m. Today is the biggest day of my life and there is no hot water in the flat. After waiting for Yuri to come out of the bathroom, he told me that work was being done on the pipes somewhere in the building, and hot water would be restored some time later in the morning. I pray this is not a prelude to a day full of catastrophes.

9:10 a.m. If all goes well this afternoon at the court hearing, I will officially become the mother, chief diaper-changer, and keeper of all-important toys for Rupert Sergei Schwartz and Nickolas Rudolph Schwartz. I will cease to exist as a single entity, and my life will never be the same again. I am both excited and very nervous. To accept sole responsibility for these two little boys, whom I didn't even know existed two weeks ago, scares the heck out of me, yet I am thrilled to be given the opportunity to share all my love and experiences with them. I wish the rest of my family could be in the courtroom today. I am very grateful that my sister will be there for me.

The boys will most likely be the last—and the youngest—grandchildren for my parents, bringing the new count up to 15. I pray to God that I will grow wise and learn patience. I'm really new at motherhood, but I am prepared to give it my best shot.

12:45 p.m. We have just returned from our daily visit to the orphanage. The first thing we did was to find Natalie and get a copy of their daily schedule. It seems fairly regimented, which I guess is necessary when dealing with so many children. I still can't believe I will have them with me all the time in a few short days.

6:30-7a.m. Wake-up and get dressed

7-8 a.m. Potty/play

8 a.m. Eat breakfast

8:30-10 a.m. Potty/play

10 a.m. Snack (juice, apple)

12 noon Lunch

12:30-1p.m. Potty/play

1-3 p.m. Nap

3-4 p.m. Potty/play

4 p.m. Second lunch

7 p.m. Dinner

8-8:30 p.m. Go to bed

I wonder if the boys have any clue as to what will happen later today? I think Rupert understands that I am different from the other caretakers but how different he has yet to learn. This will be our first day as a family. There is a term in the adoption community—it's called the "gotcha day." It means the day one can look back to as the first day as a family. I know this will always be a special day for me.

We made several stops on the way back from the orphanage so we could take pictures of the landscape. We won't be making this daily trip much longer, and I want to have a record of the countryside we have traveled each day for the past two weeks. The sky was blue and cloudless, and the air was cold. We didn't linger outside any longer than we had to in order to take our pictures.

Yuri is still worried about this afternoon's court hearing. He is making me more nervous than I already am with his talk of potential problems with the prosecutor. My stomach is growling with hunger, yet I can't think about eating lunch. Right now I just want to be alone. Ina and her family are here, and Yuri is talking with them in the living room. I need silence. I feel like crying but no tears will come. Everything around me seems so normal.

1:30 p.m. Only an hour left before we will leave to walk down to the courthouse. This is why I have traveled half way around the world, dragging my sister with me. I will try to relax until it is time to get ready for the court hearing.

8:45 p.m. The day is almost over—and now I am a mother! What a melodrama it was at the courthouse. Oxana and Sonia were both supposed to be there at 3 p.m. sharp. Sonia finally showed up at 3:15 p.m., but there was no sign of Oxana. It was freezing cold inside the courthouse lobby and I had to sit on my hands to keep them warm. There was no heat in the building, and everyone who walked down the hallway wore their coat. Yuri called Oxana on her cell phone to no avail. He finally reached her around 3:25 p.m. and learned she was in Lugansk on business. Why she was there instead of with us I do not know. Yuri went into the judge's office to speak with him and then called Oxana again. She finally agreed to drive back to town for the hearing. It's a miracle that everyone agreed to wait for her—especially the prosecutor who had the week off but had agreed to come in for the hearing.

At 3:15 p.m. Yuri, Sonia and I went in to the judge's office for my adoption interview. Donna was not allowed to go in with me. It was a sad little room with no official trappings or fine furniture. It was cold in there, too, and I was beginning to wonder how long this process would last. I was asked my name, address, age, occupation and income. In addition to the judge and prosecutor, there was a court recorder who wrote down the questions and answers. Earlier in the afternoon, we had prepared a gift bag for the female prosecutor at Yuri's suggestion. In addition to putting in a small bottle of perfume, I had inserted a crisp, new $100 bill. Yuri left the bag with the judge after the interview was over. I can only assume he will hand it over to the prosecutor, but I'll never know for sure.

The judge was a small man, about 5 foot 7 inches. He wore a sport jacket, a striped blue tie and nondescript slacks. He looked as if he hadn't shaved since yesterday, and he didn't make direct eye contact with anyone in the room. He looked uncomfortable and had a sense of uncertainly about him. He even took several phone calls during the interview. This was not the grand and solemn event I had envisioned. Once I had answered all the questions, we left the judge's room and returned to the lobby.

While we were waiting for Oxana to arrive, Donna took out the photo album of family pictures she had put together for me and showed them to Sonia and Alex. Sonia was especially interested in the pictures that showed Donna's new house. She lives north of San Francisco in a new, upscale community, which must be like heaven to people who live in Ukraine.

Oxana finally walked through the door around 4:30 p.m. and offered no explanation, excuses or apologies. The judge formally opened the hearing and read the petition for adoption out loud. Then I was asked to stand up and Yuri acted as translator for me, the judge and the prosecutor. He and I had prearranged that I would ask for the 30 days to be waived because both boys needed urgent medical treatment and that I had already arranged for them to be hospitalized upon my return. This wasn't quite true, but according to Yuri, I had to say this or I wouldn't get the 30 days waived.

Here is a list of the questions I was asked as best as I can remember. Most of the answers were in my dossier, which the judge had a copy of, but I'm sure he asked these questions just to satisfy the prosecutor that he was being diligent in his duty.

Why do you want to adopt from Ukraine?

Do you have any health problems?

Why don't you have any children of your own?

What is your salary?

Do you own your house?

Who will care for the children when you return to work?

Why is your sister with you on this trip?

Do you have any debts?

Do you have medical insurance?

Why are you asking for the 30 days to be waived?

The prosecutor asked several more questions, and then the judge and the prosecutor talked for a few minutes. The judge then told me he would waive the 30-day waiting period, and the adoption hearing was over. No hand shakes, no congratulations—nothing. Just like that I was now a mother. Everyone quickly left the room. The hearing had lasted a total of 30 minutes. Yuri went with the court recorder to make copies of the decree, and I went out into the lobby to give Donna the good news. Oxana smiled at me and showed me a piece of paper indicating the items she had bought with the money I had given her. She asked me to sign it at the bottom and then she was gone. I never saw her again.

We were all exhausted by the time we returned to the flat. Yuri had not been eating well and I thought his ulcer was acting up. He was so worried all day long, first about the prosecutor and then Oxana when she didn't show up. She was the last person we had expected to cause a problem. Yuri told us that just because you gave people money there was no guarantee that they would do what had been agreed upon.

Ina congratulated me with a kiss when we entered the flat and exclaimed, "New mama!" I'm sure the look on my face was radiant, and I felt as if I were floating on air. Yuri made a quick trip to the market before dinner to buy more milk and sour cream. He returned with a present of a dozen diapers. Donna and I both gave him a big hug and kissed him on the cheek. It was finally over.

We were all hungry and exhausted. After we finished with dinner, we sat around the kitchen table and discussed our plans for the rest of the trip. During our conversation, Yuri mentioned that he had overheard Oxana tell Sonia that the Canadian couple who was going to adopt Tamara had decided against it after consulting with a physician in Canada. Yuri feels confident that she will be adopted although I'm not as sure as he is about this. One of the things I regret not doing before I came here was setting up a relationship with a U.S. physician whom I could contact about health concerns for the boys. I don't know if it would have made any difference, but it might have eased my concerns about Nicki having FAS symptoms.

I'm sure once we have picked up the boys on Friday and have left this little town, it will finally sink in that these are now my sons, my pride and joy—and my responsibility for many years to come.

Thursday, December 11

Dear Journal: I had a really tough time getting to sleep last night. My mind was still reeling from the events of the day. I think I finally fell asleep from sheer exhaustion.

Today was one of the busiest days we have had since arriving in Ukraine. Yuri told us to be ready to start our errands at 8 a.m. sharp. Our first stop of the day was to the passport office in town which, unfortunately, didn't open until 9 a.m., so Yuri went to the post office to make copies of the adoption decree and fax a copy of it to Victor. I have yet to meet anyone in this country who has a home office with a PC and fax/printer/scanner. Everyone uses Internet cafes, the post office, and other public facilities to make copies and communicate with each other.

While Yuri made his rounds, Donna and I rambled through a small, outdoor market. We needed to outfit both boys completely and had a list, as well as a piece of paper with an outline of their feet for shoes to help us on our mission. We spied a table with children's slippers—they had little rabbit heads and looked perfect for wearing inside when shoes weren't needed. I bought two sets, blue for Nicki and brown for Rupert. They cost $3 each and I'm sure I was paying the "I'm a foreigner and I don't speak your language" price. Further down the road, we stopped at a stall that was selling footwear. I pointed to a shoe and asked the woman "How much?" The woman wrote down 240 hryvnia (which converted to $60). That was a month's salary in this small town. We quickly moved on and finished walking through the rest of the market. The sun was shining brightly, and there wasn't a cloud in the sky. It was also very cold, and my fingers, covered in thin leather gloves, were losing all sensation. After we had reached the end of the stalls, we hightailed back to the warmth of Alex's car to wait for Yuri.

Once Yuri returned, we took off for Lugansk. Our first stop was the train station to secure our passage out of this tiny little town. As he came out of the station we held our breath, hoping there was no problem getting the tickets to Kiev. Yuri sat down in the front seat, turned around and with a sad face he said, "No tickets." We both let out a cry, and then he smiled and said, "Just kidding!" He has a wonderful sense of humor, but he has been so worried these past few days that we haven't see too much of it.

Our next stop was the notary's office to have copies of the boys' birth certificates stamped. Yuri then headed off to see his contact, Lara, at the Department of Justice to work on expediting the boys' Ukrainian passports. Lara was to call her friend, Svetlana, at the registry office, where births, deaths and marriages are recorded. The office is open only on Fridays, Saturdays, and Sundays. I couldn't believe it when Yuri told me this place was open only three days a week.

Svetlana does a nice side business working on her days off to accommodate folks like me who can't wait another day to get their documents recorded. I had to go with Yuri to get the new birth certificates typed up with my name as their mother. It seemed strange to erase the boys' birth parents from their records. I felt like an interloper, removing all traces of the link between the boys and their birth parents, yet, according to Yuri, this is the way it must be done.

The registry building was an imposing structure. The lobby and offices were by far the nicest I had seen since coming to Ukraine. There were wooden carvings on the wall, carpet on the floor and heat—glorious heat pouring in from all directions. One of the walls was adorned with photos from weddings that had taken place in the office, with picture after picture of the smiling brides, dressed in ornate, white gowns standing next to their new husbands. Most of the parents were holding bouquets of flowers, and only a few of them were smiling. I asked Yuri about this last week when I saw his passport photo. He told me that the officials did not like people to smile when they were getting their photos taken. He said you would be admonished if you smiled. I guess a life-long habit is hard to break—even on happy occasions.

I asked Yuri about his wedding. He said it was a very simple affair with no big reception or fancy dress. He told me that honeymoons are for wealthy people. He and his wife spent a weekend somewhere, and then went back to work on Monday. Yuri has been married for 15 years, and I can tell from the way he talks about his wife that he loves her very much.

Yuri strikes me as a very moral and decent human being. He has a strong set of standards that he adheres to, and he has worked tirelessly for me—someone he didn't even know a month ago. He has made these past weeks, albeit trying and frustrating at times, more enjoyable than they would have been otherwise.

Svetlana interrupted our conversation, telling Yuri it would take about 30 minutes to complete the certificates. Since there was nothing more for me to do, I left with Alex to pick up Donna from the Internet café so we could go shopping for the boys while Yuri waited for the certificates. Alex took us to a store where we could buy everything we needed for the boys. It was very upscale for Lugansk and would have fit in any location in Manhattan or downtown D.C. We had a list made and we checked it over—hats, jackets, undershirts, tops, pants, socks, shoes, tights, bibs, bowls and spoons, and my first purchase of disposable diapers and wipes. The shoes were the most expensive at $30 a pair, but they were thick, leather boots that will wear well. The total came to just under $200.

We had overextended our time allotment, so we hurried back to rendezvous with Yuri near the café where we had stopped earlier for coffee. He scolded us as if we were errant schoolgirls. Then just as quickly he smiled and tossed us a bag with a delicious smell emanating from it. There would be no time for a leisurely lunch today, so Yuri had bought some cooked sausage and bread for us to eat. Our dessert was a bag of crumbled cookies that we had packed for the boys but forgotten to give them. I think it was the best meal I had eaten since we arrived in Lugansk. Yuri refused to eat anything until we had returned to the notary's office to get the new birth certificates stamped.

As we were driving down one of the main streets, a cop flagged us over. Alex got out and walked to the back of the car to talk with him. The police officer claimed that the car's left wheel had crossed the solid center line a few meters ago. This time Alex had to go to a parked police car and pay a fine. I asked Yuri later how much the fine was, and he told me it was 20 hryvnia or $5.

The notary at the first office we had been to was too busy to stamp the documents so Alex took us to another notary's office. The secretary at that office ruined one of the copies, and, since the second notary had already left for lunch, we had to find a third notary before everything was done. I felt as if I were in a Marx brothers comedy routine by the time it was all over.

By mid-afternoon we were on the road again heading towards the orphanage. Yuri had to collect the boys' medical papers, including immunization records, and send them along with the other collected documents to Victor in Kiev. When we arrived at the orphanage, it was strangely quiet. I followed Yuri into the children's playroom but no one was there—the children were all napping. A woman wearing a white dress and cap handed me a pen, and Yuri told me to sign the medical book for each child, acknowledging that I had been given a copy of their records. I had no idea there were any written records, or I would have asked for them before I made the decision to adopt the boys. I can't wait to read the English translation of these documents.

Alex dropped us off at the flat while Yuri worked on getting the passports. We darted over to the local market for what we hoped would be our last visit, and then Donna and I took the opportunity to launder the rest of our clothes. We're not sure what our abode will be like in Kiev, but it's always better to arrive with clean clothes—so says the seasoned traveler.

Yuri returned early in the evening from Lugansk, where he sent all the documents to Victor via the train. He said the woman at the passport agency in town had refused his $100 offer to expedite the process. The manager told him to contact Sonia tomorrow morning to find out what the fee would be to get the passports completed in one day. We couldn't believe it—Sonia had her finger in many pies as we would later learn. Yuri also told me that a single woman from Ireland had been offered Tamara for adoption and she, too, had rejected her. I felt such sorrow in my heart for this poor little girl. She had done nothing wrong, yet she was being denied the chance to become part of a loving family because her mother didn't know or care that too much alcohol during her pregnancy would permanently damage her unborn child. I don't think I'll ever forget the children I have seen here. I can still recall their pictures from my visit to the NAC, and it makes my heart heavy to know that I cannot bring them all home with me.

By the end of the day, we were exhausted. Donna desperately wanted to go out to dinner at the local café. Yuri said he wasn't hungry but decided to join us anyway. The moon was just shy of being full, and it guided us on our short walk across the town square. It was a clear, starry night, and I could see Orion, my favorite constellation. I have always felt safe in his presence and tonight was no exception. I will not miss this town at all; for me it was like a prison, keeping me isolated and confined for two weeks while I shuttled back and forth to see the boys every day. After tomorrow, it will exist only in my memory.

After we returned to the flat, it was time to settle up with Ina. I wrote a receipt for $420 and asked Yuri to get Ina to sign it. It wasn't until after she signed it that she confessed to Yuri that she had to split the rent money with her boss, Sonia. That woman certainly knew a good thing when she saw it, and she was in a position to take full advantage of the situation.

Later on in the evening, Yuri called me into his room where he had his blue plastic binder in which he kept all the important adoption papers. He gave me copies of a number of documents, including each boy's original birth certificate, as well as the paper signed by Rupert's parents turning custody of him over to the state. Nicki's mother had left the hospital before the papers could be given to her, so there was a different document for him that was signed by the police declaring him to be a foundling. Seeing the names of the boys' birth parents gave me a sudden sense of reality, and I wished there was a way I could let these people know that their sons had found a good home with someone who would love and care for them as her own.

Tonight I will say a special prayer of thanks to the boys' birth parents who cared enough to surrender their children so that they could find their forever home. Dear God, please bless these people and give them comfort. Let them know in their hearts that their sons are safe and will always be loved. Tell them that they are going to live in a beautiful country with unlimited opportunities. Let them know that their children will be part of a large and caring family with lots of cousins, aunts and uncles. And lastly, tell them that I will always be grateful for the gift they have given to me, and I will treasure their children until my dying day. Amen and good night.

Friday, December 12

Dear Journal: I had butterflies in my stomach from the moment I woke up this morning. Today was the day we were going to pick up the boys from the orphanage and take them on a 16-hour overnight train ride to Kiev. Today was the day I was going to become a mother to these two children and take them away from everything they had ever known.

Yuri left early in the morning to meet with Sonia to find out how much it would cost to get the boys' passports completed by today. He returned around 9 a.m. and gave me the news. She wanted $200 per child to get their passports completed. Since I really didn't have any choice in the matter, I got out my money belt and handed over the money. I will be so glad to leave this town.

All morning long I kept telling Donna that I was scared to death that I was going to fail as a parent, but she kept me calm—bless her heart. We played cards to pass the time away while Yuri traveled to Lugansk to pick up the passports. Yuri had shown me the boys' passport photos earlier in the week. Rupert had a terrible scowl on his face, and Nicki had a small bruise on his forehead. Not exactly the pictures you want to use when sending out family holiday greeting cards.

Donna and I lay down to relax for half an hour before we had to leave for the orphanage. By 1:50 p.m. our suitcases were all packed. Last night's laundry had dried and I hoped we could survive the rest of the trip without any major washing efforts. Trips like these help you appreciate all the conveniences we have in the States that are not enjoyed by people in many countries, including Ukraine. Washing machines, dryers, home PCs and full showers are just a few of the things we missed having these past two weeks.

Well, the appointed time arrived and, by some miracle, we were able to fit three suitcases, two backpacks and a camera bag into Alex's little hatchback. Everyone was quiet in the car as we made our last trip to the orphanage. Once we arrived, we went straight into the playroom and met with the caretakers. The children were napping, so the women went into the adjoining room and brought the sleepy boys to us. I had made up two large bags of clothes—one for Rupert and one for Nicki. Part of the adoption ritual is that everything the children are wearing are removed and they are dressed in their new clothes. Donna and I undressed the boys as quickly as possible. Even though the boys were supposedly potty-trained, we felt it would be better to put diapers on the boys for the rest of the trip due to our chaotic schedule. Nicki started crying first and then Rupert joined in.

We didn't waste any time dressing them in their new, matching outfits, and, when they were completely dressed, they looked so cute. The boys finally stopped crying, and, after taking some pictures, we put warm winter jackets and hats on them and got into the waiting car. It was mid-afternoon as we pulled out of the dilapidated parking area for the final time. The boys were very quiet. I'm sure they were scared even though they knew us from our daily visits. Rupert and Nicki finally began to relax as we entered Lugansk and they stared with rapt attention at the moving trucks and large buildings.

Alex dropped us off in the parking lot at the train station, leaving Yuri to lug our heavy suitcases into the waiting room in the station. We had an hour to wait before the train arrived, so Donna and I took turns walking the boys up and down the aisles. There was a little girl in the seat next to us in the waiting area. She was very sweet and wanted to play with Nicki, but he was too interested in exploring every nook and cranny of the large room. Everything fascinated him. It's easy to forget that he has lived his whole life in a small, isolated compound. He has probably been in a car only three of four times before today and certainly has never been on a train.

Yuri was nervous again—or more probably anxious. He couldn't wait for the train to arrive, and, as soon as it did, I helped him take the luggage on board. Our compartment seemed smaller than it had been on the trip to Lugansk, but, in reality, it was the same size with two bunks below and two above. We were all firmly ensconced in our bunks well before the final departure whistle blew, and the train chugged out of the station heading west towards Kiev. Slowly all the food and toys came out of their respective bags. We started eating and fed the boys bananas, bread and cheese. We also gave them some pineapple juice and a hard-boiled egg. Nicki in particular can't stand seeing someone eating unless he can have some of the food, too, so Yuri gave him several pieces of salami from his sandwich.

The boys were quite a handful in our little home away from home. Yuri had a great time playing with them, especially with Nicki. I told Yuri he should consider adopting a little boy, and his eyes were twinkling as he replied, "Yes, I love to spoil children, but it is very expensive to raise them and my wife and I work very long hours." Some things are the same regardless of where you live. Yuri made up the beds, and the plan was for Donna and me to sleep on the lower bunks with the boys, and Yuri would take one of the upper bunks. The bunks were so narrow it was impossible for me to sleep side by side with Rupert, so I tried to stretch out on the opposite end of the bed. Nicki was fussing with Donna, so Yuri picked him up and laid him down beside him.

We finally turned the compartment lights off around 8 p.m. Both boys cried as we laid them down, but Rupert soon found his thumb and quickly went to sleep. It will be a very long and sleepless night for the rest of us. Morning (and Kiev) cannot come soon enough.

Saturday, December 13

Dear Journal: Today was my indoctrination into Motherhood 101. No one had slept very well, and there was much commotion as we hurried to feed the boys breakfast on the train while we packed up all the toys and clothing. We arrived in Kiev around 8 a.m. It was cold outside and the sky was only a slightly paler shade of gray than we were used to seeing these past two weeks.

We soon made contact with Slava, our host for the next few days. Yuri had told me Slava and his wife, Tamara, could provide us with accommodations as well as cook all our meals while we completed the final portion of our paperwork before leaving for Warsaw. It sounded like a great deal. Yuri told me that Slava and his family had converted to the Baptist faith. It seems Ukraine is a prime prospecting land for new religious converts since the fall of the Soviet regime.

Slava is in his mid 40s. He is rather short but very solidly built and slightly balding. His car has a luggage rack (thank goodness), but even so, we had quite an ordeal fitting everyone and the luggage into his tiny Russian-made car. I have yet to see a car in this country that isn't completely covered with dirt and grime on the outside. Most of the interiors have several jerry rigged systems with missing window cranks and blankets covering the seat upholstery. People keep their cars forever and end up becoming amateur mechanics to save on repair costs.

We drove about 20 minutes and ended our trip in a residential neighborhood. Most of the homes in Ukraine have solid gates facing the street, either in front of or on the side of the house. Either way, you must go through the gate into the yard in order to enter the house. Once the luggage was unloaded, we were quickly transported upstairs. The room we will be sharing with the boys is about 20 feet square with large rugs, tapestries and posters decorating the wallpaper around the room. There was a nice carpet on the floor and a large window overlooking the street. Two double beds flanked the walls and a small cot was set against a large bookcase. There were several small dressers. A door led out to the open balcony on the front of the house.

But best of all, there was a feast waiting for us to devour in the kitchen right outside our room. There was a heaping pan of kashi for the boys and a large plate of buttery scrambled eggs, cheese, bread and hot tea for Donna, Yuri and me. I felt I had died and gone to heaven after having endured that hellish train ride from Lugansk. We made short work of the food. We then unpacked a few things and started to settle into our little room.

I was anxious to get to the Internet café to let everyone know what has been happening to us. It has been ten days since I was able to log on to my e-mail account and send messages. Yuri, who will not be staying with us, took me downtown via the metro to the underground mall where the Internet café is located. I was surprised at the lack of people and Yuri explained that the clothes in these stores were much too expensive for most people. The majority of Ukrainians did their shopping at outside markets where clothing and other items are much cheaper.

Once we were assigned computers at the Internet café, I started researching hotels in Warsaw since we will be leaving Kiev in a few days. I found a reasonable hotel near the American Embassy, but I want to wait until Monday to book it in case there is any problem getting a flight out of Kiev.

I was amazed at the poor condition of the roads and sidewalks as we walked between Slava's house and the metro stop. Huge chunks of asphalt were missing everywhere and people seemed to accept this as the normal state of affairs. Some of the streets in downtown Kiev were still paved with cobblestones although large sections had been patched over with asphalt. We also walked past a number of nice, new homes either under construction or recently finished. I asked Yuri who lived there, and he told me the houses were owned by the "new Russians," people who had learned to use the system in the new government to make millions in real estate and other businesses.

It was early afternoon by the time we arrived back to the house. Lunch was ready so Donna and I fed the boys rice and meatballs and then we ate. Donna had quite a story to tell us upon our return. It seems all the new foods Nicki enjoyed last night created a lethal bowel movement that took half an hour to clean up. I know this is terrible to admit, but I was grateful I hadn't been around to see it happen. I am slowly adjusting to the diaper-changing routine, but there are some things I can wait to experience. Yuri soon took his leave of us—I teased him that he was weaning us from our dependency on him as he will be leaving for home in the next day or two.

Donna suggested that we take the boys outside for some fresh air and exercise. Nicki took off like a bandit, exploring the sidewalk and grass. Rupert, who is ten months older, was petrified and started to cry as soon as we opened the gate to the front of the house. I picked him up as we crossed the street to walk down a wide pathway that was in a park-like setting. I carried him for several minutes before I had to surrender to my tired arms. He was a solid bundle of 25 pounds wrapped in a thick winter jacket. I stopped at the first bench and sat down to rest. Donna continued on with Nicki who showed no sign of slowing down.

It wasn't hard to understand why Rupert was so frightened. He had never walked down a city street with lots of cars and people before. His orphanage was surrounded by a complex of buildings in a small rural town in the middle of nowhere. If that wasn't enough to scare him, consider that in the past 24 hours he had been plucked from the only home he had ever known and was now living with strangers who didn't speak his language.

However, children are very adaptable, and, within 15 minutes, Rupert was strolling down the walkway holding my hand. We took turns with the boys since Nicki walked slower but could take off like a rocket when you least expected it. We had been outside for an hour when it started to get dark so we headed back inside. All our food and lodging cost $50 for the three days we were planning to be in Kiev. This was quite a difference to Ina's rate of $30 a day for lodging with no meals. An added bonus was Slava's extended family, who lives in the same house. His only daughter, Victoria, lived in the room next to us with her teenage daughter Julia, and Tamara's parents, Babushka and Papa, shared a room across the hall from us. Everyone welcomed us with open arms, and it felt great to have so many people helping out. The only downside was that no one in the house spoke much English, so our conversations were very limited.

In spite of all they have been through, the boys did pretty well today. Donna was still instructing me on how to provide guidance when the boys misbehave, and we made good use of a sheet of Russian words and their English equivalents, words such as don't hit, don't cry, don't throw, lie down, stay and good boy. We tried to repeat each

Russian word in English so they would begin to understand us.

Our last major event of the day was to give the boys their bath. I had read that children from orphanages disliked baths because of how they were washed by their caretakers, but from the way Rupert howled when we put him in the tub with only three inches of water you'd have thought we'd just dipped him in freezing cold snow. Nicki's cry wasn't much better, and we had every member of the family upstairs within two minutes to see what we were doing to them. We quickly washed the boys and dried them off, and only then did the tears abate. Bedtime soon followed and the boys were asleep within minutes. We had to create a makeshift barricade with pillows for Nicki to make sure he didn't roll off the bed. I'm going to sleep on the cot tonight, and Donna will share her bed with Rupert.

I can't believe how tired I am and it's only 8 p.m. There is no TV or radio here but I doubt we would have the energy to turn them on, much less listen to anything. So tonight ended my first full day as a mother although it's a title I feel I have yet to earn.

Sunday, December 14

Dear Journal: Boy do I have a lot to learn about raising children. Donna was so patient with me as she explained how to handle everything from toys to tantrums. She ran a day care business in her home for several years as well as raised three children as a stay-at-home mom, and she has seen it all. I can't even begin to think what I would have done without her, even if I had adopted only one child. I thank God every day that she agreed to come with me on this trip.

We made plans with Yuri for him to take us to the souvenir market this afternoon in order to buy gifts for our friends and family back home. I joked with him that I already had the two best souvenirs of any trip I had taken—my new sons Rupert and Nicki.

It was pouring rain outside, so Yuri called a taxi to take us downtown. Tamara lent us umbrellas and we grabbed two empty bags to carry all our purchases. Babushka graciously agreed to watch the boys, and we left them napping in her care. The drive downtown seemed to take forever, but we finally arrived on a street that was littered with two long rows of tiny stalls, all covered in plastic to protect the wares from the rain. Yuri suggested we do a quick walk through and then go back and start making our purchases. It was obvious he had done this before, and I must say that today, as with every day, he had the patience of a saint.

It was a most miserable day, but we managed to laugh and make jokes as we strolled from stall to stall, trying to keep our umbrellas under control while passing the other tourists. By the time we had made our purchases, Yuri was teasing us about how no Ukrainian home has such things as we had bought. But how could I pass up the two hand-painted metal trays, a steal at $10, or the amber earrings for Meg and Pat Mary, both of whom have done so much to make sure my house is ready to move into when I return? The Christmas ornaments will be keepsakes to give to the boys when they are grown up, and the decorative plates, well, I've always enjoyed displaying items from my travels, and they were so pretty and inexpensive that I just couldn't resist buying them. My bargaining efforts were somewhat successful although I must admit I felt guilty trying to negotiate with the vendors knowing they were working so hard to make a living. I told this to Yuri and he just smiled. He knows very well the difference in the standard of living between Ukrainians and Americans. It must be hard for him to travel with his clients knowing how easy and inexpensive it is for us to buy electronics, clothing, cars and other items, yet I cannot remember any instance of bitterness in his voice. On the contrary, he is very proud of the gifts he has received from other clients, and he has mentioned several times that he has a standing invitation to visit them in the States.

The boys were still napping when we returned to the house. Donna was not pleased as she had asked that the boys be awakened after two hours so they would be able to sleep that night. For myself, I will have no problem falling asleep. My experience with the cot last night was a total disaster. Tonight I'm going to share the bed with Nicki, and Rupert will sleep on the cot. We opted for a quick face, neck and hands wash for the boys tonight instead of a bath. Both boys still cried, but it was nothing like last night's howl fest. I'm already brainstorming how I will introduce them to the pleasures of bathing in a tub.

Both boys had a slight cough and nasal congestion so we gave them a small dose of decongestant medicine. After wasting several doses, I learned that there is a right way and a wrong way to hold a small child when dispensing medicine. Rupert went to sleep quite easily but Nicki kept fussing. He is teething and we think his new tooth is hurting him. I didn't have any medication to ease the pain so we resorted to the age-old remedy of a few drops of cognac on his gums.

Tomorrow will be our last day with Yuri. He has a ticket for a train that leaves late in the afternoon. Donna and I sat down tonight, and we each wrote a letter of thanks to him for all he had done for us. Our letters were very different in prose, but the message was essentially the same. Yuri was no longer a paid worker. He had become our friend and confidant. We will be sad to see him leave, but the excitement of going home in a few days is more than enough to keep our spirits up. Here is my letter:

Dear Yuri: You have shared so much of yourself with us these past weeks—helping me through the adoption process, taking us sight-seeing and shopping and helping me understand what the country and people of Ukraine are really like. I cannot help but wonder what my life would have been like had I been born here. Would I have become someone like Sonia, a "new Russian," or would I be more like you, working to help others, yet struggling at times with the inequities of life? I guess I'll never know the answer.

I have been very fortunate in my life, and I will always be grateful to you for helping me find my darling little boys. They have filled a missing place in my heart, and I know they will bring much joy and happiness to my life. I will carry home many memories our trip—the long train rides, dinners at the little café and playing cards at Ina's. These images will stay with me forever. I hope you will accept my gift to you as a thank you for everything you have done, but more than that, use it to enjoy some of life's little luxuries. Travel, spoil your daughter and wife with presents and eat well.

I would like to think we have started down the road to friendship, and I hope that we will meet again one day. Until that time, I wish you and your family health and happiness. May God keep you and bless you always.

> Your friend,
> Margaret

I inserted a generous tip into the envelope along with our letters. Then Donna enclosed a Polaroid taken of the four of us and sealed the envelope. I put it inside my binder and will give it to Yuri tomorrow before he leaves for home.

Monday, December 15

Dear Journal: Last night's experiment of sleeping with Nicki didn't work too well. I couldn't fall asleep listening to his breathing as he was so close to me. I guess I was just too wired. I grabbed my pillow and blanket and lay down on the floor next to the bed. When I awoke this morning, I was very surprised to see Nicki lying beside me—on the floor. I don't know how he fell out of bed without my hearing him, but I was scared to death that he had hurt himself and was unconscious. Fortunately he was fine. I'm sure this is only one of many mistakes I will make now that I have these two little boys to raise.

I had made an appointment with the consular at the U.S. Embassy for 8:30 a.m. this morning to get a letter confirming my adoption of Rupert and Nicki so I could apply for a Polish visa for the boys. Last fall, Poland decided that all Ukraine citizens, even adopted children, must have a visa to enter their country. The U.S. Embassy in Kiev will soon be able to complete all the INS paperwork. Once that process is in place, adoptive parents won't have to travel to Poland, but for now I must follow the current process.

There was a huge crowd of people standing in line to enter the Embassy when I arrived. I felt as if I were walking by a parade stand, looking at all the people who wanted to secure a visa to travel to America. I felt a bit guilty as I cut through the line and walked right into the security trailer. Once inside the main building, all I saw were hallways and a sign that led me to a small waiting room with two teller windows. I went up to one of the windows and introduced myself to Lilia, the clerk who handles all the foreign adoption paperwork. I handed her the packet of photos and documents along with the boys' new Ukrainian passports.

I sat down to fill out the applications and to wait for the letter I needed to take with me to secure the Polish visas. Sitting next to me was a middle-aged man who was working as a missionary at a children's orphanage in Simerophl in Crimea. As we started talking, he told me that many of the donations made to the orphanage had disappeared, never making it to the children. So now, instead of simply giving boxes of new clothes to the orphanage, his team opens all the boxes and tells the children to put the clothes on right there. Food, especially ice cream, is also opened up and an instant party is created. I told him how important his work is and I have never been more sincere.

As I was waiting for my letter to be typed up, I saw a couple walk into the room with a boy and girl. I asked the woman if they were adopting the children, and the smile on her face was all the answer I needed. The boy was five and his sister was three. I must admit I felt a tiny pang of envy as I looked at the little girl. Why hadn't I found a little girl like that instead of two boys? But then I looked at the photos of Rupert and Nicky on the applications I held in my hand, and I instantly knew the answer. God had directed me to these two adorable little boys because they needed someone to love and care for them. It's that simple.

I soon had the necessary letters and quickly exited the building. I will need to return here tomorrow for my interview to get all the necessary papers for my visit to the U.S. Embassy in Warsaw. Paper, paper everywhere. Governments live and breathe by the number, size and color of stamps they apply to any official document.

Slava then drove Yuri and me a short distance to the LOT Polish airline offices. They fly directly from Kiev to Warsaw every day. I had the option of taking a seventeen-hour train ride ($40 for the four of us) or flying an hour and a half (approximately $700 for all of us) to get to Warsaw. It cost a lot of money to fly, and Donna had said she would be okay with either the train or the plane. But the thought of spending countless hours in a tiny compartment with the two boys was more than I could handle, so I pulled out my credit card and booked a Tuesday afternoon flight.

We then walked a short distance to the Polish Embassy. The line outside was half what I had seen at the U.S. Embassy but long enough to make for an uncomfortable wait in the cold weather. Fortunately, we were allowed in without having to wait in line, one of the few times it pays to be a foreigner in Ukraine. After turning in my paperwork, I was told to return between 1 and 2 p.m. to pick up the visas.

Our next stop was to the British Airways office. I needed to change our return flight home from Warsaw, as well as purchase seats for the boys. A very polite young man at the counter told me with a pleasant smile that my tickets could not be changed because they were non-refundable. I knew he was wrong, but instead of arguing with him, I asked to speak with the airline's office in Warsaw. He gave me the phone number, and Yuri and I went to a telephone office where you pay to use a phone to make international calls. I paid the cashier in advance and was assigned a booth that was just large enough for Yuri and me to squeeze into. It was then I got the bad news. British Airways had no seats available on any flights out of Warsaw on Thursday. In fact, they didn't have any seats at all until the following Tuesday, which was when we were scheduled to return home. There wasn't anything I could do, so I went ahead and ordered the tickets for the boys. I requested bulkhead seating so we could lay Nicki down during the flight from London to D.C.

So with this piece of bad news I had to return to LOT and exchange the tickets for a flight on Sunday instead of tomorrow. Our hopes for an early return were dashed, but at least we had a safe and comfortable place to stay until we left. We passed the Romanian Embassy on our way to a cafeteria for lunch, and there was no one standing in line in front of the building. I told Yuri about my friend, Judy, who had tried to adopt a little girl from that country. Part of me wanted to walk up the steps and bang on the door until they let me in to talk with the Ambassador about the travesty of allowing orphaned children to suffer through life without the opportunity to be adopted by a loving family. But I didn't. I walked right past the building in silence.

After lunch we returned to the Polish Embassy, and I quickly secured the boys' visas. By then it was mid-afternoon and Yuri had to meet Victor to sign some papers and then go to the station to catch the train home to his family. We walked several blocks to a local Internet café. We stood together in a dark and noisy room that was full of people and said our good-byes. I gave him a big hug and kissed him on the cheek. I handed him the envelope and told him not to open it until he had returned home and had a chance to sit down and relax. He looked at me and his eyes told me that he, too, had enjoyed our time together. I told him we expected to see him next year on his trip to the States, but only time will tell how long our new found friendship will endure. Then he was gone and I was alone again.

Back at the house, Donna took the news about the delay better than I thought she would. She has been remarkably flexible for someone who has never traveled abroad before now. Our dietary and bathing habits in Ukraine are a far cry from what we are used to, and I can't recall her ever complaining about the hardships we have endured. I am truly grateful, not only for her companionship, but for everything she has done to help me get through this process.

The rest of the day passed quietly enough, and, before I knew it, we were getting the boys ready for bed. They howled again during their bath, and it took several attempts and two more snacks before they would both settle down for the night. Donna and I are switching beds tonight, and I'm going to sleep with Mr. Wiggly Worm, my new nickname for Nicki, and Rupert will sleep by himself on the small cot. I'm the only one left awake now, and I must catch up on my journal-writing before today's events fade from my memory.

Sweet dreams Yuri and God's speed to your home and loving family.

Tuesday, December 16

Dear Journal: I am writing this entry on Wednesday evening, the 17th of December. Yesterday, I was sick to my stomach and couldn't deal with doing much of anything. Here is my recollection of yesterday's events:

We were served mashed potatoes and bratwurst for breakfast today. Donna refused to eat any of it, and I managed to eat only a spoonful of potatoes and a small sausage. We left the house at 10 a.m. for my interview at the U.S. Embassy. The boys were required to come although the staff at the Embassy didn't seem particularly interested in them other than to acknowledge their presence.

We were at the Embassy by 10:30 a.m. but had to wait for Victor who was bringing the translated court decree and other necessary documents for the meeting. The other reason I was meeting him was to pay the additional fee for the adoption of a second child. I must admit I don't believe it cost him anywhere near $1,000 for the additional paperwork, but those were the terms to which I agreed, and I didn't feel it was fair to complain about it now. I also gave him $150 as an expediting fee for his contact at the Ministry of Justice to get the adoption decree processed in one day.

Victor's car had broken down and he was late for our meeting. I told him it was time to buy a new car. He just smiled and said that he was used to having it around after so many years—just like a wife. Yuri had told me something of Victor's past, although I'm not sure how much of it is true. I wonder if people like Victor are afraid to spend the money they earn in such a cash-oriented business. People may start to ask questions....then before you know it the tax authority is knocking on your door. I must admit that, during our limited contact, he has been very efficient which was what he was paid to do.

Once we arrived at the waiting area inside the embassy, I opened the packet of documents from Victor and began to read through them. There was a lot of information that I had never read before (in English), and I wanted to make sure I had everything I needed before I met with the U.S. official for my interview. One of the documents had additional medical information about the boys, including diagnoses for Rupert's fluid build-up and Nicki's eye problem. I wish I had known this information existed. I could have done more research but it's too late now. Rupert and Nicki are my sons, and nothing I read in those papers would make any difference. Once my name was called, I walked up to the window and handed over the packet of documents along with the boys' passports and additional photos. Then I was asked to complete and sign two affidavits, one relating to their health and the other dealing with immunizations.

While my paperwork was being processed, a man entered the room with his son. Frank was from Austin, Texas and had arrived on December 2 to adopt a young boy. He, too, had worked with Cathy Harris. The child he had adopted, Vitaly, a slender boy of six, was sitting quietly by his side. Frank had found Vitaly in an orphanage in Lugansk that housed only 53 children. Why they keep these orphanages so decentralized I don't know, but I have to believe that when they close the orphanage in Lotikovo where Rupert and Nicki were living, the rest of the children will be placed in the existing orphanage in Lugansk.

Frank told me the director at the orphanage hadn't wanted to show Vitaly to him, saying the boy was developmentally delayed. Frank kept insisting and they finally brought him into the office. He said he thought the director was afraid to let any of the children get adopted for fear that his job would be eliminated. Vitaly's mother had abandoned him at the age of four in a shopping market with his birth certificate tucked in his pocket. Can you imagine how difficult it must have been for his mother to do that to her own child? What a sad story. When he told me he had hoped to adopt a boy as young as two or three, I smiled at him and, pointing to Rupert and Nicki, said I had come here looking for two young girls.

Vitaly was very skinny and didn't smile at all, but once we showed him where the box of toys was located, he immediately found a truck and started playing with it. Frank said his facilitator's husband had driven them from Lugansk, instead of their traveling on the train, an experience I couldn't believe he wanted to miss. They were leaving for Warsaw this afternoon after Vitaly's medical exam and would be back home on Friday. I wish that could have been our travel plan instead of being stuck in our increasingly small room for another week.

After I collected my packet of documents, I was asked to answer about a dozen survey questions about the adoption process. The questions were fairly general. Did I use an agency? Did I pay more than expected in fees? How long did the process take? Was I pleased with my translator/facilitator? I should have asked how this information was used, but, by this time, I just didn't care. Then I had to enter a small, private room with a glass window. The gentleman behind the counter asked more questions about the boys' history and their health, and then he reviewed my survey answers. He asked me to raise my right hand and swear that the information I had written on the affidavits was true. Once that was done, he told me I could use the phone on the wall to call the U.S. Embassy in Warsaw to arrange my final appointment. I called and got a 9:30 a.m. appointment for next Monday, the 20th of December.

I had to make one last visit to the window in the main room to collect the checklist for next Monday's appointment along with information on how to register the boys with the Ukraine Embassy in Washington D.C. I find it ironic that a country that spends so little money on these children is so stringent about monitoring the children's well-being after they are adopted. I am also obligated to provide annual reports on the boys' progress.

It was around noon when we left the Embassy compound. Victor asked me if there was any trouble with the paperwork. I looked at him with a straight face and said "Yes." Then I paused before I told him, "They wanted to know how it got to be so perfect." He laughed, then he translated what I had said to Slava. We said our good-byes and drove away.

It was time for lunch when we arrived back at the house. The meal consisted of soup and shredded carrots that had some type of marinade on them. By the late afternoon I was not feeling well at all. My stomach was doing somersaults, and my neck and back were aching. I had no energy and could barely stand up. Donna was a real trouper, giving me time to rest while she dealt with the boys. We took a quick walk to the market late in the afternoon, but I could barely stay upright. Slava and his family knew I wasn't feeling well, and they all pitched in to help watch the boys.

I took some medicine for my stomach and prayed that all I needed was is a good night's sleep to feel better. Donna agreed to sleep with Nicki tonight so I could get some rest.

Wednesday, December 17

Dear Journal: This has been the longest and toughest day of my trip. I've been sick, and I've been sick away from home, but I've never been sick and away from home and cooped up with two very active little boys in a small room.

I knew I still wasn't feeling well when Donna and I sat down to a delicious looking breakfast of scrambled eggs, ham, cheese, and bread. I ate two bites and then pushed my plate away. Not another mouthful could I eat. As sick as I felt, I didn't have the luxury of curling up in my bed and pulling the covers over my head. I had things to do and could not delegate these tasks to anyone. So I got dressed and followed Victoria to a local Internet café about 15 minutes from their home. During our walk we cut through a park where people were lining up to fill their water bottles from a tap that was fed by a local spring. There were several old women with bent backs sweeping the snow off the sidewalk with homemade twig and straw brooms. It looked like a scene from an old movie, but I didn't stop to admire the view. All I wanted to do was find the café and sit down.

The best part about the Internet café was that it was blissfully quiet inside and the connection was pretty quick. After I finished sending all my e-mails, I sat there with my head in my hands, waiting for Victoria to return so we could walk back home together. I felt awful and dreaded the afternoon ahead.

I returned in time to help Donna with the boys' morning snack of yogurt and bananas. They are voracious eaters and devour everything in sight. The kitchen, just like Ina's, is tiny. There are small stools that fit under the table instead of chairs. Every nook and cranny is used to store pots, pans and supplies. I know people whose food pantry is bigger than this kitchen. Right next to the kitchen is the bathroom, which looks like it was last remodeled in the 1930s. The exposed hot water pipes dominate the one wall and we have been using them to dry the boys' clothing, which must be washed every evening.

It snowed last night and we took the boys outside before lunch to burn off some of their ever present energy. We stayed inside the courtyard and let them do some exploring on their own. Rupert likes to have his hand held, but Nicki is quite the opposite. Both boys are making many more sounds now and Donna is working with them to sound out words. They are both enchanted with the snow. I'm just glad there was some diversion that didn't require much energy from me.

Almost everything we have in our backpacks has been converted into makeshift toys for the boys. Fortunately, we have two of most things. Donna found a baseball cap I had brought, and it instantly became Rupert's favorite possession. He loves to wear a hood or hat on his head. We're not sure if it has something to do with his wanting to protect his head or is just an idiosyncrasy.

After lunch I lay down with Nicki and we napped together. He likes to suck on two fingers on his right hand and twist the ends of his blanket under his chin. Rupert, on the other hand, is a dedicated thumb sucker. I am beginning to notice their little quirks and habits. This would be much more enjoyable if I were feeling better. I'm still stressing about the rest of our trip. There is much that needs to happen between now and when we leave for home. I keep re-checking my documents to make sure I have two of everything for my appointment at the U.S. Embassy in Warsaw.

It was dinner time before I finally felt ready to get off my bread and tea diet and try some soup. It tasted delicious, and I'm cautiously optimistic that I will feel better in the morning. Donna has been such a good teacher these past few days. Now she's starting to push me into making more of the decisions about discipline, food and schedules. This morning I learned a new use for Q-tips. It's great for removing boogers from the boys' nostrils. I can only imagine the inventive uses I will find for things once I am on my own with the boys. I have to believe that my time here in Kiev is a good adjustment period for all of us. Once we are back in the States, Donna will fly home to California, and it will be just me and the boys—my boys.

Thursday, December 18

Dear Journal: The good news is that I am feeling better. After breakfast this morning, I took out two small toothbrushes and gave one to each of the boys. They immediately put it in their mouths and tried to imitate me as I was brushing my teeth. I was sitting on one of the beds and had one boy on each side of me. Donna took some pictures of us as we were sitting there. We were all laughing and the boys were having such fun.

The INS requires that the children receive a medical exam before I can get their visas, so Victor scheduled a morning appointment for the boys to be examined at the American Medical Center here in Kiev. It turned out to be quite an experience. Slava drove us there and agreed to wait until we were finished. While we were waiting in the reception area, I started talking to an American who was sitting next to me with his wife. She was expecting their second child and was at the clinic for a routine checkup. They were either Amish or Mennonites—he had a beard and she wore a plain dress, and her hair was in a bun with a white cap. They were missionaries, distributing Bibles and ministering to the community in a city about two-and-a-half hours south of Kiev. They have been in Ukraine for a year and had 18 months to go before they returned to the States. Our conversation made me think about all the humanitarian efforts carried out by Americans around the world and their outpouring of support in times of crisis.

Once we entered the exam room, Dr. Mathews started his examination of Nicki. He was weighed and measured for height. His mouth was checked and his heart and lungs were tested. Everything appeared to be fine. He didn't check Nicki's eyes, but, at that point, I decided to be quiet and get this over with as soon as possible.

Then came Rupert. Same drill. When I asked Dr. Mathews about the shunt inside Rupert's head, he said, "I'm not a specialist and I don't know about such things." After he reviewed Rupert's medical file from the orphanage, he started making phone calls. Apparently Rupert's last TB test indicated that he had been exposed to the bacteria. Dr. Mathews was advised to take a chest X-ray to confirm that Rupert did not have tuberculosis. The clinic only had equipment to X-ray adults, so we had to bundle up the kids, get back into the car and drive about 15 minutes across town to a local hospital. Dr. Mathews, Rupert and I went into the building and up four flights of stairs. We entered a large office that had an X-ray machine on the right side of the room. I was told to remove Rupert's shirt. Two nurses strapped a small shield around his groin and gave Dr. Mathews and me full-sized lead aprons to wear. We held Rupert, who was standing up against a small metal plate, and they took the pictures. Rupert was very good during the whole process. A few minutes later, the film was developed, and I got the good news—no tuberculosis. When I asked Dr. Mathews how much the X-ray cost, he said it was included in the exam fee. So, they include an X-ray in the exam fee, but they don't have equipment at the clinic to perform one, and he never suggested we take an X-ray of Nicki at the same time as Rupert. My confidence in his medical proficiency was greatly diminished, and I was thankful the boys didn't require any treatment from him. Each exam cost $100.

We returned to the house where the boys had a hearty, late lunch. I stuck to my soup routine even though Donna raved about the mashed potatoes and fried chicken. We now have our mealtime routine down pat. First the boys are fed. Then we barricade the kitchen with one of our suitcases to keep the boys out so we can both eat in relative peace.

Julia and her cousin spent several hours with the boys this afternoon, and it was a welcome break. I took the opportunity to review the U.S. Embassy checklist for my appointment in Warsaw and noticed that the staff at the U.S. Embassy in Kiev stapled different papers for each boy's birth certificate to the certified copies. I didn't think it would cause any problem but I was still worried about the possibility that something could go wrong and cause us to miss our flight back home.

The NAC will close tomorrow for the holidays and won't re-open until January 12. Ukrainians celebrate Christmas on January 7 in accordance with the Russian Orthodox religious calendar. This means that all of the families who had appointments in December but haven't completed their paperwork will either have to fly home and return in January or spend the next few weeks in limbo. That thought makes my week-long delay seem trivial in comparison.

Tonight I lay down with Nicki until he fell asleep. He nodded off against the side of my body, and, as I watched him breath, I thought about how different his life will be with me. Each day I feel a little closer to the boys. I showed Rupert how to kneel, and we said our evening prayers together before he went to bed. It was the first time he didn't cry as he climbed into his cot and laid his little head on the pillow to sleep. They are both such sweet children. I pray to God each night that I have the strength to raise them to be good, strong men.

I have to keep telling myself that everything is now in God's hands. For my part I am going to work on staying healthy for the rest of the trip.

Friday, December 19

Dear Journal: It was a wet morning but it stopped raining long enough for us to take the boys on a long walk to the park. I think we were all going a little stir crazy, and it felt good to get some fresh air. As I was walking along the sidewalk, I started thinking about the blue and yellow colors in the Ukrainian flag. I believe they're supposed to represent the blue sky and the golden grains grown in the fields. It would have been nice to come here in the summer time and enjoy more of the natural beauty of the country. The only colors I have seen are the gray, streaked skies and the brown dirt and mud that cover the ground. Never have I been so homesick to see green grass and well-manicured lawns.

During our walk, we saw stray dogs, pigeons and a cat. Each creature was thoroughly examined by the boys, who love to make dog sounds and stop to listen any time they hear a dog barking. Yet, last night Tamara brought her little dog upstairs to show the boys and they freaked out. They started crying and wanted nothing to do with the poor creature. Perhaps they've never seen a dog close up, and it will take time before they can enjoy playing with animals.

The neighborhood surrounding Slava's house is typical for Ukraine. The street has single-family homes, some more cared for than others. The city of Kiev is full of old, brick apartment complexes that would fit right in with tenement housing in the center of any major U.S. city. All along the main thoroughfares are small food vendors, usually women, selling everything from oranges to soaps and cookies. Cookies are big in Ukraine. Instead of buying them in boxes, they are displayed in large bins; some have jam or chocolate decorations while others look more like tea biscuits. It's a nice treat to sit down in the afternoon with a large cup of hot tea and freshly baked cookies.

I headed to the Internet café after lunch to check my e-mails. Pat Mary sent a message telling me that some of my friends are planning on welcoming us at the airport, and she is concerned we won't be prepared for such a large celebration. I told her that, even though it will be a long journey back home, it will feel good to see familiar faces after being away from home for so long. Reality is starting to set in with e-mails flying back and forth about car seats, bedding, changing tables, high chairs and more. Thank goodness I have a few months off before I need to go back to work. I feel as if I've been living in a bubble with everyone else dealing with the day-to-day affairs of my life, and now that bubble is about to burst.

During my walk to the Internet café, I noticed several men standing in the street with open bottles of beer in their hands. It was the middle of the afternoon, but no one gave them any notice. I saw one young couple; the woman was pushing a baby carriage and the man walking beside her had a bottle of beer in one hand and a cigarette in the other. I thought about little Tamara and how innocent she looked as I held her in Natalie's office at the orphanage. I pray every day that she finds a family who can accept her disability and provide her with a loving home.

I need to buy baby books when I return home so I can start to document the boys' firsts in life. I got my first real neck hug from Nicki today. Another first was teaching him to clap his hands as I sang "Patty Cake" to him after lunch. I was so excited and proud.

Six p.m. could not come fast enough today. That's when dinner is served, and food has a guaranteed calming effect on the boys. Rupert still puts too much food in his mouth, but he has started taking smaller bites when I use hand signals to remind him. He now gets a smaller spoon, and, if we give the boys cookies, I cut them up first so Rupert can't jam the whole cookie into his mouth. Nicki still cries when we put him down from the table, even if he's so full he can't finish the food left on his plate.

We had a delightful evening with the boys, mainly because Julia, Babushka and Grandpa spent time entertaining them. Julia gave the boys a small ball to play with, and Grandpa was trying to teach them how to kick the ball. Nicki didn't have the coordination to put his weight on one foot and kick with the other, but Rupert could do it if I helped him. He and Grandpa had a fun time kicking the ball back and forth across the room.

It was bath night again and Rupert started crying the minute I took off his shirt. His howling pitch has decreased in duration but not in decibel. Donna noticed that both boys had a small red rash across their chests and backs as we dressed them after their bath. We speculated that it must be a reaction to either the cheese or processed meat we mixed in with their scrambled eggs for dinner. Neither child is used to processed foods of any kind, but we don't know for sure if this is the cause of the rash. They also started eating boxed cereal yesterday morning, so that could also be the culprit. We put some cream on their skin to help dry up the rash.

Nicki had a terrible time falling asleep tonight. Usually he is down for the count in 20 minutes, but tonight it took over an hour. Donna was watching him and noticed that he kept scratching his left arm. She brought him into the kitchen, and we could see the rash had spread to his arm. I smeared hydrocortisone on his arm, and we gave him some cough medicine to quell his raspy breathing. He settled down shortly afterwards and was soon sound asleep.

The kitchen table has become our little haven—a place away from all the clutter and toys where we can sit and write or just talk. Sometimes Babushka and Grandpa eat late at night, and we suspect it's because he has a part-time job. I can't begin to imagine the hardships they must have suffered under the Soviet regime. Yet they have managed to retain their humanity in spite of everything they have endured. The walls in their house are covered with religious images and quotes from the Bible. It is reassuring to me that people like this still exist in the world and that I was fortunate enough to be placed in their care.

Saturday, December 20

Dear Journal: The first thing Donna and I did this morning was to shout with glee—whoopee! Today is our last full day in Ukraine. Tomorrow we are on a plane for Warsaw and then home sweet home. I've never been so anxious to get home in all my life.

The morning was pretty quiet. Most of the family members slept in or stayed in their rooms, so we tried to keep the boys from making too much noise. I've learned the Russian word for quiet, pronounced *tisha*, and must have used it a hundred times before 10 a.m. After a mid-morning snack, we decided take the boys for a walk outside.

Donna spotted a tiny park, and we made a slight detour to check it out. It had a nice playground and we put the boys on a seat swing. Nicki loved being pushed really high, and he protested greatly when it was time to leave. I was pleased to see that Rupert enjoyed it as well. I think they will be good for each other; Rupert is more cautious and Nicki loves to explore. Donna and I have been working with the boys to teach them how to play nice—not to hit each other and to hold their own if the other steals a toy. I suppose these lessons will continue for a very long time.

We had borsht and meat blintzes for lunch today. I will miss the hearty, homemade soups we have been eating. The folks at the Food and Drug Administration would be outraged if they saw how foodstuffs are sold and stored in this country. Yuri told us that some food distributors in Ukraine have been known to sell counterfeit foods, substituting margarine for butter and putting tea in recycled cognac bottles. We were amazed at this revelation, but, to him, it was just one of those things that people deal with every day.

This afternoon I had a rare hour to myself. I must admit there were times during our trip when I longed for a quiet corner, especially this week. I took this time to review the checklist for my Monday appointment at the U.S. Embassy in Warsaw, and I filled out what I hope will be the last form I will need to get the boys' visas. Babushka and Grandpa played with the boys after dinner. Donna and I organized our luggage and started separating out the items we wanted to leave behind, such as extra soaps and shampoo.

It has now been a month since my sister and I, full of anticipation and excitement, left the States. In a few days we will be leaving to return home, and I will become the boys' full time mommy. This morning as I watched them sleep, I felt so blessed that I was somehow chosen to find these boys and provide them with a loving home.

I told Donna that I won't be able to really relax until I have the boys' visas in my hand, and we are safely on board the plane home. But I also know that I have to take care of myself. Getting sick while Donna was here to help me was a real wake-up call. Tomorrow we pack up, say good-bye to Ukraine and head west towards Warsaw.

Sunday, December 21

Dear Journal: Donna and I spent the morning washing up and packing. Babushka kept the boys busy while we sorted out all the clothes, toys and medicines and decided what we would need to carry in our backpacks for the long flights ahead. Slava was going to take us to the airport at 12:30 p.m. to catch our 2:35 p.m. flight. I should have insisted that we leave earlier, but I just assumed he knew how much time was needed to catch our flight. It's never a good thing to assume, and this time was no exception.

We left the house a little late and didn't arrive at the airport until 1:15 p.m. Slava had to park quite far from the terminal, and I was already nervous about making the flight. By the time we found a luggage cart and got inside the building, it was 1:45 p.m. I had mistakenly thought that no one would be traveling on a Sunday, but, as we entered the building, it looked like the entire population of Kiev was fleeing the country. Our first hurdle was getting the luggage examined. Then we had to get in line to clear customs. Of course, we needed the forms we had filled out when we arrived in Ukraine. I had found mine two weeks ago, stuffed in my coat pocket, and, fortunately, did not throw it out. Donna had packed hers away in one of the suitcases and had to retrieve it while Slava and I held on to the boys. Then we had to fill out new forms. I had to redo mine because I had printed my name on the wrong line—more delays.

The longest line was at the airline counter. We were behind a man who was arguing with the ticket agent about a large, flat package that he wanted to take on the plane with him. Our business class line was still shorter than the economy class line (LOT doesn't sell one-way tickets in coach class), but as the minutes ticked away I was thinking to myself we might as well be back at the flat given the slim chance we had of making our flight.

We finally dragged the boys and our luggage to the counter to check in for the flight. By this time I was sweating both from the heat in the building and from fear that we were not going to catch our flight. It was now 2:20 p.m. and I thought we had a clear path to the departure gate. We went up the escalator and walked smack dab into another line, this time for passport control. Once I handed the woman our passports, she wanted to see the adoption papers. No problem. Then she told me she needed to take them to someone to be reviewed. I told her our flight was leaving in ten minutes and she kept smiling and said "Don't worry." But I did not believe her and I silently cursed myself for not making Slava leave earlier. It was 2:28 p.m. when she handed me our boarding passes. I really didn't have any time to review the documents she returned to me; I just shoved everything in my backpack and went through the checkpoint. I couldn't believe it when I saw another line of people. There had to be at least 30 people in line to go through another luggage check. My heart was pounding and my mouth was as dry as the desert. I had to do something quickly if we were to have any chance of leaving on our flight. I looked straight ahead and saw a nice looking, middle-aged man in line. I managed to somehow convey my desperation, and, by the grace of God, he let us cut in front of him and his companions. I literally threw my coat and backpack at the security attendant, and we whisked the boys through the last security gate. I couldn't even look at my watch to see if we were past our departure time.

Our gate was directly in front of us. One more stop to process the boarding tickets and then we ran—each of us with a boy in our arms, down a long ramp that landed us outside the airport on to the tarmac. A crowded bus was waiting and we were the second to last to get on board. My heart was beating so fast I could hardly breathe. "Deep breaths," Donna kept saying, "Take deep breaths." I have never been so relieved as I was at that moment, knowing we were going to finally leave Ukraine. As soon as the bus started moving, I noticed a couple with a young girl who looked as if they were from the States. It turned out they were from Norfolk, Virginia, and we were all staying at the same hotel in Warsaw. It was so nice to speak with someone from back home.

The plane was not very big but I didn't care. We had seats in the first row, and I sat with Rupert while Donna sat with Nicki across the aisle. Susan and Paul Jones, the couple from Norfolk, sat with Larissa, their seven-year-old adopted daughter, in the row behind us. The plane ride was just short of two hours, and both boys did very well for their first flight. I was so happy to be in Warsaw I almost kissed the ground as we left the plane. I felt that I was back in the real world again.

As soon as we arrived in the baggage claim area, a very neat and polite porter offered to help us with our bags. I immediately accepted his offer. We zoomed through customs with nothing to declare and were soon in the main part of the terminal. Nancy, my travel agent, had found a great deal for us at the brand new Marriott Courtyard directly across from the airport. Our porter took us outside the airport and across the street into the reception area.

The hotel looked like the Taj Mahal after our experiences in Ukraine. Our room had a huge, king-size bed with two cribs. I almost cried when I saw the bathroom. It was perfectly clean and hygienic, and the bathtub was sparkling white. The boys were in fine spirits as they explored all the nooks and crannies of the room. Donna and I soaked up the English-speaking TV news, but even the German-speaking programs were a joy to watch.

We had dinner with the Joneses in the restaurant in the hotel lobby. Susan and Paul were delightful and I really enjoyed their company. Susan had considered adopting as a single woman several years ago but decided to wait until she was married. A few years later, she met Paul and they have now been married for three years. They used an agency to facilitate their adoption, and our time-lines were very similar. I was shocked when they told me they had paid $3,000 through their agency to a contact at the NAC to get an early appointment in December instead of waiting until February. They had also been promised a referral for two healthy, younger children.

Their saga was heartbreaking. It had taken them three trips to the NAC to find their two daughters, each of whom was located in a different region. They didn't have enough time to complete the process and schedule the court hearing for Olga, their new 15-month old daughter, so they will return to Ukraine in January to complete the process. Larissa, who was traveling with them, was a darling little girl with dark hair cut in a page boy style and a very serious looking face. Her mother's boyfriend had been drunk often and physically abusive. Larissa and her four siblings were removed and placed in an orphanage about 18 months ago. Despite the NAC's official policy of not separating siblings, a couple from Spain adopted two of Larissa's younger sisters. Larissa did not know any English except the word no, and neither Susan nor Paul spoke much Russian. Susan told us of Larissa's dramatic performance when she play-acted getting drunk and passing out. Susan said her performance was very comical, but it was obvious that Larissa needed to act this out as her way of dealing with the pain and loss of her family.

I could sense a fragile bond that had developed between Larissa and the Jones. I asked if Larissa had been given the opportunity to say whether she wanted to be adopted, and Susan said she had consented to the adoption. I could tell that Susan was waiting anxiously for the day when Larissa would call her Mother. The look in her eyes when she stroked Larissa's hair told me she would make a great parent.

We had a very frank discussion about the politics of adoption in Ukraine. Susan told me about a rumor that the NAC director is married to the head of the KGB in Odessa. There have been many personnel changes at the Center over the past 18 months. Every adoptive family seems to have a different experience at the NAC, and I'm sure there are many secrets we will never uncover as to why some people find exactly the child they are looking for while others return home childless.

Dinner at the Marriott was a real treat with English menus, sparkling water, crisp, white linens and very attentive waiters. I am finally starting to relax and cast off the heavy weight I have been carrying on my shoulders these past few weeks and it feels really good.

After we returned to our room, it was time for a long soak in the bathtub. I told Donna to go first, and I would watch the boys. Donna came back into the room five minutes later and told me to come into the bathroom. She had filled up the tub with steaming hot water that was full of bubbles. Then she said to me, "This is for you, to celebrate becoming a new mom." I must admit I didn't protest one second longer than it took me to disrobe and slip into the tub. I was in heaven. I scrubbed myself from head to toe—twice to make sure I had removed every last piece of dirt and sweat from my body from the past four weeks. After drying off, I felt like a newborn baby, safe, secure and squeaky clean. I am so grateful everything went so well today—making the flight with only minutes to spare, meeting the Joneses, and finding this splendid new hotel. Praise the Lord we have left Ukraine and have landed in paradise.

Monday, December 22

Dear Journal: Today took us through the final hurdle before returning to the States—collecting the boys' U.S. visas. I had left a wake-up call for 6:30 a.m. to make sure we finished breakfast in time to travel with Susan and Paul to the embassy. We had decided to travel together since our appointments were only 15 minutes apart. Once we arrived at the embassy, we walked straight in—past all the foreigners waiting in line. We were each given a number and entered the waiting room. We managed to find a row of seats and settled in to wait for our numbers to be called.

As I approached the clerk at the window, I prayed that all my paperwork was in order. After a quick review, my documents were given a stamp of approval and I was directed to the cashier's window to pay a $1,135 processing fee. For some unknown reason, it costs more to adopt two children who are unrelated than if they were siblings. The last step was an interview with an immigration agent who looked at the boys and asked a few questions about their medical conditions. There was one more form to complete, and I had to swear again that everything I had written was the truth. By 11:30 a.m., we were finished for the morning and grabbed a cab back to the hotel.

After a brief rest, we went downstairs for lunch. The restaurant had the Christmas menu out and had decorated the area with a huge Christmas tree. The whole lobby looked festive, and we thoroughly enjoyed ourselves. There were only a few guests in the restaurant, probably because it was Christmas week. The staff was polite and attentive, and they spoke excellent English. If I weren't in such a rush to return home, I could easily see myself staying here for a week or so to recuperate from my long journey.

My next task was to go to the airport and visit the British Airways office to pay for the boys' tickets. Donna stayed in the room with Rupert and Nicki while they napped. I quickly found the airline's administrative center on the top floor of the airport. It was just before 2 p.m. when I entered the office. I introduced myself to the agent and explained to him what I needed to get done. Well, you would have thought I was buying two tickets to the moon. It took him forever to find the reservation and confirm the seats. Then the agent began to hand-write the ticket. I was beginning to get nervous about the whole process. Finally, it was time to pay for the tickets, and I gave the agent my credit card. He entered the number into the computer, and it spit back a message saying that my credit card was invalid. He tried again and got the same result. I told him that I knew my card was valid and asked him to call their main office, but he insisted it was my problem and that I should call my credit card company. This went on for over five minutes, and I was getting very frustrated. I was not going to leave that office without getting those tickets.

After taking several deep breaths I calmly asked him to try processing my credit card one more time. He mumbled something in protest, but I insisted nicely and he finally complied. This time the computer gods smiled upon me and provided an authentication number. I looked at my watch again. It was after 3 p.m. It had taken an hour to pay for two tickets. I kept telling myself that like Dorothy in *The Wizard of Oz*, there's no place like home, and I intend to get there as soon as I can.

I went back to the hotel and made arrangements with Paul Jones for us to return to the embassy to pick up the children's ' visas. We had the taxi wait for us and had no problem getting the visas. Driving through downtown Warsaw was a stark change from Kiev. I now understand why it is such a popular destination for Ukrainians as it looks so clean and prosperous. Earlier in the day I had seen a brochure at the hotel for a three hour city tour. I showed it to Donna thinking she might want to see something of the city while I ran my errands. I would have liked to tour the city as well, but as it turned out, neither of us had the time or the energy to play tourist.

Once I returned from the embassy with the visas, Donna and I decided to take the boys for a walk through the airport. We found a luggage cart and put them both in it, making it easier to get around. It was fun pushing them around the concourse, and there weren't many people to get in our way. The airport was beautifully decorated for the holidays, and the workers were putting the finishing touches on a huge Christmas tree in the lobby. There was a small section of nice shops that were filled with beautiful amber jewelry, handmade items and toys. We stopped at one of the shops that had a huge array of stuffed animals. The clerk put some of the toys on the counter, and all the sights and sounds of the musical animals properly impressed the boys.

It's hard to describe how I felt this afternoon. Part of me wanted to extend my stay at the hotel and stave off the harsh reality I knew was waiting for me back home. I wanted to freeze this moment in time—between when I've completed the multitude of tasks to find the boys and when we return home to start our new life together. I guess I really just wanted to enjoy and celebrate this moment while Donna was still with me.

Dinner was a splendid affair with the Joneses. We were the only ones in the restaurant and thoroughly enjoyed having a private dining experience. We had plenty of time to chat about the children and discuss what our lives would be like once we returned to the States. Everyone was in a joyous mood, so happy that this ordeal was finally complete. We celebrated with delicious desserts that left my stomach feeling as if I had just finished a big Thanksgiving dinner.

Once we had put the boys to bed, Donna and I packed up everything in the room. I left a wake-up call for 5:30 a.m. to make sure we could have breakfast and still make our 8:30 a.m. flight to London. I am so excited that we are finally going home. But once again, I won't be totally relaxed until we are safely on board and winging our way back to the U.S.

Tuesday, December 23

Dear Journal: Today was a long, long day. The flights from Warsaw to London and London to D.C. were quiet and uneventful. We had a five hour layover at Heathrow and did our best to keep the boys fed, amused and rested. Once we arrived at the airport we snagged two luggage carts to carry the boys, but it was difficult to travel between terminals with stairs, escalators, buses and long, long corridors to navigate. Again, I don't know what I would have done without my sister's help.

Once we reached Dulles, I surrendered the visas I had so carefully guarded to the clerk at the U.S. Immigration office. Every minute we had to wait for clearance seemed like an eternity after our long day of traveling, but we finally got permission to leave the waiting area. I had to fight back the tears as Donna and I pushed our carts with the luggage and the boys towards the exit door. I knew this moment marked the end of one journey and the beginning of another longer one for the boys and me. Our little duo was about to be disbanded. I looked at Donna and thought to myself. . .deep breaths. . .just keep taking deep breaths. We propped up the boys on the luggage carts and just kept moving forward.

We sailed through the doors into the terminal like conquering heroes. I spotted our welcoming committee almost immediately. Jack, Pat Mary and her family, and our good friends shouted at us as we wheeled the boys and our luggage across the room. It was a very happy reunion with lots of hugs, kisses and a few tears of joy. The boys took it all in stride as I proudly introduced them to everyone. After about ten minutes of celebrating, we were carted off to the parking lot and headed back to my apartment. The next few hours were pure bliss. We had a grand time talking about our adventure, eating pizza and relaxing. I made sure to say a prayer to thank God, my Mother, and the universe for guiding me to the boys and returning us safely home.

Part III

The Harvest

Wednesday, December 24

Dear Journal: Donna and I called my Dad this morning. I could hear the relief in his voice, and, after I hung up the phone, I reminded myself that parents never stop worrying about their children, even when they become parents themselves. Goodness knows I have a lot to learn about what parenting is all about.

After we got the boys fed and dressed, I took Donna to see my new home. I couldn't believe all the work that had been done while I was gone. I had furniture, a beautiful bedroom for the boys and boxes of donated clothing and toys. I was thrilled beyond belief. Of course, much more remains to be done, but it was fair to say that my house was now livable.

After a quick inspection of the house, we headed back to the apartment for lunch before taking Donna to the airport to make her flight home. I half jokingly asked her if she was ready to move back to the east coast. She has been my confidant, friend, advisor and teacher for the past few weeks and I will miss her. But the time had come for this student to graduate and strike out on her own.

I'm sure I'm still feeling the effects of jet lag, but the boys appear to be doing just fine. They ate all their food at dinner, and then it was time for their bath. Rupert is beginning to enjoy bath time, once the initial cry of fear dissipates. I tried something new with Nicki tonight. I had a small plastic dish, and I used the soap to make some bubbles in it. He was fascinated with them and, for the moment, forgot all about his crying. So ended my first full day back home.

Thursday, December 25

Dear Journal: Merry Christmas to us all. Today went by so fast, between changing diapers and doling out snacks to my two little bundles, I barely had time to relax and enjoy the day. The boys are exploring the apartment and making good use of the toys we brought from Ukraine. The ownership of any item, especially a toy, has already been the cause of several fights. I am trying to stay out of the squabbles so they will learn to deal with these issues without my getting involved. Needless to say, nap time was a welcome event, and I took the opportunity to replenish my energy level with a quick nap of my own.

We spent the afternoon visiting with friends and then headed to Pat Mary's for Christmas dinner. Everyone welcomed the boys with open arms and they behaved wonderfully. It has been a long day, and I am ready for 20 hours of continuous sleep.

Friday, December 26

Dear Journal: I am going crazy. The boys are bored and I am not up to amusing them all day long. I am learning the difference between whining cries with no tears and real crying, one of the many fine points of child care. Nicki doesn't understand the concept of no or time-out yet, but all Rupert needs is a stern look from me when I scold him and he starts to cry. Fortunately, these moments are short-lived and we are all getting along very well.

On the plus side, I have been getting phone calls and e-mails from friends and church members with messages of congratulations and offers of help. My top priorities right now are getting time to do laundry, pay my bills and organize the office in my new home. It's hard enough going to the bathroom without making it a major event.

My friend Jack and I took the boys and two carloads of clothes to my house this afternoon. The boys napped in their new room for the first time while we unloaded the cars. Pat Mary and her two children painted the room a cheery yellow, got the crib for Nicki assembled and even managed to find a rocking chair for the room. It was so nice to be able to close the door and let them sleep while we got some work done. Thank God for nap time.

I took an hour before dinner just to sit and relax, but the boys did not want to leave me alone. I tried to get them interested in their toys, but all they wanted to do was play with me. I have to start reading some of the child development books I have been given to learn what the boys are going through. I can't begin to describe how ignorant and helpless I feel right now. I know absolutely nothing about raising children, and my patience is wearing thin. How can I possibly survive the next year all by myself?

Today has been one long whirlwind. It's 9 p.m. and I am totally exhausted. Donna called this evening to check up on me, and I told her that I really missed her. I can't believe how much work it is to handle both boys by myself. It took an hour to give the boys a bath and put them to bed. Nicki is slowly getting over his fear of taking a bath. I made more bubbles in the tub, and he stopped crying long enough to smile. That's the first positive sign I've seen and I'm very encouraged.

Saturday, December 27

Dear Journal: My day is now made up of losing my patience and praying for patience. I pray I have the patience to play with the boys until they get used to being with each other and can amuse themselves. This morning was a whirlwind of getting dressed, fixing breakfast and finding toys to entertain the boys. A friend had given each boy several books, one of which plays Christmas carols. That quickly became the most desirable toy in the room after I decided that the balloons they had been playing with were ready to be retired. I couldn't get Rupert to stop putting the tied end of the balloon into his mouth and I was afraid he would pop it and swallow the plastic.

Each boy pushes the envelope with me a little bit more each day. Nicki seemed to be very needy this morning. Thinking he was bored, I got out the Play Doh, and we had fun with it for about half an hour. That's about the limit of Nicki's attention span. After lunch, Jack and I took another load of clothes to the house, and I started to organize my office. At least I will have my own bedroom again, something I really missed in Ukraine.

This afternoon I took the boys shopping so I could pick up a potty seat and a booster chair for Rupert. I ran into Mary Ellen from work and introduced her to the boys. Neither of us had much time to talk, and I promised I would call her once things settled down. It felt strange rolling a cart through the store with two little boys in it. I was waiting for someone to walk up to me and say "Where did these children come from, and what are you doing with them? They don't belong to you."

It's hard to explain this feeling. When I saw women without children walking in to the store I thought to myself, I used to be like that—footloose and fancy free. Part of me envied them their freedom, but, when I looked at the boys, I knew I had made the right decision. They desperutly needed someone to love them, and I do care for them more than I could have ever imagined.

I wanted to give them a quick wash up tonight and put them to bed a little early. Nicki absolutely screamed as I started to undress him, and he clung to my neck as hard as he could to keep me from taking off his shirt, yet once I stood him up in front of the mirror and let him play with the soap while I washed him, he was just fine. Rupert behaved fine until I laid him down on the cot. Suddenly he started wailing with tears streaming down his face. After a few minutes of this, I was afraid he would wake up Nicki, so I brought him into the bedroom with me. Rupert finally started nodding off to sleep. I took him to his bed, but the same thing happened again. He got up on his own this time and started knocking on the bedroom door. I tried coaxing him to sleep with pillows spread out on his bed, but he just started crying again. He finally fell asleep in my room lying on my stomach.

Each day brings new challenges to me. I am constantly second-guessing myself every step of the way. Neither of the boys can speak, making it hard to figure out what they want. They just point and grunt when they need something.

Sunday, December 28

Dear Journal: I was invited to participate in the Mass today as the congregation celebrated the Holy Family. I arrived at the church shortly after Mass had started and as I stepped into the hall, everyone rose and started to applaud. I tried hard not to cry as I carried the boys to the front of the church. The celebrant priest introduced us to the congregation and gave a wonderful homily about what it meant to be a family. I have never been surrounded by so many caring people. I believe now, more than ever, that opportunities to better your life present themselves to you every day. You just have to be willing to say, "Yes, I do need your help," and all the good things in life will flow into your arms. I know this because for many years I thought of myself as a self-sustaining island who needed no one else to survive, and now I am surrounded by so much love I can't stop smiling.

There are so many people I need to thank for their gifts and donations, but it's hard to find the time. I keep forgetting that, as a new mother, I need to make sure I don't wear myself out. I talked to Donna this afternoon and gave her an update on my progress. How I miss her company. I shared with her all my trials and tribulations about potty training and toy stealing.

I decided to give the boys a bath this evening and see if I could calm Nicki's nerves. I added a bathing sponge and a rubber ducky to the bathtub toys and was delighted with the results. The boys played very well together, and I was able to wash them with no crying.

It's now just past 10 p.m. and I am completely exhausted. I'd better start doubling up on my daily dose of vitamins.

Monday, December 29

Dear Journal: I actually slept in until 7:30 a.m. this morning. The jet lag must be wearing off and not a day too soon. Pat Mary and her 17-year old son Charlie agreed to watch the boys for the day so I could get some work done at the house. I got the boys dressed in record time, but it looked like I was going away for the weekend as I loaded up my car. I had a toy bag, a diaper bag and a food bag—and I still managed to forget their bibs. Rupert and Nicki quickly made themselves at home at Pat's, and I quietly left so as to not make a scene. I had a mountain of mail to open and several important calls to make, including scheduling an appointment with the pediatrician for the boys. After a quick lunch, I took another load of clothes to my new house. It was a beautiful day outside—warm and sunny. I felt that the day had been made to order just for me.

I returned to pick up the boys around 4:30 p.m. after a full day of housework and shopping. They were playing outside and it was great to see them smiling and happy. I must admit I felt pretty good myself. My day off was just what I needed, and I gave my sister a big hug before I left the house with the boys.

While undressing the boys this evening, I noticed they both have a slight rash—Nicki's is worse than Rupert's and is concentrated around his chest and left arm. I gave them a dose of children's Benedryl to stop the itching, but I am very anxious to get them to the pediatrician and have them thoroughly examined.

I was able to entice Rupert onto the potty this evening after dinner. Both boys have bowel movement two to three times a day, and it's generally right after eating. I'm hoping the new pull-up diapers I bought for Rupert will encourage him to use the potty. Everything went smoothly until it was time to put the boys to bed. After I put Nicki in the crib, I knelt down with Rupert to say his prayers. When he climbed into bed he started to cry. I went into the bedroom to watch TV, and within two minutes, Rupert was banging on the door. I put him back to bed three times, but he kept getting up. I decided to stay with him and sing him lullabies until he went to sleep.

Friday, January 2

Dear Journal: The days are beginning to blur together. I can't begin to explain the range of emotions I have felt these past few days—frustration, anxiety, desperation and gratitude. The real adjustment period for all of us has just begun. I'm learning how much time the boys need to eat and get dressed. Also, how short their attention spans are, something that is clearly related to how tired they become. One thing I know for sure is that it takes them no time at all to get into trouble.

Rupert is very susceptible to head injuries due to the shunt in the back of his head. He has already bumped his head several times this week. Nicki, on the other hand, is so quick and speedy that I'm concerned he can grab things that might harm him before I have a chance to put them out of his reach. I am trying to be very productive during their nap time—checking e-mail, making phone calls and doing laundry, but the two hours don't last nearly long enough. I am running on the fuel of good wishes and prayers from my friends and neighbors, and I'm due for a maintenance overhaul.

Everyone who meets the boys tells me how cute they are, but all I can think of is the plight of the children left behind at the orphanages. I continue to think about Tamara and the little mute boy whose picture I saw at the NAC in Kiev. I wish I had the resources to go back and bring them both home with me. It's a haunting feeling, knowing that there are children who may never feel the love of a mother or father and will spend every night of their lives praying for someone to take them home. I must admit that tears well up in my eyes when I think about all the love I have received in my life and how much that is lacking in the lives of the children who are still at the orphanages.

The good news is that my energy level is rising but so too is my realization of the tasks ahead. I am still several days away from moving into my new home, and I am anxious to get settled in. The holiday season is fast disappearing, and I know that next week will bring many challenges. I am grateful that I don't have to return to work right away so the boys and I can get used to being with each other.

Rupert is still having problems going to sleep. He obediently climbs into bed at night but then he starts to cry, gets out of bed and wants to come into my bedroom. I've tried singing lullabies to him, but as soon as I stop, he starts crying again. I don't know why this is happening. I'm not sure if I should be stern and send him back to bed alone or coddle him and stay at his side until he falls asleep. I'm afraid if I stay with him, it will become a habit that will be hard to break. I can't begin to imagine what is going on inside his mind right now. He has been through so many changes these past two weeks, and I wish I were better equipped to handle these situations. I guess that's what all parents say.

Monday, January 5

Dear Journal: I feel as if I have turned the corner today. My energy has returned and I feel more in control than I have since I returned home two weeks ago.

I am getting ready to move into my new home in a few days, and I welcome the thought of not living out of a suitcase. I can't wait to get settled in with the boys. They have lots of new toys, including little cell phones that they simply adore. We play a lot and I am trying to work in concepts, colors and words. They love to climb all over me, and I feel that my pants have grown Velcro as they continue to attach themselves to me.

Jack and I took them to a local restaurant for lunch today and they behaved beautifully. It's hard to believe that these children were in an orphanage in a tiny little town in rural Ukraine less than a month ago. They have adapted so well and everything is such a wonder to them. Yesterday at church, Rupert and Nicki were in the playgroup and Rupert learned how to use a straw. I was so proud of him.

I am slowly realizing what I mean to these little boys. I am their new caretaker—when they hurt themselves they look to me to comfort them; when they are hungry I am the one to feed them, and when they are tired I am the one to pick them up and hold them. It is such an incredible experience to have these little strangers depend upon me for everything. They have accepted me unconditionally, and I have to admit I love it when they need me. I e-mailed photos of the boys to my friends and family today, and I'm sure I sounded just like every other proud parent.

Rupert seems to be settling down better at bedtime. Depending on the day's events, I've decided to either not give him an afternoon nap or let him sleep only an hour. I want to make sure he has one-on-one time with me each day. Nicki is much more demanding than Rupert. Yesterday, while Nicki was napping, I put Rupert in the high chair to eat his lunch, and he sat there contentedly for over an hour enjoying his sandwich and milk.

I am blessed with good neighbors, family and friends. I believe I am on the right path in my life, and I am more excited about what the future will bring than I have been for a long, long time.

Wednesday, January /

Dear Journal: It's just before 11 p.m. and I have come from the boy's bedroom. They are fast asleep ensconced in their warm pajamas. We made the big move today, and tonight I will be sleeping in my new home for the first time since I bought it in August. I am tired but feel good.

My daily schedule gives me little time for myself. I usually get up between 7:30 a.m. and 8 a.m. and Rupert is generally already awake. Breakfast is chaotic to say the least. I usually end up eating cold eggs or soggy cereal, the result of chasing Nicki down to change his diaper and getting Rupert on the potty so he can do his thing.

By the time I have the boys and myself dressed, they are already bored and clinging to me like peaches on a tree. I have been playing a cassette of children's songs which Nicki really likes. After of few rounds of "Old MacDonald Had a Farm" and "Row, Row, Row Your Boat" it's time to make the morning snack. Out come the cleaned bibs from breakfast; I usually give the boys some plain yogurt and bananas. After the clean-up my little charges demand I return to the play area. Lunch is served between noon and 1 p.m., and nap time starts between 1:30 p.m. and 2 p.m. Nap time can last from one-and-half to two hours, just enough time to eat lunch, read the mail and make some phone calls. Then the routine recycles itself with an afternoon snack, more playtime, dinner, bath and bed.

Dinner was very quiet tonight. It felt strange being alone with the boys. It was the first time we had eaten dinner without Jack. Talk about one-way conversations. After dinner, Rupert wanted some time with me, so I picked him up and held him while Nicki continued to attack the plastic containers I had put into a special drawer in the kitchen. Earlier in the afternoon, I had to reprimand Nicki for climbing into the drawer and sitting in it. I swear he gets into everything. Bath time came quickly, and by 8:45 p.m., the boys had quieted down in their beds.

I had a few chores to complete, including making up my new bed for the night. The house is very quiet, and it looks totally different from when I bought it. I am so relieved that I am finally home. I can honestly say that I would like to take my suitcases and store them up in the attic for a long, long time. I simply want to enjoy being with the boys, entertain my friends and neighbors, and catch up on all the projects I had started last fall.

Saturday, January 10

Dear Journal: It was only a month ago today that the court hearing took place whereby I legally became the boys' mother. It seems light years away right now.

I picked my Dad up at the airport yesterday morning. I was pleasantly surprised last week when he told me he wanted to visit us and meet his new grandsons. He is such a natural with children. He loves to play with Rupert and Nicki, and they really enjoy the attention. It's really nice having him in the house. Not only do I have someone to talk to, but he can watch one of the boys while I am changing the other's diaper. This morning we were all in the living room and there was such a cozy atmosphere.

It's funny the choices we make in life. My father got married at 32 and raised seven children. He was a devoted husband to my mother and has been married for over 20 years to Bee, his second wife, whom he married several years after my mother passed away. Between them, they now have 15 grandchildren, and he enjoys spending time with all of them. I compare him to some ex-boyfriends for whom the idea of making a commitment meant agreeing to make plans for a weekend more than two weeks in advance. And here am I—the ex-world traveler who has traded her suitcase for a diaper bag. It is so easy to let life carry you along like surfing a wave. You can surrender yourself and let the energy of the water carry you onto the beach, or, like me, you paddle against the current and decide for yourself in what direction you will flow.

I can't deny there have been moments in the past few weeks when I would have loved to hand the boys over to someone and say—here, just take care of them while I get my life organized, and I'll come back for them when I'm done. However, life doesn't happen like that. This is truly the greatest challenge I have ever faced. I continue to ask God each day for the strength and health to carry on and to give these boys all the love and attention they deserve.

Tuesday, January 13

I took both boys to the pediatrician for their check-up today. Rupert and Nicki tested positive for exposure to tuberculosis; apparently BGC, one of the immunization shots they are given in Ukraine, often creates a false positive with this test. The doctor ordered chest X-rays for both boys just to be sure they don't have TB, and he prescribed an antibiotic that both will have to take for the next six months to kill any latent TB cells. He also ordered a host of tests to check for everything from AIDS to parasites.

Other than that, their examination went well. Each boy has gained two pounds. I'm especially glad to hear that about Nicki, who is so skinny. There were no physical problems noted by the doctor, but I had to admit I'm not sure how experienced he really is in dealing with issues specific to internationally adopted children.

Nicki has a minor ear infection, although you'd never know it from his behavior. The doctor prescribed some antibiotics and told me that it should clear up in a few days. I got the name of a well-regarded pediatric ophthalmologist from Karen and will call tomorrow for an appointment to check out Nicki's left eye.

Friday, January 16

Dear Journal: This week has gone by so quickly. I took Dad back to the airport on Wednesday and called home that night to see how he was doing. Bee told me he was exhausted, but she also said he had a great trip and had very nice things to say about the boys.

My friend John from PAX came over this afternoon and installed child-proof locks on the two kitchen cabinets that have all the cleaning supplies. I can deal with Nicki getting into the pots and pans, but it's the chemicals I'm worried about. Another friend, Virginia, came over this afternoon and helped me sort through all the donated clothes. She has several grown children, including twins, and she was invaluable in helping me figure out what size clothing the boys wore. Nicki is a true 18 months and Rupert is a 2T (toddler) although most American children wear a size above their age.

I can tell this is going to be a long haul, and I understand why some women who are not able or willing to devote 110 percent of their time and energy to their children see motherhood as a drain on their life. You are your children's primary, secondary and backup provider for food, love, security, entertainment, educational stimulus and the list goes on. I can't remember when I have been more tired at the end of each day. I'm eating more than I have in a long time and am still losing weight.

Yet, there are moments I wouldn't trade for the world. When I get a hug or can stop a cry it makes me feel great. When I see them doing something for the first time, I am thrilled that I can be part of their accomplishment. I am also relieved when nap time and night time roll around. I think of my single friends and, yes, there is some envy. To have the freedom to do what I want when I want is something I won't experience for a long time.

On Thursday I arranged for a friend to come over to spend a few hours with the boys so I could run errands. It felt so good being able to crank the music up in my car and go about my tasks unencumbered, yet it was nice to come back home and see the boys' smiling faces. Everything takes so long with them—getting them dressed, getting in and out of the car. Even a simple trip to the drug store can be a stressful event. I try not to make more than three stops during a single car trip. Nicki really fusses about getting in his car seat. I know it's hard for them not to stay close to me when there is so much that is new to see.

This afternoon when I held up a pair of overalls that were a size 4T (for a four year old), I wondered how the boys would look when they were big enough to wear them. It seems they will never grow up, but I'll settle for a two-way conversation with them and getting rid of the changing table. Oh, how my goals have changed.

Monday, January 19

Dear Journal: The days are all running into each other. I keep looking at the piles of laundry and the mess in my room, and I wonder if they will ever get cleaned. I start the day with so much energy, but, by the time the boys are in bed, I am totally exhausted.

Rupert had a major meltdown at dinner tonight. I'm not sure if it was the beef I put in the rice or the green beans. I think he has problems chewing food that isn't fairly soft. I tried to get him to eat some vegetable soup, but he wasn't interested in eating anything. I wanted to end the meal on a positive note, so I brought out some peach slices and he slurped those right up. Nicki, who has only four teeth, continues to devour everything I give him. Right now, he is eating as much as Rupert, and I've noticed another tooth has broken through Nicki's gums.

On a positive note, Jack and I took the boys out to lunch yesterday, and Nicki learned to use a straw. It was very exciting—he is such a mimic. However, sometimes his enthusiasm works against him. The other night the boys were in the bathtub, and Nicki took a huge bite out of the Ivory soap bar. I couldn't help but laugh at the expression on his face; then I helped to get all the soap out of his mouth.

My friend Liz came over for dinner Saturday night. She's in her late 40s and single like me. I've known her for a number of years, and I can honestly say she has more motherly instinct in her than almost anyone I know. She has lots of pets and plenty of nieces and nephews, but I don't think she will ever have kids.

It's a lot of work—more work than I ever imagined. Planning for meals, changing diapers and trying to throw in some learning along the way is a lot tougher than it would appear. It's been hard to keep the friendships I have with my single women friends. Some of them, like Liz, have responded warmly to my new family. But I can sense that I will probably lose the friendship of others who are more focused on their work or other activities and don't have the time to spend me with me now that I have the boys.

I can't believe January is almost over. One of my precious work-free months is slowly slipping away from me. I still haven't started my research into child care, and I am praying that I can finish the renovation on the bathroom before the beginning of April. We'll see. Right now I would settle for a neatly folded pile of clean clothes and fresh, clean sheets on my bed.

Tuesday, January 20

Dear Journal: The reality of my new lifestyle is slowly sinking in. Every morning when I wake up I lie in bed, and listen for the boy's voices. At night when I walk by their room I tread a little lighter just to make sure I don't disturb them, although that same silence in the daytime is dangerous. When I don't hear their voices or some noise, I know they are up to something and I'm usually right.

I keep thinking how much fun it would be to have a husband to share all of this with me. At times, I am so busy I can't pay as much attention to the boys as I would like. Just cleaning up after dinner, getting them ready for bed and then having enough energy to work on my correspondence or organize a closet is exhausting. I often think of my mother and what she must have felt all those years when she had seven children to tend to and still had time for her husband and household. I've made a little list to compare what her life was like versus mine, and it's quite an eye opener:

MOM	ME
♣ New mother at age 24	♣ New mother at age 45
♣ Had a wonderful husband	♣ Going it on my own
♣ Stayed at home with like-minded neighbors	♣ Taking several months off then going back to work full-time
♣ Had no car of her own	♣ Have my own car
♣ Had milk delivered to the house	♣ Am buying organic milk at the store to eliminate concerns about hormones

MOM	ME
❧ High school degree	❧ MBA in Int'l Business;
❧ Never traveled abroad until later in life	❧ World traveler
❧ Used cloth diapers	❧ Regrettably have gone over to the dark side and am using disposables
❧ Dependent on husbandfor income	❧ Dependent on self for income
❧ Had parents, in-laws and relatives within 30 minutes drive	❧ Have one sister with two teenagers 30 minutes away

My house has been such a blessing to me. As much trouble as it was to clean up and make into a home, I couldn't ask for a better layout. All the living space is on one floor, and it's very functional. I can go from the boys' room to the laundry room to the kitchen to the breakfast nook in just over a minute. We usually stay in the back of the house where the kitchen is during the mornings and then move to the front of the house where the living and dining room are located in the afternoons and evenings.

I admit to getting lonely, but my family and neighbors have been very supportive. I know that I have many people still praying for me, and for that I am truly grateful. I can only guess at what my life would have been like had I chosen to stay childless, yet I do not regret my decision. On the contrary, I am growing to love these little boys a little bit more each day.

Wednesday, January 21

Dear Journal: Today was another milestone for me and the boys. We attended our first group activity at the local community center. I had signed us up for a class entitled "Tales and Tunes." It was promoted as a stepping stone to prepare children for pre-school. It lasted 45 minutes, and there were eight children in the room plus the boys. I was the only one with two children, and I definitely had the most active little ones. All the other kids sat quietly on their mom's lap during the song session. The class was fun and it got us all out of the house for a few hours.

Since I had walked the mile or so to the community center with the boys in the stroller, I decided to stop by the park on the way home. The boys really enjoyed themselves on the swings and had a great time going down the slide. Nicki is a daredevil. He went down the big slide on his stomach and tried to go down standing up. He shows no fear when climbing up or going down stairs. Rupert is more cautious but still seems to enjoy himself.

Rupert has been very clinging today. He has refused to do anything on the potty for several days and fussed over his dinner again last night. So today I spent some time alone with him while Nicki napped, hoping that would give him some comfort. I think he's jealous of the time I spend with Nicki. I am trying to pay more attention to Rupert, but there are times when I can't carry him, such as when we went for a walk this afternoon. When I said no, he threw a major temper tantrum, crying and kicking his feet.

I am still trying to fold the laundry I washed three days ago, but there is always something that gets in the way. I have to register the boys with the Ukraine Embassy and figure out how to get their citizenship squared away. Everyone I talk to tells me I need a different form, so I have sent an e-mail to the adoption newsgroup hoping someone can help me.

I made an appointment for a CAT scan and shunt survey for Rupert after speaking with Dr. Magrum, the neurologist and have scheduled an appointment for Nicki to have his eye examined. I had an appointment this week with Dr. Scott, my eye doctor, and brought the boys with me to meet him. He told me about a colleague who specialized in making eye prostheses and went to Ukraine specifically looking for a child who needed his special skill. He and his wife adopted a six-year-old girl who had been shunned by her playmates and the orphanage personnel because she was missing an eye. She is now happy in her new family in the States. When I hear about people who open their homes up to children with major disabilities, I wish I had the energy and the resources to handle a child with more physical challenges.

I called Mary Ellen this afternoon to thank her for sending a care package with several wonderful children's books, including two about adoptive children. We ended up having a long conversation about some of the challenges she has dealt with as a single parent. She also gave me good advice about how to handle questions from the boys when they get older and ask about their birth parents. I told her how I ended up with two boys even though my preference had been to bring home two girls. She shared some funny stories with me about raising boys versus girls. Her advice to me was that raising boys will break your house, but raising girls will break your heart.

Thursday, January 22

Dear Journal: Lists! Lists! What did I ever do without them? I've never used a grocery list before, but God help me if I forget something now. Today I had four hours to run my errands while a friend watched the boys. I made it to the pool office, copy store, picked up my PC and the last of my boxes from my friend's basement and bought 16 bags of groceries. I spent over an hour at the grocery store, mainly checking prices and reading labels. I have decided to buy organic fruits and milk and to avoid using prepared foods as much as possible. It seems everything has either corn syrup or artificial flavorings, and I am trying to minimize the boy's intake of preservatives and artificial ingredients.

This afternoon Ellie and Virginia, two wonderful ladies from my church group, came over to help me organize my kitchen while the boys napped. It was great fun talking with them about their child rearing experiences. I asked a lot of questions and got some great advice. My main concern was how to deal with Rupert's constant demand to be held. Ellie suggested two things—first, when I was holding him I shouldn't be doing anything else, like cooking or talking on the phone. She said to give him my undivided attention and secondly, smother him with hugs, kisses and soft words. Another great piece of advice I got this week was from my friend Kate who suggested that I start reading a book to the boys as part of their bedroom ritual, even if they don't appear interested or want to sit still. I still feel like such a newbie when it comes to being a mother.

I am working very hard to have the patience to deal with the boys—especially Nicki—when they do something I have told them not to do. He is so gregarious that even when I reprimand him he just smiles and giggles at me. Even Rupert, who is so sweet, is starting to challenge me when I tell him not to do something. I can see the look in his eye as he sees me watching him. I am trying to be as even-handed as possible and to make sure that I am giving them more than their daily dose of love.

Friday, January 23

Dear Journal: Just a short note to remind myself that it was one month ago today that Donna and I brought the boys home. I remember that moment just before we walked into the airport lounge where everyone was waiting for us. I can still feel the elevated level of excitement and nervousness as I realized I was going through the door into my new path in life. It's still hard for me to use the words mother and son in a conversation.

Today I took the boys to their first public play group at the local community center. There is open playtime from 10 a.m. to 12 p.m. every Friday morning, and it's held in a huge gym. The room is full of balls, bikes and tumbling mats. Rupert took quickly to a little bike while Nicki couldn't get enough of a big ball that he could sit on as I bounced it up and down. I met several parents, including one father who told me he had taught his baby sign language to encourage the ability to communicate. He said she could signal when she was thirsty or wanted a toy. I guess if it works with chimpanzees it would work for babies as well. What will they think of next?

Sunday, January 25

Dear Journal: Dad called yesterday to see how I was doing. It is so heartwarming to know that I am in his thoughts and prayers. I tell everyone that I need their prayers now more than ever before and I really mean it.

The boys continue to challenge me and I am the first to admit I don't always think through my actions. After a fun half hour outside, we came indoors, and I prepared a hearty, vegetable soup for lunch. Instead of giving the boys some bread to hold in their hand, I broke it up and put it in their soup. I don't know if that's what made Rupert decide he didn't want it, but he rejected it flat out without even taking a spoonful. So I took off his bib and set him down. Well, he had a little foot stomping, lying on the floor, crying session that lasted a full two minutes. He then came back to the table and said, "Upa," so I put him on my lap instead of back in his chair and he ate every drop of soup in the bowl. Just this week I've probably made over 100 mistakes, but as long as I learn from them I figure I'll be okay.

I now have all the photos back from my trip, and I still can't believe I was in Ukraine for a month. Some of the pictures are priceless. I am so grateful that I will have mementos of our trip for Rupert and Nicki when they grow up. I have no idea how interested they will be in their heritage or the adoption process, but I want them to have as much information as possible.

Tuesday, January 27

Dear Journal: If I had any lingering doubts about Nicki and FAS, I can happily state that this is no longer the case. He is very bright and inquisitive. He has great eye contact and remembers everything. I am so grateful that neither of the boys have any long-term behavioral or attachment issues. There are moments when I reach back into my memory and remember little Tamara. I wonder how she is doing and whether she is walking on her own now. Perhaps she has been adopted by a loving family who can provide her with the support and therapy she needs.

It snowed yesterday for the first time since we returned from Ukraine. I bundled the boys up in snowsuits, and we spent two hours outside visiting neighbors and having fun.

The boys looked so cute in their outfits I just had to take pictures. I know they saw snow in Ukraine, but I don't think the boys had ever been out in the snow, and, after they figured out how to walk in it, they had a great time.

Saturday, January 31

Dear Journal: It's just after 8 p.m. and I'm sitting here by myself eating leftover rice with chicken and carrots from the dinner that the boys barely touched. The house is quiet and the front room is full of gift bags from friends who attended a shower Kate threw for me this morning.

I was very excited with the anticipation of seeing many of my friends. I put on nice clothes and make-up to show them that I haven't surrendered totally to the pandemonium that normally reigns in the house. The shower was scheduled for 11 a.m., and I had given Kate the names of about 30 friends to invite. As pleased as I was to see some people from former jobs and consulting assignments, I must admit I was disappointed that more of my longtime friends did not attend. I can understand conflicts, but it would have been nice to get a card or a call to arrange a visit in lieu of attending the shower. It's funny the expectations we have of friends and family. In retrospect, I have had more support and help from people at my church whom I didn't even know six months ago than from people I have known for years.

I did have some good news from Meryl today. She told me that Alison, her friend from California, was selected by a Chinese couple to raise their infant daughter. They had given her up for adoption for economic reasons, and the little girl is already in Alison's care. I am very happy for her and wish her all the best. I have met so many people during this past year who have yearned for the love of a child in their life. It's nice to know that you don't have to be married to experience the joys of parenthood, although it would be nice to have a partner, especially on bath nights.

The boys have been doing very well. There were more firsts this week. Both boys learned how to zip and unzip their pajamas and Rupert is starting to form parts of words like banana and apple. Rupert continues to test me—if I tell him something, such as "Don't close the door," he will touch the door and act as if he is going to close it to see my reaction. He's had several time-outs this week, which is unusual for him. I know it's a normal part of a child's development to start acting more independent.

Potty training for Rupert has been put on hold for the time being, partly because his system is not cooperating from a timing perspective—most of his bowel movements are made during breakfast or nap time, so unless I can get him to urinate, there's not much he can do on the potty. I feel partly responsible. I'm not getting up early enough in the day to start their breakfast, and, consequently, all their meals, naps, and play times are 30 to 45 minutes later than they should be. Part of the problem is that I'm staying up too late to get my work done, such as organizing taxes, answering e-mail, and unpacking boxes.

Nicki, on the other hand, is driving me crazy with his curiosity. He has climbed on to the kitchen table, chairs—you name it he has climbed it. And he keeps doing it, even after I have done a time-out with him. He also can't keep his hands off the kitchen cabinets. I think I'm going to have to surrender and get the child-proof locks for all the doors, since I can't get anything done because I have to keep after him. He is, however, becoming more affectionate. Several times a day he will take my hand and place it on the side of his cheek and snuggle up to it.

Cooking continues to be a challenge for me. I've always been better at collecting recipes than I have been at

making them. After my umpteenth meal of mashed potatoes with carrots and ground turkey this week, I decided
that I had to start adding some variety to the dinner menu.
So dinner on Wednesday was pancakes and applesauce,
and we had sea bass and rice for dinner on Thursday. Spaghetti and homemade sauce was on the menu last night;
sautéed chicken and rice with carrots are planned for this
evening. I can't even imagine what I'm going to do for the
next 18 years. Just the thought of having to cook 365 meals
every year is too much to contemplate.

I took a look at my hands today, and I couldn't believe
how dry and cracked my skin was and how sad my nails
looked. I have spent very little time on myself this past
month, and I guess that's par for the course when one becomes a mother. Between changing diapers, cooking and
cleaning up I must wash my hands at least 15 to 20 times a
day. I know I need a hair cut, and I don't remember the
last time I shaved my legs. On the other hand, I've gotten
more hugs from my children in the past month that I have
from anyone else in a whole year.

I spent almost an hour preparing and cooking dinner
tonight. The boys didn't eat much this morning and their
afternoon snack was some cookies in the car. When Rupert
took only a few bites I felt like saying, "Don't you realize
how much I worked to make your dinner?" But instead I
just acknowledged that he wasn't really hungry and got
the boys started on their bath a little early.

Every morning when I walk into their bedroom, Rupert
greats me with a big smile, holds up his arms and says
"Upa." How can I refuse to pick up this little boy whose
only desire in life is to be loved? Of course, my arms get
quite a workout when Nicki also wants to be held, but I'd
rather get my exercise holding my two precious children
than go to a gym and sweat it out with weights.

I desperately need to organize my adoption expenses and other financial paperwork so I can complete my taxes. There's enough money in the bank to pay the bills for now, but it's been a long time since I've been on a budget, and I'm not as good at it as I should be. I know that I need to start up my meditation and yoga practices again. I need to focus on what I will be doing once I return to the work force and concentrate on what my path in life will be.

Monday, February 2

Dear Journal: I've received the boys' passports back from the Ukraine Embassy, and today I went to the post office to apply for their U.S. passports. I had to wait an hour in a small waiting room until my number was called. The boys behaved fairly well, especially since it was past their lunch time when I got to the counter. I had all the necessary documents, including their Permanent Resident Cards (courtesy of the Department of Homeland Security), new passport photos, and the original adoption decree. I'm hoping I get the passports back soon so I can then apply for their social security cards. The government passed a law several years ago that automatically gave citizenship to all children who were adopted abroad by Americans, but there is still much confusion about the process.

Tuesday, February 3

Dear Journal: I am so tired of changing dirty diapers, washing dishes, making meals, wiping faces and bottoms, cleaning bibs and washing clothes. The only thing I'm not tired of is giving hugs. I guess that's the reward you get for doing everything else.

It rained all day which meant the boys stayed inside. They were pretty good at playing by themselves although Nicki wanted to be held more than usual; he must have sat on my lap for almost half an hour after getting up from his afternoon nap. He had a runny nose and may have a slight fever. I couldn't face cooking another meal today. I defrosted some mashed potatoes and ground turkey for the boys and they ate it all up.

I have been dealing with medical bills the past few days. Little did I know when I signed up with my healthcare provider that they do not cover any preventative services for members under the age of 19. Obviously I wasn't thinking that I might one day have children when I selected this carrier. The pediatrician's office has given me a break on some of the charges from the boys' first checkup, but I will still have to deal with the cost of all the blood work that was done for each boy. Those charges were over $500 per child and some of the rates were astounding— including $70 for a lead paint exposure test.

I got a call today from the agency I work with to find contracting assignments. They have been so wonderful to me, and I am very grateful for all their support. They wanted to know when I wanted to return to work, and I was quick to let them know that I would be ready, willing, and able to do so by the first of April. Every day brings more bills, and I am starting to look closer at what I can live without to keep my expenses down until I return to work.

Donna called this evening to see how I was doing. She is such an inspiration to me and always has good advice. I still don't know what I would have done if she hadn't agreed to go on the trip with me. For all the little problems I have, I know that I am blessed with a loving family.

Well, it's 9:30 p.m. and I'm going to treat myself to a big bowl of ice cream before sliding into bed.

Friday, February 6

Dear Journal: I used to love rainy days, especially if I got to stay home and cuddle up with a good book and a nice cup of hot tea. Well, these days if it rains it just means I am cooped up with two little boys who are driving me crazy, and I can't take them outside for some fresh air. It was pouring rain today, and the roads and walkways are full of mushy slush from the last snowfall.

Nicki had a slight fever the past two days and is teething like crazy. The upper tooth that we first discovered while we were in Ukraine is still coming in, and another one has appeared on the other side on top. As a result, he isn't eating or drinking as much as he does normally, and he wants my attention a lot more. Rupert has a slight cold, but it really hasn't affected his behavior or his eating habits.

I decided not to give Rupert his afternoon nap so he wouldn't wake up Nicki before he was ready to get up. It was so nice just to have Rupert sit and play quietly by himself. Then, once Nicki woke up, I called my next-door neighbor, Connie, to see if Devon, her four year old son, wanted to play with Rupert for a few hours. It worked out perfectly, and while Rupert was next door I spent time with Nicki, playing some music and dancing. Nicki loves to rock side to side whenever he hears music. He's especially fascinated by the instruments used by the musicians at church.

Sunday, February 8

Dear Journal: It's a bit of a struggle, but I am making a commitment to get to Mass every Sunday. The service starts at 9 a.m., but that is usually when I'm leaving the house. As I was driving my car to church, I was trying to count the number of crying jags each boy had this morning, for reasons ranging from not wanting to eat to being hit on the head. I have long given up trying to count the number of times I say no in a day. I think it would be too depressing.

Everyone at church has been so generous with their attention, and the boys really enjoy listening to the music and playing with the other children. It's nice to hear that what I'm going through is normal and that it will get better as the boys get older.

My friend Nancy came over for lunch today. The boys gravitated right to her, especially Rupert. He has opened up so much since I brought him home. He is more outgoing and affectionate with other people, especially women. Nancy and I had a great chat, and I was so grateful for her visit. It was nice to be able to talk with someone from my former life. We have a lot in common, and I'm sure I talked non-stop from the moment she walked in the door. I can appreciate how people who are shut-ins or prisoners must feel when they don't have much adult contact. I can't wait until I can have a two-way conversation with the boys.

I'm starting to think about what type of child care I want to have for the boys. February is almost half over and I really haven't started my research. Part of me would love to stay home and have a child care provider or mother's helper part-time. I really enjoy being with my sons and watching them grow. I do feel guilty that I don't spend more time playing with them, but I have to accept the fact that, as a single parent, there will be some things I just can't do as well as if I were married.

Tuesday, February 10

My friend Bud brought lunch to me today. He is such a model dad. I feel encouraged that there are men out there who aren't afraid of commitment and hard work to make a family and a relationship work. We had a delightful conversation, and then the boys opened some of the presents he had bought for them. He had such fun watching them play with the toys. Later, we took them for a walk outside. I know it sounds silly, but it was so nice to have someone with me as we took a walk with the boys. I started daydreaming about what it would be like to have a husband—someone I could partner with as we raised the boys together.

The rest of the day went smoothly enough. The boys really love their bath time, now, and no matter how long I let them play, Nicki still cries when I take him out of the tub. Rupert holds on to all his toys to the point that he doesn't play with them for fear of losing them to Nicki. I'm trying to reinforce the fact to Rupert that he can't always take Nicki's toys away from him just because he is bigger. Of course, this triggers a little tantrum, but it is short-lived and soon forgotten.

The last thing I do before I leave their bedroom at night is to lean over and softly stroke their heads, telling them how much I love them and that they are good boys. It's such a sweet moment that I wish it could last forever. I would love to know what was going on inside their minds. I'm still waiting for the day they start to call me Mama.

Thursday, February 12

Dear Journal: I took Nicki to the doctor today to have his left eye examined. Of course, I was running late from my morning errands, and by the time I fed them and dressed them, I hadn't thought about whether their diapers needed to be changed. Well, by the time we arrived at the office there was a noticeable scent in the air—enough for the office manager to ask if I wanted to tend to the boys' diapers before we saw the doctor. So of course I whipped out my changing pad and proceeded to change them on the floor in the little play area in the waiting room. Once I finished, they told me there was a changing table in the restroom upstairs. Well, so much for office decorum.

It appears that Nicki's condition is not quite as simple as having a lazy eye. The doctor believes there may be a problem with his retina, and he called a colleague who is a specialist to arrange for an ultrasound of Nicki's eye on Monday morning. I'm not too worried, but I am anxious to know what is causing the problem with his eye. The doctor said his vision is blurry in his left eye, and I can't bear too think how this disability would have hurt him had he not been adopted. I feel so much love for this little boy that I would do anything to make sure he has every opportunity in life.

I got a call this evening from one of my stepsisters. Mary is close to me in age and was married several years ago to a doctor. They live on a farm near a moderate-sized town in the south where he is slowly building a practice. She had sent me a lovely card a few weeks ago and called to find out how I was doing. I think she would like to adopt children, either domestically or abroad, but they both have so much going on in their lives right now. After speaking with her, I felt so good about having made the decision to find my forever children. I know it was the right thing for me to do, although I know it's not for everyone.

Friday, February 13

Dear Journal: Today is another landmark for me. It was exactly two months ago that Donna and I traveled to the orphanage for the last time as I officially took Rupert and Nicki into my care. It has been two of the most exhausting and exciting months of my life. I'm not sure if it's the warm (50 degrees) and sunny weather today or not, but I am beginning to relax more with the boys and have some fun.

I find myself playing with them when changing their diapers or putting on their clothes—tickling their toes and doing the "Little Pig Goes To The Market" rhyme with them. I'm not getting as upset if they don't eat all their food or misbehave. I have stopped worrying about Rupert's lack of interest in potty training and am trying to interact with them more by playing with their toys and making up games.

Nicki is back to his old self and both boys are eating up a storm. They finished all their oatmeal at breakfast and, after a hearty snack of banana (for Nicki) and apple (for Rupert), they each ate a big sandwich of peanut butter and jelly for lunch.

I received an adorable gift yesterday from the folks at my marketing agency—a big basket of homemade cookies inside a small rocking horse imprinted with each boy's name and birth date. So for dessert, we all enjoyed one of the cookies. Then it was nap time while I washed the dishes and opened the mail.

It's 3:30 p.m. in the afternoon, and I am sitting here at my desk listening to the silence in the house. It sounds beautiful. In the old days I could sit at my computer for hours and work on projects, but now I have a very short window of two hours to complete my work. As we were walking in the door from our errands today, the UPS truck pulled up and the delivery man gave me some books I had ordered. He said "Have a nice weekend," and for a moment I didn't understand what he was saying. Since I've stopped working, the concept of weekends versus weekdays has dissipated, and I didn't really think about this being Friday. Oh, it would be so nice to figure out a way to stay at home with the boys. I'm working on making it happen, but I'm still way short of my goal.

Sunday, February 15

Dear Journal: Today was a nice, typical day for us. After church I brought the morning paper into the boys' room while they played and I read (or tried to read). I feel so fortunate that they want to be wherever I am—I know in ten years time that will change!

I called an old girlfriend this afternoon while the boys were napping. I have known Kathy since I was in high school, and we have continued to stay in touch through career changes, moves and boyfriends. She recently opened up her first retail establishment, a gourmet food shop, in a small town outside of New York City. I hadn't talked to her in over a year, so we had a lot of catching up to do. She told me how demanding her work at the shop is as she is the sole proprietor with only her boyfriend to help out. I told her I knew exactly what it felt like to work seven days a week with no time off. Kathy has never been interested in having children, and there were times when we joked mercilessly about what a pain it was to be on a plane with crying babies or how they should outlaw strollers in malls. Now I can't imagine going to the mall without my little umbrella stroller, but as for planes, well, some things don't change.

I took the boys to the park down the street this afternoon after they awoke from their nap. It was sunny outside but still quite cold—around 37 degrees. They climbed on the jungle gym and had lots of fun on the swings. There was a couple in the park with their little girl and a large dog that they had on a leash. Rupert is extremely afraid of animals—even stuffed ones. Nicki is very curious about dogs and cats, but he feeds off of Rupert's fear and usually won't approach a small cat, although he did pet one several weeks ago at a church gathering. I don't know if Rupert's fear is because he had never seen animals while in the orphanage or if he became frightened after a particular incident. I'm hoping that with time Rupert's fear dissipates, but for now I have to be careful about where we go.

I talked to Donna tonight for the first time in over a week. We had a nice chat, and I gave her an update on how the boys are progressing. I asked if she and her husband Bob would agree to be Nicki's godparents and she said yes. I want to arrange the boys' baptism during a trip to Buffalo this summer to attend my sister Janet's wedding.

Monday, February 16

Dear Journal: We went to the eye specialist, Dr. Deegan, today and he confirmed that Nicki has a detached retina in his left eye. He said that, based on the sonogram, it started happening last summer. This means that Nicki probably has little or no vision in his left eye since the blood vessels have stopped the flow from his brain to his eye. The recommended course of action is laser surgery—performed as soon as possible. Dr. Deegan wasn't very positive about how much of the vision in his left eye will be restored, but I have decided that I will begin my prayers and affirmations that the blood vessels strengthen and his vision returns. Nicki is a very tenacious little boy and will be up to the challenge, regardless of the outcome.

It really isn't possible to know why he developed this problem. It could be due to an injury or something called Coats disease. When I look at Nicki, all I see is a loving little boy who has a great zest for life. His big brown eyes are so tender and innocent. Every time I look at him, I pray that the surgery will be successful. The good news is that there was no evidence of a tumor although the doctor has ordered a CAT scan just to be sure.

Wednesday, February 18

Dear Journal: The "Tales and Tunes" class this morning went very well; Rupert is still very much the observer. He rarely joins the activities and stays close to me. Nicki is slowly learning to follow the teacher's lead (sit down, wait his turn, put the toys away) although he wanders around the room more than the other children. I've started chatting with some of the other moms and feel more comfortable around them now than I did at the start of the session. I still catch myself when I introduce the boys as my sons. I'm not used to referring to myself as their mother. It still feels odd—this new role of mine.

My church ladies, Ellie and Virginia, came over this afternoon to finish painting the breakfast nook and help me clean out the spare bedroom. I did get a surprise today when I went into the boy's room to get them up from their nap. Rupert was sitting in Nicki's crib. He had apparently climbed up the outside railing into the bed. I couldn't believe it. I didn't think Rupert was that nimble but, as Ellie reminded me, he's probably been working on it for some time. I had mentioned to Ellie that after feeding Nicki a grilled cheese sandwich I noticed a rash on his body. She asked me what kind of cheese I gave him, and I told her it was extra sharp cheddar cheese. She said he may be too young to digest that type of cheese and that may be why he developed the rash. I feel so clueless about these things.

Rupert hasn't been eating much food these past two days. This afternoon I gave them both a protein drink, and tonight he woke up crying with a stomach ache. I don't know if the drink was the culprit or not, but after an hour of crying, he let out a big fart and then had a huge bowel movement. That seemed to resolve the issue. I did talk with Donna tonight after Rupert went back to sleep, and she gave me some advice about what to feed him tomorrow. She said to remember BRAT (bananas, rice, apples, and tea). These are easily digestible foods for children with upset stomachs.

Other than the occasional upset stomach or teething, both boys are flourishing. They are still very curious about things, and it's so much fun to show them something new. The other day I introduced the boys to their shadow and they were just entranced. Things like turning the light switches on and off really intrigue them. They are making more sounds and have started forming words like apple, banana, all gone, and uh-oh. But they still aren't saying yes or no except with hand signals.

The boys are challenging me in ways I never expected. I have to be an arbitrator, judge and jury, monitor and nurse all within a matter of minutes. But at the same time I have so much joy in my life when I am with the boys—even when I get frustrated by Nicki's incessant need to raise the toilet lid and stick his hand down into the water or Rupert's penchant for closing the door to every room.

Friday, February 20

Dear Journal: Everything has been arranged for Nicki to have his eye surgery next Wednesday. I sent out several e-mails to my friends and family asking them to pray for Nicki's full and speedy recovery. I'm not worried about the surgery, but I am anxious to know the results. I feel guilty that I haven't had more time to pray for Nicki, but I decided the next best thing was to ask everyone I know to join me in sending him healing energy.

I got an e-mail today from Carol, a woman living in Bronx, New York, who is leaving in ten days for Ukraine. She read my post-trip e-mail and wanted to find out how to get a copy of FRUA's medical booklet. I told her to e-mail her address to me, and I would send her my copy. I also told her to stay in touch with me and let me know if I can do anything for her while she is in Ukraine. I feel that is the least I can do after all the help I received from Karen prior to and during my trip. It's amazing how the circle of love winds its way through your life. You never know when a complete stranger will perform an act of kindness toward you. It makes it so much easier to do the same for someone else.

Meg and Michael came over for dinner tonight along with two of Meg's children. One of them, Tucker, has just finished his captain's certification and hopes to crew on private yachts. It seems like such a long time ago that I first thought about casting off all my belongings to spend a few years sailing on a boat in warm waters. Now I have a house, a mortgage, two children and a handful of never-ending projects. Perhaps I will still have my life at sea, but it will have to wait a few years to be fulfilled.

Saturday, February 21

Dear Journal: This morning when I walked into the boys' room I found Rupert had climbed into Nicki's crib again. I don't know how long he had been in there—it's possible that he spent the night with Nicki. I decided it was time to lower the crib mattress and secure the drawer underneath the crib that Rupert was using to gain a foothold. Jack helped me to lower the frame and move the bed away from the window to remove any further temptations to play with the mini-blinds.

I also noticed a pungent odor in the air. I checked their sheets but didn't notice any wetness. Then I looked at Rupert's pajamas and knew something had happened. He had had a mini-explosion in his diaper during the night that had covered half his body. So I stripped off his clothes and put him in the bathtub to clean him off. Then I opened up the window. I decided it was time to wash all the sheets and blankets. He had been suffering from diarrhea for several days, so I called the nurse practioner at the pediatrician's office. She gave me the same advice that Donna had given, as well as some other dietary tips such as keeping him away from milk and sticking with white bread and applesauce.

The weather was nice again today, so I took the boys outside to play after lunch. Nicki found a small red ball and played with it for the longest time. Rupert stayed occupied with the wheelbarrow that Michael had used last night to bring over some firewood. If there's a tool with a handle around the house, Rupert will find it. He loves to push brooms and play with toy lawnmowers and is always there to carry a pail or bag.

Tonight was a big night for me. Two neighborhood girls, Millie and Elyena, came over this afternoon to spend time with the boys before Jack and I left the house to go to dinner and a movie. The girls were wonderful with Rupert and Nicki. They gave the boys all their attention, and it was so much fun to watch them laughing and giggling—yes, both the boys and the girls. I had all the instructions written down along with my cell phone number. I must admit I checked my phone several times throughout the evening, even keeping it on during the movie, but no calls came in.

When we returned home at 10 p.m., the girls were watching TV and said that everything went fine. The boys ate their dinner and went to sleep on time. It was a funny feeling knowing that the boys did so well for these girls. Part of me felt sad that they didn't miss me, but most of me was glad that the boys behaved so well. When I went in to check on the them, Rupert woke up and wanted to get out of bed. I held him for a minute before putting him back into bed. He cried for a minute or two and then went back to sleep. I guess I am needed after all.

Monday February 23

Dear Journal: I still can't believe how quickly these two little boys have become the center of my life—and I didn't even know they existed three months ago!

Rupert had another major explosion in his diaper this morning. I guess it was the result of the food I gave him yesterday afternoon after he didn't have any bowel movements for the day. The result was worthy of Mt. Etna. It took me over half an hour to clean up the sheets and Rupert got an early bath. I opened the window in the boy's bedroom to air it out.

I called the pediatrician's office again, and they told me to continue the BRAT diet for another few days. So it's back to applesauce and rice with bananas thrown in for good measure.

Nicki took an early nap, so I decided to take the boys to the park after lunch. It was a warm day and I was surprised to find we were the only ones there. However, by the time we left, there were half a dozen children and their moms. The boys played in the sandbox for the first time. It took them a few minutes to figure it all out, but once they did, it was great fun.

I feel that I'm slowly starting to understand the boys' moods and behavior. Rupert certainly comprehends the concept of time-out and will improve his behavior at the mere mention of sitting in the chair. Nicki, on the other hand, doesn't pay much attention to me when I tell him no, but he is getting better about staying away from cupboards and kitchen drawers. Rupert continues to enjoy being on my lap—he still takes my hands and wraps them around his waist. The only time Nicki wants to be held is when he's tired or bored.

Tuesday, February 24

Dear Journal: Today was a very busy day for me and the boys. They both had CAT scans at the local hospital and the process lasted the whole morning. The boys were put to sleep with a small dose of medication to keep them still for the scan. Both of them were very woozy when we left the hospital. I kept them in Nicki's crib until late in the afternoon, so they wouldn't fall and hurt themselves.

The good news is that each boy has gained another two pounds. That's four pounds in two months. At this rate, I'm going to have to redirect some of my financial portfolio into grocery stocks. I can't seem to leave the store for less than $100 no matter how hard I try. Never before in my life have I bought so many groceries, yet no matter how much I bring home, by the end of the week I find that I need to return to the store for more food.

I got an e-mail from Judy today. She finally returned from Guatemala last week with her baby girl, Olivia. I am so happy for her. She has struggled so hard and long to become a mother. I remember last year when I first met her; she had already completed her home study and was planning on adopting from Ukraine. What a difference a year can make in our lives.

Wednesday, February 25

Dear Journal: I took Nicki to the hospital at 8 a.m. for his eye surgery. The nurses at the outpatient ward were terrific. They had to give Nicki several doses of eye drops, and they worked extra hard to make him comfortable. I spoke with Dr. Deegan before the procedure, and he explained what he was going to do. I stayed in the post-op room during the surgery soaking in the silence in the room. I felt very comfortable that everything was going to be all right. I told God I was putting all my fears and worries in his hands so I could take care of the day-to-day challenges.

I feel God has been testing me lately to see if I really know the value of my children's health compared to all my possessions. Last week someone backed into my one-year-old car; then I found out that my second car, which I was keeping for use when I needed to haul things, has a burned out transmission. And today, I found a rip in the new hall carpet I had bought last month and the list goes on. Oh, how I miss having someone with whom I can share these challenges.

The good news from the surgery is that Nicki's right eye has not been affected. Dr. Deegan did a lot of work on

Nicki's left eye to reattach the retina, but only time will tell if he was successful. Nicki has a patch over his eye (which he hates, of course), but otherwise he came out of the surgery with flying colors. Nicki was very sleepy this afternoon. That meant he spent a lot of time on my lap. He doesn't usually do that, so it was nice to have him cuddle up so close to me. We are a family, my boys and me. I know that whatever obstacles lie ahead can be dealt with if I just keep everything in perspective.

I just finished reading an e-mail from a couple in one of the adoption e-mail newsgroups. A chill ran up my spine as I read how they had returned home from Ukraine without finding their child. They left Ukraine to return home on the day I went to the NAC to begin the task of finding my two little angels. I feel so guilty now about how I complained that I didn't get the two girls I thought I wanted. Why does it take someone else's tragedy to make you appreciate what you have?

The couple made five trips to the NAC to find a child. The first two referrals were for children with cerebral palsy, and the third child had Hepatitis B. Their fourth referral was for siblings, but the boy had obvious fetal alcohol facial features. Their fifth referral was for sibling girls, but one of them had facial features of FAS. They also wrote about the excessive drinking and alcoholism they encountered in the streets and restaurants. There was such obvious pain in their letter that I felt like reaching out to them with a big hug. I think I will keep this letter as a reminder to me that no matter how hard my life has become, it would be even harder if I had returned empty-handed.

Tonight when I put my children to bed, I whispered to Rupert and Nicki that I loved them very much. I've told them that every day since I adopted them, but now I have more feeling behind the words when I say them.

Friday, February 27

Dear Journal: I called the pediatrician's office again this morning (fourth time in ten days) and decided it was time to bring Rupert in to deal with his diarrhea. It hasn't been getting any better, despite his being on the restricted diet, and I didn't want to wait any longer to have him checked out. His energy level is fine, but it pains me to keep him on such a strict diet. The doctor who read his chart (a different doctor than the one he saw in January) decided that he needed to have additional tests run for guardia and a highly contagious virus that is going around that causes long-term diarrhea.

Tonight at dinner, Rupert pointed to me and said, "Mama." I don't know what it was, but, when he said it, there was something that touched my heart in a way it has never been touched before. Usually when the boys want my attention, they just grunt or cry out. It felt as if he really knew who I was—the person who would love him and take care of him forever. It's moments like this that make it all worthwhile.

There was a great e-mail today from one of the adoption newsgroups. One of the couples in Kiev has found two little boys, and they described their emotions as they finalized their adoption hearing. Why do people have such different experiences in Ukraine? I don't know. I wish I did as there are so many children in Ukraine still waiting for loving parents to bring them home.

Saturday, February 28

Dear Journal: Happy Birthday to me! I feel so complete and genuinely happy today. I have the loving family I have desired for so long. I'm 46 years old today. I live in a house

surrounded by nature, and I have a fulfilling and reward-
ing life-style. I have two wonderful, healthy children and
an abundance of loving family and friends. I have money
in the bank and a sailboat in the water. What more could a
woman ask for?

It was a glorious day outside. The temperature broke
50 degrees with blue skies. After a hectic morning, I took
the boys outside to play for an hour before lunch. It's wonderful to watch them play with their trucks and throw the
ball. They are so happy. We took a short walk down the
gravel street in front of our house where I found a tarnished
penny on the ground. I was about to make a wish but then
I stopped. I felt so blessed that I decided it was unfair to
wish for anything else.

Jack arrived in time for lunch, and Millie and Elyena
came over around 1 p.m. to baby-sit the boys. After a quick
shower, I piled into the car with Jack and we headed towards the water. We arrived at the marina where I keep
my boat during the summer months. After visiting with
some friends, we drove to where my boat is stored for the
winter to check it out. I started to daydream about all the
adventures the boys and I will have on the water this summer. Then we headed to a local restaurant overlooking the
water for dinner.

It was a great day for so many reasons. I feel I have
been given blessings upon blessings. Life is good and it
will only get better. Bring it on, God, I'm ready for all the
wonders of the world you can show me.

Monday, March 1

Dear Journal: The weather has been unseasonably
warm these past few days, and I have tried to get the boys

outside as much as possible. Nicki continues to find the dirtiest places. Yesterday he plopped down in a mud puddle and proceeded to kick his feet until his pants were the same color as the mud. Rupert is more reserved and didn't get nearly as dirty as Nicki. I start thinking about what their life would have been like if they hadn't been adopted, and I can't bear to imagine it. I am so glad they are with me.

Rupert did the cutest thing yesterday afternoon. We took a walk with the little stroller, and the boys took turns sitting in it. On the way back to the house, Nicki was in the stroller and Rupert was pushing it. Rupert stopped the stroller and went over to Nicki; he bent over and put Nicki's hood onto his head and then gave him a hug. Now all I have to do is say to Rupert, "Give Nicki a hug," and he will grab Nicki and give him a big neck hug. He also has started kissing me on the lips, and it is the sweetest thing in the world.

I dropped off Rupert's stool samples to the pediatrician's office this morning. He had another explosion this morning, and I feel guilty for having waited so long before I took him to the doctor. He has a very healthy appetite but was complaining of stomach pains at dinner tonight. It may be as long as three days before I know what the problem is with his stomach. In the meantime, I can feed him only rice, potatoes, carrots, bananas, and soy milk. I had to make another run to the grocery store today because I ran out of bananas again. Both boys love them and I can't buy enough of them.

Tuesday, March 2

Dear Journal: Today was magical. The weather was uncommonly warm again and it was a wonderful day. The boys and I went over to Connie's house to have coffee and cake with Kate and her two boys. On the way over there, I saw some worms on the driveway. I thought this would be a good opportunity to introduce the squiggly creatures to the boys. Nicki was terribly intrigued and wanted to pop the worm into his mouth within seconds of holding it. Rupert, on the other hand, wanted nothing to do with the worm. Such different personalities.

After we left Connie's, I invited Kate and her boys to spend some time at our house. We decided to have lunch on the front porch. The boys ate peanut butter and jelly sandwiches, and life could not have been sweeter. Kate and her boys stayed until around 2 p.m. As soon as they left, I took Rupert and Nicki into the bathroom, washed them and changed them, and put them to bed. I had just enough time to make a few phone calls and pay some bills before they awoke from their nap.

I felt so relaxed today. The boys were so happy, and it felt great to be outside in the warm sun. Rupert is beginning to say words in English, and I know it will be only a few months before he is really talking. On the down side, Nicki has now come down with diarrhea. That means both boys are on the BRAT diet now. I decided I wasn't going to wait until Rupert's test results came back before I took Nicki to the pediatrician, so I made an appointment for early Thursday morning. The good news is their appetite and demeanor are still very positive.

Wednesday, March 3

Dear Journal: Today was another pleasant day but much busier than yesterday. We went to the "Tales and Tunes" class this morning and I was pleased to see that Nicki is now beginning to accept direction from the teacher.

Rupert is also getting better at becoming involved in the group activities although he still spends much of the time sitting on my lap.

After an early nap for Nicki, I drove the boys to the local elementary school for developmental and speech delay evaluations by Child Find, a free, government sponsored service. After spending some time with the boys, the educators decided that I should bring the boys back in July in order to give them a few months to develop their speech patterns. I feel grateful that there are services out there that can help me if the boys do need assistance.

Thursday, March 4

Dear Journal: I now have the medicine that I hope will cure both boy's diarrhea. Rupert's results came back indicating that he has a benign parasite in his intestine. I took the prescription to a local pharmacy and asked them to add apricot flavor to the medicine, since the doctor told me it wasn't very pleasant tasting.

We started out today at the pediatrician's and then drove to Alexandria for an eye checkup with Dr. Deegan. He has a wonderful manner with Nicki. He told me that his primary focus was to ensure Nicki didn't lose his eye due to glaucoma build-up. I feel guilty that I haven't prayed more for the boys.

Our next stop was at the Social Security office to apply for the boys' social security numbers. Once I signed in, it took over two hours before my number was called. There I was, stuck in this small, packed waiting room trying to entertain and control two little boys. Rupert was pretty good, but Nicki was all over the place. I was so glad I had packed their diaper bag with cups and snacks and a few toys but it was not an experience I ever want to repeat. One of the security guards began to admonish me about controlling the boys, and I came very close to making a big scene about how long the process was taking. Instead I took a very deep breath, and calmly walked away.

I haven't touched any of my projects this week. It seems something always comes up in the afternoon, whether it's making phone calls or running errands. I need to start going to bed earlier so I have more energy to get things done during the day. Maybe I should just clone myself so one of me can take care of the boys while the other me can spend the day organizing my office and making progress on my projects. What I really need to do is get out and have more adult interaction.

Friday, March 5

Dear Journal: Another nice day. I took the boys to the park this morning and met a group of women who belong to a mom's club. I never knew such a thing existed, but from what I have learned, they are very popular. These women and their children get together on a regular basis to socialize and network. One of the women, Charisse, is going to send me their newsletter and contact information. How I wish I could stay home with my boys. Most of the moms are slightly younger than I and are married. It would be nice to find some single moms close to my age, but I guess it doesn't really make that much difference.

Nap time was another struggle today. Rupert just would not settle down. The last straw was when I went in to quiet them down, and there was Rupert, standing next to Nicki's crib with no diaper. Its soiled contents were smeared all over his bed linen, which of course I had just changed that morning. Nicki had also taken off his diaper and tossed it on the floor. I was not happy. I took Rupert's hand and led him into the bathroom where I made him sit on the floor until I returned. Then I went back into their bedroom and put Nicki's diaper back on him. After cleaning up Rupert, I took him to the couch in the living room and told him to stay on the sofa. These boys seem to find new ways to challenge me every day.

My friend Martha came over for dinner tonight. We were on the phone this morning confirming our plans, and she asked if she could bring anything with her. I blurted out "Why don't you pick up some Chinese for dinner?" I felt so bad for asking her to bring dinner, but, with the day I was having, I don't think I could have managed anything except a phone call to the local pizza parlor for carry-out.

Martha brought two books with her that she has kept since childhood. One of them is *Tell Me About God* and the other one is *Tell Me About Jesus*. They are wonderful primers to introduce the children to the concept of God and the role He plays in our lives. It's obvious that they meant a lot to her, and I was very touched that she would give me the books for the boys.

Sunday, March 7

Dear Journal: Today started out with a lovely Mass at church. I actually arrived on time this morning and got to listen to the whole service. After we returned home, the boys and I spent an hour outside getting some exercise before it was time to go in for lunch.

After I got the boys quieted down for their nap, I set about completing the last minute preparations for Nicki's birthday party. His actual birthday isn't until March 14, but we will be out of town next Sunday. It turned out to be a wonderful affair. All the neighbors came, along with some of Jack's friends, Pat Mary, her two children and some friends from church. We all sang happy birthday to Nicki as he sat in his high chair in the dining room, wearing a party hat. Even though I had practiced blowing out candles with him, he still needed help but he handled all the attention very well. It was hard to keep from crying as I brought the cake into the dining room where we all sang to him, a little boy nobody had wanted, who just three months ago was languishing in an orphanage half the world away.

It's 9:30 p.m. now and the house is perfectly quiet. I can't begin to explain how exhausting it was to do everything by myself for this party. I've decided it's time to focus on a plan for a partner to enter into my life. I am looking for a man who will focus his energies on me and the boys, someone who will make us the first priority in his life. I know that the right man is out there for me.

Monday, March 8

Dear Journal: After getting the boys dressed this morning, I got out the hair-cutting kit that Ellie had purchased for me. It has every tool you could possibly need, including several that I had no idea how to use. I thought it would be helpful to cut their hair in the bathroom so they could watch me do it, but I think I would have been better off using a stool in the kitchen.

I put Rupert up on the countertop and showed him what I was going to do by snipping off a piece of my own hair. I then trimmed his bangs and the hair around his ears and the back of his neck. He wasn't thrilled with the idea of getting his hair cut, and it's possible some of the anxiety stems from his treatment at the orphanage. It's a good thing I did it though, as a small section of his right ear lobe had a patch of dry, red skin. I treated his ear in January when his hair was much shorter but I hadn't looked at it lately. I guess that's another good reason to keep his hair short.

Rupert's hair is perfectly straight, so I had to be careful to cut it evenly across his forehead and neck. On the other hand, Nicki's hair is quite curly, and it didn't take nearly as long to trim his hair. I took a small lock of both boys' hair and taped it to a baby book that I am putting together for them.

There was some good news today as Rupert's stool has finally begun to harden. I know this sounds trite, but he has had diarrhea for so long that I am thrilled the medication is starting to work. While we were in the boys' bedroom today, I noticed Rupert was standing in front of the door frame where Dad and I had marked their heights back in January. I couldn't believe that Rupert has grown almost an inch in two months, and Nicki has grown half an inch. These boys are making such good progress. I love to look at Nicki's chubby cheeks and see that his legs are getting some fat on them. I'll never forget how skinny he looked that day at the orphanage when we undressed both the boys.

Tuesday, March 9

Dear Journal: I took Rupert to see Dr. Magrum this morning to review his CAT scan results. The good news is that his shunt appears to be working properly. The bad news is that there are two small cysts in his head. So, it's back to the hospital for an MRI. I never really knew what the difference between a CAT scan and an MRI was—until now. An MRI can slice and dice a section of the body from several difficult angles whereas a CAT scan is one dimensional. I don't even want to think about what might happen when the MRI results are reviewed. I can only pray that Rupert won't need any surgery

I received the hospital bill for Nicki's laser eye surgery to the tune of $5,000 and change. I know I've complained about the costs of health care, but I am so grateful little Nicki is in a country where we have the expertise to treat his ailment. Every time I look into his eyes, I think about the miracles that can be performed nowadays. I continue to hope and pray that his left eye remains healthy and that he has no vision problems with his right eye.

Wednesday, March 10

Dear Journal: When it rains it pours. Not only was the weather miserable today, but so were the boys. They have both come down with colds, probably due to the change in temperature, although it could also be that I haven't been as careful as I should be about washing hands before meals. I knew I was in trouble when Rupert started acting up as I was trying to get his jacket on to go outside. He rarely misbehaves, so this was totally out of character for him.

The boys were so tired that I put them both down for a nap as soon as we returned from the "Tales and Tunes" class. After a late lunch, I gave them some medicine to ease their congestion and help them sleep. Jack came over around 2:30 p.m. to watch the boys. I had made an appointment for a facial and was so tired I ended up sleeping through most of it. I did have enough time to stop by a health food store to pick up some new vitamins for the boys and some Echinacea and Golden Root to help boost their immune system. The salesperson, who was helping me read the dosage instructions on one of the labels, made the comment, "What two-year-old weighs only 24 pounds?" After I told him that Nicki weighs 21 pounds, I could see the look of surprise on his face. He told me that his five-month-old daughter already weighs 17 lbs.

After a quick dinner of leftover spaghetti, I gave the boys a bath and put them to bed. I spent the rest of the evening packing for our trip to the outer banks of North Carolina. Wally, a friend of mine, has offered us the use of his beach house for a few days. The plan is to leave early tomorrow morning and let the boys sleep in the car during the five hour trip. I must admit I never realized the amount of paraphernalia one needed when traveling with children. Besides the portable crib, the booster seat, and the backpack full of diapers and wipes, I also packed toys, towels, and enough clothes, socks and shoes to deal with wet puddles and forays into the ocean.

I spent only five minutes deciding what to bring on the trip for myself. I have to be more mindful about spending time taking care of myself since I have been feeling very run down lately. If there is one thing that I am truly sick and tired of it's the clothes I have been wearing. I usually just grab whatever is in the clean laundry basket. That means I keep wearing the same clothes over and over again. Whatever made me think I could raise two boys by myself?

It's 10 p.m., and I'm finally packed and ready for the trip. I just hope I don't forget to pack the boys before we take off in the morning.

Thursday, March 11

Dear Journal: Jack, the boys and I arrived at the outer banks this morning just before 8 a.m. We stopped at the local supermarket to stock up on food before heading out to Wally's house. As soon as I took Rupert out of the car to go into the store, I could tell there was trouble in his diaper.

By the time we had arrived at the house and unpacked the car, it was too late to prevent a terrible case of diaper rash on his little bottom. I now know I should have changed him at the supermarket, but he was still wearing his pajamas, and all of his clothes were buried in the trunk. Note to self: Always keep a spare diaper and change of clothes handy when traveling.

I tried to put the boys down for a morning nap, but they had already gotten their second wind and were creating havoc in their room. I brought them upstairs, gave them a snack, and we headed down to the ocean which was only a five minute walk from the house.

It was high tide and the surf was tremendous. The water was foaming brighter than the snow on the mountains against a clear blue sky. It was an amazing picture, and, with a temperature in the mid 50s, it was a perfect day to introduce the boys to the Atlantic Ocean. I was amazed that Rupert wasn't scared to death of the roar of the waves. Nicki was slightly apprehensive and didn't even try to challenge the approaching water. As soon as we reached the sand, the boys planted themselves on the ground and started digging and scratching the surface with little twigs. We spent most of our time scouting for pretty shells and collecting trash that the boys picked up on the beach.

We headed back to the house around 1:15 p.m. for lunch and to settle the boys down for an afternoon nap. They quickly got into some hi-jinks in their room so I had to put Rupert in a separate room so they would both go to sleep. During this brief interlude of about an hour and a half, Jack and I enjoyed a late lunch on the outside deck watching the waves blow into the wind as they pounded against the shallow sand near the shore.

After a noisy dinner, I gave two very tired little boys a quick bath and then put them to bed. They didn't make a peep once I closed the door, and I immediately said a prayer of thanks to the Saint of Happy Vacations. Jack and I read our books and had a pleasant, quiet evening. I continue to pray that we have good weather for our trip and that the boys' health continues to improve.

Friday, March 12

Dear Journal: Today marks another anniversary with the boys. It seems so hard to believe that it was only three months ago since Donna and I drove away from that isolated orphanage in the middle of nowhere in a third world country with the two little boys sitting on our laps. I was talking to a friend the other day who said that children teach us as much about ourselves as we share with them. I know I have learned many lessons already, mostly about controlling my anger and finding patience and compassion for others.

It was another glorious day on the beach with bright sunshine and calm winds. Rupert's cheeks looked very ruddy by the end of the day, and I think it's time to put on the sunscreen. I want to make sure that neither of the boys gets over-exposed to the sun. I have seen firsthand the effects of skin cancer and melanoma on family members and I want to avoid that with the boys.

After a hearty breakfast, we dressed the boys and headed to the beach. We must have spent three hours playing in the sand and taking short walks. I brought my camera and took an entire roll of film. I want to make sure I have enough so I can start putting a scrapbook together for each of the boys. While we were playing on the beach, I noticed that Nicki was sitting down, rocking back and forth. At first I was worried that something had frightened him. I haven't seen him doing this since shortly after I brought him home. Then, it dawned on me that he was rocking to the rhythm of the waves. He was singing softly to himself and then wanted to climb into my arms. It felt so good see the boys enjoying themselves. I said a special thanks to God, my mother, and the universe for the blessings I have received in my life.

Sunday, March 14

Dear Journal: Happy second birthday, Nicki! My poor baby spent the entire morning acting up and crying for his mama. At first I thought he was just tired, but when I checked his mouth I found that he had two more molars poking through his gums; one on his upper left side and another one on his upper right side, just starting to pierce the gum. That means when they are all in, he will have nine teeth. Thanks goodness I brought some pain medication for him.

It wasn't as windy today as it was yesterday. I packed up the diaper bag and we headed down to the beach. I took the stroller out of the trunk, and Rupert insisted on pushing it himself. It took three times as long to get to the beach, and I tried to be patient with him as he pushed it in all the wrong directions. Rupert is exhibiting his independence more and more each day. Some of it is good, such as being able to put on his slippers and socks all by himself, but part of it is defiance, such as when I tell him to leave the bedroom door open and he continues to push it closed.

We had a grand time at the beach, even though the wind, which was blowing due east, was 10 degrees colder than it was on Friday. Jack found a piece of plastic string and took the boys on a hunt to find shells they could thread on the string. Jack tried to make a sand castle with a large plastic cup, but the sand was not cooperating. I guess some things will have to wait until summer.

My energy level is still not 100 percent. I lay down to rest this afternoon and was out like a light within minutes of putting my head on the pillow. Anyone who says they are taking their kids on vacation is doing just that—the kids have a great time, but Mom has more than her share of work to do each day. I think the boys and I are trading cold germs as I can't seem to get rid of the stuffy head and sore throat I have been suffering from for the past week. Perhaps I have a mild case of the flu, but, whatever it is, I wish it would go away.

Monday, March 15

Dear Journal: It rained all day today. I decided we needed to get out of the house so we drove to the North Carolina Aquarium on Roanoke Island. It was only 25 miles away and very kid-friendly. The boys were absolutely fascinated with the fish in the large tanks. In one of the rooms, you were allowed to touch the rays and skates that were in a shallow, round tank. Nicki touched one of them (with my help) and howled with dismay. Rupert did put his hand in the water but wanted nothing further to do with the fish.

Even with Jack's help, I can't count the number of times I lost sight of one of the boys at the aquarium. Thank goodness there were only a dozen people there and few rooms to visit. I had to change both of them in the ladies' room, and, between watching Nicki to make sure he didn't stick his hand down every toilet, and wiping Rupert's derriere, I must have said a hundred prayers to God. I don't know how single parents can watch more than one child at a time in public places. As much as I enjoyed the outing and took delight in seeing the boys experience something new, I must admit I don't think I will ever be ready for Disney World.

Tuesday, March 16

Dear Journal: We spent most of the day traveling back home in the rain. It took a while to pack everything and clean up, so we didn't hit the road until 10:30 a.m. The trunk was absolutely stuffed with bags, suitcases, Nicki's crib and Rupert's booster chair. We had to fit the stroller, the boys' coats and the diaper bag into the back seat with the children. It was cramped in the car and we were all looking forward to being in familiar surroundings again.

The drive home took almost seven hours because of several stops for food and diaper changes, but I would have driven ten hours to get back to my own house. Although it was nice to get away, I've decided it was not something I would ever call a vacation. Being away from home meant I had to deal with limited clothing and food options, fewer toys and the worry that the boys would break or damage something in my friend's house. It was a good lesson for me about what to expect when we travel to Buffalo this summer for Janet's wedding.

Wednesday, March 17

Dear Journal: We went to our last "Tales and Tunes" class for the winter session today. Both boys have made great progress—Rupert is becoming more engaged in the group activities, and Nicki is becoming more compliant to requests to sit and listen to the teacher when she tells the stories. I am very proud of both of my boys.

I spent most of the afternoon going through all the mail I had received while we were away. I finally received the boys' social security cards. This was the last item on my checklist to fully integrate them as new American citizens. I may decide to re-adopt them one day so they will have U.S. birth certificates. Some adoptive parents have done this to make it easier for their children to get copies to use for school registration, but it's not a requirement.

I also received my latest copy of "The Family Focus," the FRUA spring newsletter. The articles focused on FRUA's ten years of existence, including numerous personal stories. One of the pages contained statistics on U.S. issued orphan visas for Eastern European and Russian countries. In 1993, there were 273 visas issued for Ukrainian adoptions; in 2001 there were 1,246 and last year there were only 702. I can attribute this decline to the growing frustration felt by prospective parents with the increasing risk of returning home without a child, additional paperwork requirements, and extended lead times to complete an adoption. I felt so sad as I looked at last year's number, knowing there are thousands of children in Ukraine who need loving homes. In contrast, Russia had only 746 visas issued in 1993, and last year there were 5,209 visas issued. I wish I could charter a fleet of jets and take all the orphaned children out of Ukraine and bring them here to the States. I believe I could find a home for every one of them within a year or at least improve their quality of life with the proper medical treatment.

We spent several hours running errands this afternoon including a stop to the pediatrician's office to drop off Rupert's stool sample and a visit to the local pharmacy for a refill of the medicine for his diarrhea. I was trying to find another bottle of Echinacea for children, but none of the drug stores I visited stocked it. It's a shame more outlets don't carry homeopathic remedies for children. I hate the idea of giving them cold and pain medicines without first trying more gentle herbal and natural remedies.

Logging on-line tonight, I discovered that my e-mail account was overloaded with messages. It is interesting to read the notes from folks who have yet to travel to Ukraine. It's so heartwarming to read about how anxious they are to bring their children home. I can't begin to describe how big a hole the boys have filled in my life. Rupert and Nicki just can't get enough hugs and kisses each day. I thank God every chance I get for these two precious gifts I have been entrusted with, and I pray each morning for the strength, wisdom, and energy to give them all the love, guidance and affection they will need in life.

Friday, March 19

Dear Journal: The past two days have been pretty quiet. Nicki has developed a viral infection in his left eye and I am concerned it might delay his second surgery, which is scheduled for next Wednesday. I talked to Dr. Deegan yesterday morning, and he told me to finish using the eye drops I had been given after Nicki's first surgery to see if that will help clear up the infection.

I did get some good news from Rupert's pediatrician today. He called to tell me that his stool sample did not show any sign of the parasite. Hurrah! He recommended I give both boys yogurt with acidophilus to encourage the good digestive bacteria which may have been killed off along with the parasite by the medication. The best news, though, is that Rupert's stools are no longer runny messes, and I can now start to broaden his diet to include more foods.

The boys spend a lot of time playing together and most of the time they get along very well. However, Rupert continues to take toys away from Nicki whenever he sees him playing with something he wants to have. If I'm around, I tell Rupert to give the toy back to Nicki. His usual reaction is to cry and then get on all fours and bang his head on the floor. Both boys will do this when they are really upset, and I am trying to find ways to redirect their frustration. This is the only vestige from their orphanage behavior that I have seen, and the good news is that it doesn't happen very often. Initially, Nicki would do this more than Rupert, but now it's reversed. Fortunately, the tears don't last very long.

Rupert has developed a set routine that he will now follow before going to bed. All the toys have to be off the floor and put away, and all the clothes have to be off the top of the dresser. Sometimes I also take the changing pad off the table and put it in the hallway. He is very fastidious and will pick up every little piece of paper or scrap off the floor and hand it to me. His vocabulary now includes "I do it," and he is getting much better at putting on his slippers and pulling up his pants by himself. I'm starting to plant the idea that big boys make "kaka" in the potty. Both boys are pretty good about telling me when they've had a bowel movement, and I think Rupert may be ready in another month or two to start potty training.

I've made some follow-up calls regarding my start date back to work, and it seems I may not go back until the beginning of May. On the one hand, I am looking forward to spending more time with the boys, but on the other hand, I'm getting a bit anxious about my bank account balance. I just have to keep telling myself to place all my worries in God's hands, and it will turn out all right.

Saturday, March 20

Dear Journal: I was a little late going in to the boys' room this morning to get them up. When I walked into their room, I found Rupert sitting in Nicki's crib wearing only his diaper. Nicki was stark naked—he had taken off both his pajamas and his diaper which, needless to say, had the remains of some stool in it. What to do? I tried to communicate to Rupert that he wasn't supposed to climb into Nicki's crib, but I have the feeling that it won't have any effect. I tried harder to teach Nicki that only Mama can take off his diaper. I hope I don't have a little exhibitionist on my hands.

It was quite cool this morning. I decided I would go crazy if I didn't get out of the house, so I bundled the boys up and we went outside for some fresh air. I have a box with toys on the front porch with several large trucks and balls for the boys to play with on the lawn, but today they preferred stones, sticks and the rake I was using. It seems that nothing is as desirable as that which I am using. I guess I should enjoy it while they are still young enough to want to be around me.

Nicki now understands when I tell him that his actions will result in specific consequences. For example, I told him he had to stay within the boundaries of the front lawn or he would be taken inside. His standard response is to grunt and motion with his arm as if he is pushing something away. This is the way both boys communicate to me that they don't want something or are rejecting what I am telling them. Both boys can say the word no but they still prefer to use this hand signal.

This afternoon, as I was changing Nicki's diaper, I was looking at the progress of his new teeth and noticed that he had chipped a small piece off the top, left edge of his tooth. I asked Pat Mary if she thought I should take him to the dentist, but she said as long as he's not in any pain, I might as well just wait for the tooth to come out. I have a feeling this is just the first of Nicki's little injuries.

On the spur of the moment I called my friend Joanne, whom I haven't seen since I returned from Ukraine. I invited her and her husband, Mike, to stop over and meet the boys. They arrived around 5 p.m. for drinks and ended up staying for dinner. Joanne casually mentioned that they had gone to a Chinese adoption seminar several months ago to learn about their program. Mike, who is 57, said he was told he was too old for their program. I know Joanne would like to have a child, but Mike, who has a grown daughter, is not very enthusiastic about this, and I doubt they will end up adopting. I wondered to myself if there really is an age when one is too old to raise a child. I know that I probably would not want to adopt younger children once I turn 50, but everyone is different.

Sunday, March 21

Dear Journal: Happy Springtime. I decided to stay home from church as the boys were just about over their colds, and I didn't want to risk the spread of germs, especially since Nicki's eye is looking so much better. Instead, I gave the boys a bath, since last night was a hurried affair. We spent a quiet morning in the living room while I tried to read the paper. I'm pleased that both boys are interested in books, and I try to keep several in each room of the house. Many of my friends have brought gifts of books, and I know, as my sons get older, we will have many hours of enjoyment from them.

While I was getting the boys ready for their afternoon nap, I noticed that Rupert had a nasty diaper rash. It must have hurt him terribly, as he cried when I wiped him after changing his diaper. He does have very sensitive skin, but I can't think of what might have caused this problem. I don't think it's related to the parasite problem, and I haven't given him any new foods recently—oh, when will it end? The triple dose of diapers, doctors and day care issues continue to perplex me. I hate the feeling that I am such a beginner at all this. The other day I was chatting with one of the neighborhood moms who said I really needed to get on a list now if I wanted to get Rupert into a pre-school situation this fall. Isn't there a manual somewhere for first time adoptive mothers?

This afternoon was a rare treat for me. One of the church members was having an open house so I arranged with Millie and Elyena to come over and watch the boys. It was such a liberating experience to chat with adults without worrying about what mischief the boys were getting into at the house. Jack and I stayed at the party until seven, and were among the last guests to leave. It was so refreshing to walk into the house with the boys having been fed, bathed and ready for bed.

I decided to send an e-mail to the adoption newsgroup about Rupert's head banging behavior. He does it only when he's upset, but it is so hard for me to watch him get down on all fours and bang his head hard on the floor. Then he starts crying and tells me he has a boo-boo on his forehead. I would worry more if his general behavior was disruptive or disturbing, but Rupert is such a gentle child that it seems so out of character for him to act this way.

Monday, March 22

Dear Journal: This morning, one of Jack's friends, Charlie, came over to the house with his digital camera to take photos of the boys and me. Since the lawn around my house leaves much to be desired, we went next door to Meg and Michael's where the spring flowers are blooming everywhere. I dressed the boys in the matching outfits and shoes that Donna and I had bought for them in Lugansk. The pants have pockets with bunnies and carrots embroidered on them and matching vests with hoods.

Charlie spent 30 minutes taking pictures at various places in the garden and on the door stoop in front of their house. It was very important to me that we have our first family photo as soon as possible. In some strange way this helps to validate the fact that we are now a family. I plan to send the pictures to all my friends and relatives as a formal way of introducing the boys. I also wanted a nice picture to put on my desk at home and in the office. Speaking of work, I got confirmation that my start date back to work will definitely be delayed until the beginning of May.

I spoke on the phone today with Jackie, a former coworker, who told me a story about a child that she is mentoring through a program at work. She meets with this little eight-year-old girl once a week at a local school and recently brought in cupcakes to help celebrate her birthday. She said she was surprised when one of the teachers told her that this was the first birthday they had celebrated at school this year. Jackie was amazed that none of the children's parents made cookies or cupcakes for their children to bring to school. She said it really drove home to her how influential parents are in building their child's self-esteem—not just because they make cookies for their child's birthday, but because they are in such a unique position to influence character and social skills. I told her that, as glad as I will be to go back to work, I do worry about not being with the boys every day. I want them to grow up being kind, generous, polite and honest. I've waited so long to find my children that I don't know how

I can entrust their care and well-being to a perfect stranger, no matter how capable she might seem.

I had to make a late afternoon run to the grocery store to buy more bananas. I've started calling Nicki banana boy because he absolutely loves this fruit. He would eat them at every meal of the day if I let him. Needless to say, banana is one of the few words Nicki has learned, along with more, upa, all done, ball, and hello. Rupert adds new words to his vocabulary almost daily, and I can see that he watches my lips very carefully when I am speaking to him. He babbles quite a bit, but I know in his mind he thinks he is speaking very clearly to me.

Tuesday, March 23

Dear Journal: The sun was shining so brightly this morning that I decided it was time to take the boys back to the park after having been sequestered in the house for the past few days. Nicki really enjoyed the swings. Both boys laugh so quickly, and it's fun to watch them find their way around the playground. Rupert is becoming more confident and went down the slide several times. He is more coordinated and agile now and can climb up several rungs to the play platform without any help from me.

There wasn't anyone at the park when we arrived, but a group of children and mothers entered the playground about half an hour later. I just sat on a bench and watched all the mothers interact with each other. They seemed very content with their role as full-time moms. I must admit I looked at them with envy, thinking about how nice it would be if I could afford to stay home. Then I thought about all the gifts that God has bestowed upon me—all the talents and skills I have developed over the years—and I decided that I should instead focus on making every day I have at home with the boys the best it can be and not worry about what I don't have.

As different as the boys are in personality, I really think they will be very good friends as they grow older. Nicki has an outgoing personality and will walk up to anyone if he sees they have something he wants. Rupert, on the other hand, is more reserved and observant before he will engage someone, although both of them are very warm and affectionate. I am a little concerned that they have no fear of strangers, and I'm trying to balance their need to socialize with my worst fear that they may become separated from me at the store or park and have no qualms about taking the hand of a stranger who might do them harm.

I can't believe how quickly time has passed. I spent a few moments this evening to reflect on what I have learned—and how much my life has changed since the day I brought the boys home. I've titled my list "The good, the bad, and the ugly."

GOOD

- The first really big hug and kiss I got from each boy
- The feeling I have when they call me Mama
- Carrying the boys' baby pictures in my wallet
- Being the one to take care of all the boo boos
- Singing songs in the kitchen in the middle of the afternoon, just for fun
- Knowing my children will always be part of a wonderful and loving family

BAD

- ♣ No way I can walk out of the grocery store for under $100
- ♣ Trying to figure out who is good enough to take care of my children once I go back to work
- ♣ Doing more laundry and cooking than I have ever done in my entire life
- ♣ Cracked skin from washing my hands so much
- ♣ Putting my hiking boots and skis into the back of my closet
- ♣ Moving every piece of nice china I own to a level of five feet or higher in my house

UGLY

- ♣ Waiting to change into my nice clothes right before I leave the house to keep them from getting dirty from the boys' fingers
- ♣ Dealing with diaper rash, diarrhea, and leaky diapers
- ♣ Total exhaustion by 8 p.m. every night
- ♣ Dragging a screaming child out of the store while carrying an armful of grocery bags
- ♣ Listening for the sounds of silence when the boys are playing
- ♣ Feeling guilty when I shout at them after losing my temper

I received several responses today from my query about Rupert's head banging from the folks on the adoption e-mail newsgroup. Several of the e-mails were from parents whose child ended up being diagnosed with sensory integration issues and required ongoing therapy. One of the women told me that some kids bang their heads and rock in the orphanage for brain stimulation. A single dad told me his son did it simply to get attention or act out frustration. Based on the responses, it seems like the longer and more frequent the outbursts, the more serious the situation. One woman told me that it was not unusual for adopted children to do this, and with love and attention, this behavior will soon fade away, but if not, I should seek professional medical advice.

My intuition tells me that this is not a serious problem with Rupert. He doesn't bang his head unless he is upset, and I assume this is behavior that he has seen at the orphanage and is mimicking. However, it pains me so to see him suffer, and I am going to be more proactive in taking him in my arms and holding him when I see that he is getting ready to bang his head.

Wednesday, March 24

Dear Journal: Today was one of the most exhausting days I have experienced since bringing the boys home. Nicki's second eye surgery was scheduled for this morning, and I had to deal with it by myself as Jack was unavailable to help me out. My day started at 5:15 a.m. I woke the boys up, got them dressed, and took Rupert over to Connie's before putting Nicki in the car and driving to the hospital.

I met with Dr. Deegan before the surgery, and we talked about the condition of Nicki's left eye. The surgery lasted over an hour this time, and when Dr. Deegan came back to see me, he explained that Nicki will probably never have any vision in his left eye. He said it was an advanced case of Coats disease, which can affect children as early as birth. I asked him if he knew what caused this disease; he thinks it is simply a kink in Nicki's genetic make-up, nothing more, and nothing less. The good news is that in 65 to 95 percent of the cases, it affects only one eye. I tell myself to be grateful to God that Nicki still has very good vision in his right eye.

By the time we arrived back home from the hospital, it was 1 p.m. I hadn't eaten anything since this morning and I felt exhausted. I brought Rupert home and he couldn't keep his hands off me. This was the first time I had left Rupert by himself, and I prayed that he didn't think I was leaving him and not coming back. Nicki was still woozy from the anesthesia. I put both boys in their beds for an afternoon nap as soon as I could manage it. I probably should have taken a nap myself, but I had too many other things to do.

Nicki was still very groggy when he awoke from his afternoon nap and demanded all of my attention. I just couldn't cope with Rupert's need for attention as well, so I sent him back to Connie's for an hour or two. By dinner time, I realized that I was never going to make it through the evening by myself. I called Meg and asked if she would come over to help me feed the boys and put them to bed. She agreed and I don't know what I would have done without her. I handed Nicki over to her as soon as she arrived, and gave Rupert some much needed attention. He still needs more hugs and attention than Nicki does on a good day, so it makes sense that on a day when I haven't spent any time with him, he would act up and want me to hold him.

Thursday, March 25

Dear Journal: I've changed my mind about how exhausting yesterday was, and I've decided that today was much worse. Don't ask me why, but I had scheduled an MRI for Rupert today, never thinking that it would take a few days before everything got back to normal.

Nicki hadn't eaten or drunk anything yesterday, so I knew he would be starving this morning. Conversely, Rupert wasn't allowed to eat or drink anything this morning because he was scheduled to have an MRI at noon. So once again, Meg stepped in and offered to take Rupert on her morning walk. I could then feed Nicki without Rupert seeing him getting food.

Even with Meg's help, I really struggled through the morning. Nicki was so helpless and wanted me to hold him every second. Rupert would cling to my legs and wouldn't let me sit down, demanding to be held. I had called another neighbor to see if she could watch Rupert for a few hours this morning but she wasn't available. She suggested using the TV as a distraction, something I have tried to avoid. Since this was an extreme situation, the three of us spent the morning on the couch watching TV. I let Rupert play with the cordless phone and Nicki got to play with the TV remote—big mistake. Later in the morning, I couldn't find the remote control anywhere in the living room. Well, as I emptied out the clothes from the washer I found it—Nicki had managed to slip the remote into the front loading washer before I put the clothes in to be washed. I guess I am lucky it wasn't the cordless phone in there instead of the remote.

Jack arrived around 11 a.m. to watch Nicki and take him to his follow-up eye exam. Everything went fine with Rupert's MRI, but I didn't get home from the hospital until after 3 p.m. Rupert was still very groggy from the anesthesia and went right to sleep. Both boys slept until 5

p. m. at which time I went into their room to get them up. I knew they were both exhausted so I fed them, washed them and put them back to bed by 7 p.m. Jack and I had a quiet dinner, and I am going to bed as soon as I can drag myself to the bedroom.

Friday, March 26

Dear Journal: This morning started out as a repeat of yesterday; Nicki was crying and needy, and Rupert was demanding my attention. After feeding them both, I called the pediatrician's office and left a message for the doctor to call me back about Rupert's continued diarrhea. I thought the last medication had resolved the problem, but, like a bad penny, it just kept coming back. His stool is too soft, and this week he had four major explosions. The worst one was yesterday evening. The results are the same regardless of what I feed him. When the doctor called me back, he had some other ideas about what might be causing the problem. End result—I need to drop off one more stool sample tomorrow morning. I also spoke with him about Rupert's diaper rash that is becoming quite severe. It seems to get worse with every bowel movement. I feel so frustrated and helpless. I am using a cream to relieve the symptoms but the cause is still elusive.

I decided to forgo the errands I had planned for today since we all needed a day without any pressures. It felt good to relax. The boys played out in the yard after their afternoon nap and we all had a good time. The weather was very nice and several of the neighbors were outside, working on their lawns and cars.

I received an amazing e-mail today from a woman in one of my adoption e-mail newsgroups. Elizabeth and her husband had traveled to Ukraine last February and had selected Rupert for their referral at the NAC. But when they arrived at the orphanage to see him, they were unfamiliar with his diagnosis and, with only a short time to make a decision, chose to return to Kiev to seek another child. They found another little boy and adopted him instead of Rupert. While at the orphanage, Elizabeth had taken several pictures of Rupert. She wrote me that even after returning home with her new son, she could not discard his pictures. Elizabeth told me what a sweet boy Rupert was and how she felt sad that they had chosen not to adopt him. Then she had seen a picture of Rupert and Nicki that I had sent to the newsgroup and realized my son was the same child they had seen last year. I told her my story, and, the more I thought about it, the more remarkable it is that I found him, especially in light of the fact that I was never shown his profile at the NAC.

Saturday, March 27

Dear Journal: This morning was a busy one with stops to the pediatrician's office, the grocery store and the bank. The boys were both very tired after lunch as they had awakened at 6:30 a.m. Nicki's eye was hurting, and it took awhile for the pain medicine to kick in. Rupert, as usual, just wanted my undivided attention. Once I put them to bed for their nap, I left them in Jack's capable hands to meet some friends of mine downtown. It was the first time since my return from Ukraine that I had seen them, and it was very heartwarming to share the boys' pictures with them.

By the time I returned home, Millie and Rachel, my baby-sitters, were minutes away from arriving. Jack and I spent a pleasant, non-stressed evening having dinner and going to the theatre to watch a foreign film I had been looking forward to seeing. Ah, a small taste of my former life.

Sunday, March 20

Dear Journal: I was so proud of myself this morning. I actually got the boys dressed and fed in time to get to church for the whole Mass. As soon as I put the boys in the playroom and walked in to attend the service, Nicki let out a hellacious cry for his mama. I ended up spending the next hour in the playroom with Nicki and Rupert. I couldn't take the boys with me, and Nicki would start screaming if I tried to leave. This is so out of character for him, but I think it's because of the surgery he had last week. He has been more cognizant of my presence since then, but I am hoping he will, in time, return to his usual self.

It was a nice day, so after we returned from church I decided to let the boys play outside for a while before lunch. Well, it took Nicki all of two minutes to find the one remaining water hole along the driveway next to the house. By the time I reached him, he was already soaking wet. Rupert joined in the fun by lying down next to the water and getting his entire outfit smeared in red clay. Anders, my neighbor, was outside washing his car and saw the boys attack the water. I felt like saying to him "You know, this is exactly the reason why I didn't want two boys. They're too messy and are always getting into trouble." But I didn't. I just smiled and shrugged my shoulders and said to myself, "Oh well, what's another few clothes to wash?"

I had placed an ad in the newspaper this weekend for a nanny and have been overwhelmed by the calls. Most of the calls are from women with very exotic sounding names like Fatima and Luda. Many of them do not have a car, and a few of them cannot drive. I've started a checklist of questions to ask each applicant to help me screen out those who don't fit my criteria. What I really want is someone who looks and acts like Mary Poppins, right down to singing the songs at the children's bedtime. I am trying to keep an open mind when I speak to these women on the phone and not judge them solely on how well they speak English.

Monday, March 29

Dear Journal: Today was absolute madness as I tried to keep up with the deluge of phone calls about the nanny position. I eventually stopped answering the phone as I just couldn't handle the calls and take care of the boys at the same time. My energy level is really low. Nicki has been waking up at 6:30 a.m. these past few days, and both boys are going non-stop.

I did have one last trip to make this evening to my former church. In making plans to have the boys baptized, I was told that I needed to attend a class before I could schedule their baptism. The class consisted of a 20 minute video with a commentary by a nice couple from the parish. The video described the ceremony in detail and the purpose behind choosing godparents. The group of attendees consisted of seven or eight young couples who had either just had a baby or were expecting one. Meanwhile, most of my attention was focused on Rupert who was playing with a PC that was in the back of the room and Nicki who was roaming around with a set of headphones on his head. The entire session lasted a grand total of thirty minutes. By the time I arrived home with the boys, I was too tired for words.

I have now had over 50 calls on the nanny position. Mary Poppins where are you?

Tuesday, March 30

Dear Journal: I took the boys to a new music class this morning at the community center. There must have been two dozen children in the room, and then there was Nicki. My little boy stood within a foot of the teacher and her guitar throughout the entire class. He rocked side to side with the music, trying to snap his fingers to the beat. It was so obvious that he has an innate sense of rhythm, even the teacher commented on it at the end of the class. She suggested I go to the local music store and pick up a few instruments including a triangle, egg shakers, and harmonica to use at home.

The rest of the day was fairly quiet. The boys took a very long nap, and I was able to catch up on some of my paperwork. I did get a phone call from the pediatrician who said that Rupert's last stool sample came back negative, meaning the medicine he is taking for TB is not the cause of his loose stools. That means the next step is to visit a gastroenterologist. More time and more tests. All I want is for my poor baby to get better.

I have sent several e-mails to Yuri but have yet to hear back from him. I drafted another message to him this evening with an update on the boys' medical condition. I wonder if I will ever hear from him again.

Wednesday, March 31

Dear Journal: Where do I start? I drove to the music store down the street and the boys thought they had found nirvana when they saw all the guitars on display. It was all I could do to keep them from grabbing the instruments as I searched for what I wanted to buy. Thirty dollars later,

I had my little starter kit and headed home. I know it will be money well spent.

I met with Susie, the first nanny candidate, this morning. I'm not sure what country she is from originally, but she seemed pleasant enough and very interested in the boys. I told her I couldn't pay her cash and that I would have to take out taxes. Being a nanny is what being a waitress used to be before the IRS got involved. Most of the people want cash—with no paper trail.

Then it was back to the pediatrician's office for Rupert. The pediatrician wrote a prescription to clear up his diaper rash, and on the way to the pharmacy, I tuned in to a country and western music station. I don't normally listen to it, but I was in the mood for some perky music. Among the songs I heard was our national anthem, sung by a popular male vocalist. I turned to Rupert and Nicki said to them, "This is your new country's anthem. Listen to it and remember it." I thought about all the people we met in Ukraine and wondered how many of them would like to become American citizens. My guess is quite a few, and here are these two little orphans who by the grace of God were chosen to live in one of the best countries on Earth.

There are many days I wish I could take a nap, and today was one of them. Alas, I am driven to make some phone calls and pay bills. After the children woke up, I bundled them up, and we spent about 40 minutes playing outside, picking dandelions and enjoying the spring flowers. The boys like to tear things up and flowers are no exception. I have to be careful what I show them now. Picking flowers might be fine in my yard, but I doubt the neighbors would appreciate it. That's the challenge with kids. You have to watch them because they don't yet understand why it's ok to do something only under certain circumstances.

Toward the end of the afternoon I decided I needed to make a quick run to the grocery store. I had only a few things to shop for, but it's hard not to browse, especially when something is on sale. I bought several small cups of yogurt this time and put them in the cart where Nicki was sitting. Ten minutes later he had poked his finger into the top of one of the containers and had smeared blueberry yogurt all over his face and jacket. So, I did the only thing I could do—I went to the salad bar, got a few spoons and we all had a little snack right there in the store.

Thursday, April 1

Dear Journal: They say April showers bring May flowers. If that's true we should have a gorgeous bouquet by the end of the month with all the rain that fell today. We went to see Dr. Deegan this morning for Nicki's one-week check up. His eye is looking much better, and now it's a matter of waiting a few months to see whether he responds to shadows and light.

Rupert has suddenly expressed an interest in using the toilet instead of diapers. I've read a number of e-mails from folks that counsel against forcing children to potty train before they are ready. I didn't think this day would ever arrive. He still uses diapers, but I have a feeling he will be finished with them by the end of the summer. He is very insistent about using the toilet in the morning although his interest wanes as the day progresses.

I had another nanny interview this afternoon. Marie is in her late 30s and brought her young daughter with her. She seemed very pleasant and took an interest in the boys. She had been earning $15 an hour at her last position, and I told her I wouldn't be able to pay her that much. I'm a little suspicious of people who are willing to accept less than they have been earning, worried that they will stay only until they can get a better paying job.

Friday, April 2

Dear Journal: Another dreary, rainy day. I had my third and final interview this morning. Juanita is the youngest candidate and had more experience working in a day care center than working as a nanny. She seemed genuinely interested in the job and dressed very nicely for the interview, but I am concerned about her lack of experience. I have told all the candidates that I will make a decision this weekend. I hate the idea of having someone else taking care of the boys, but I really don't have any alternative.

Nap time was very productive this afternoon. I did a load of laundry, washed the lunch dishes, made phone calls, checked the mail and paid some bills. I also cooked up a batch of homemade bean and chicken soup. It's wonderful when the boys settle down quickly for their nap, but I still feel I'm running behind in my work projects.

Saturday, April 3

Dear Journal: Well, I've made my decision, and I've offered the nanny position to Susie, who has accepted my offer. She will start on the 25th of April. We will spend a week together before I start back to work. It's hard to say why I chose Susie over the other candidates. I know she really wants the job, and she received an excellent recommendation from her last employer. She is saving money to buy a car, and, until then, her husband will drive her to my house in the morning and pick her up in the evening.

Hiring a nanny has been just like interviewing someone for an office job. You meet them and check their references—but, in the end, it sometimes boils down to a gut feeling.

I had a terrible morning. Rupert was being unusually challenging. I think he's trying to exert his independence, while at the same time he craves my affection. He can now reach items on the kitchen counter, and I have to be careful what I leave there. It never fails that as soon as Nicki gets interested in a toy, Rupert will take the toy away from him. Then, when I interest Nicki in something else, Rupert will drop what he has and grab the new toy.

Nicki is still very clingy. He has developed a cold, probably because he stripped off his pajamas the other night before going to sleep. I think we all need a break. The weather improved enough today to go out for a bit this afternoon for which I am grateful. I got a call today from Denise, one of my neighbors who stays home with her children. She asked if her two daughters, Olivia and Abigail, could come over and play with the boys for an hour or two. God must be sending me lots of love today to give me this wonderful gift. The boys had a wonderful time playing with the girls, and, by 2 p.m., they were exhausted. Enter gift #2. Meg and Michael agreed to hold down the fort while the boys napped so I could run to the bank, buy groceries and make a quick stop at the drug store. What a difference it made not having to shop with two little children.

The rest of the day was blissfully uneventful. After I put the boys to bed, I broke open a bottle of white wine. I know. Terrible. It's Saturday night and I'm drinking wine and eating popcorn while I read my e-mail and visit my favorite sailing Internet sites. If anyone had ever told me 25 years ago that this is how my life would turn out, I would have laughed them out of the room.

Sunday, April 4

Dear Journal: I got myself and the boys ready by 8:45 a.m. so we would get to Mass on time to celebrate Palm Sunday. As I walked into the hall, I noticed everyone was already standing and had palms in their hands. Something was amiss. It turned out I had forgotten to move my clock ahead for daylight savings time. Oh well. That's what happens when you live alone and don't read the paper every day. Instead of going straight home, I tried to think of where I could go to take the boys to play and I remembered a conversation I had yesterday with Kate. She told me that she sometimes took her boys to a certain McDonald's where they have an indoor play center. Perfect, I thought. They had a good time playing there while I sat and relaxed with a cup of coffee.

I really yearn to have someone to talk with during the day. I love the boys dearly, but I really miss ongoing adult interaction. It's hard to imagine what it would be like to have a man in the house. Yesterday afternoon while I was outside with the boys, I noticed my neighbors were outside on their patio. The husband was tending to the grill, cooking the food for dinner. It's times like that when I really long to have someone to share the responsibilities of raising the boys as well as having a man with whom I can share the rest of my life.

I don't know if it's because there is a full moon tonight, but both boys were driving me absolutely crazy once I got them up from their nap. One of their favorite toys, a battery operated toy guitar, was the object of contention today. Nicki was playing with it, and Rupert would not give up trying to get it. He was crying incessantly and wanted to attack Nicki to get the toy from him. I finally decided I had to do something to distract them. I got two bar stools and put them next to the kitchen counter. I started making dinner and showed the boys everything I was doing, from peeling and cutting the potatoes to adding garlic to the ground turkey. I gave them scraps of potato skins and small pieces of garlic so they could taste the food as I was preparing it. Both of them were as calm as a tropical sunset as I conducted my little cooking class.

Dinner, of course, brought new battles. Nicki refused to wear his bib. Five minutes of screaming and crying ended with Nicki sitting on my lap, wearing his bib and happily eating his food. After dinner I took them into the bathroom for a quick wash-up. The phone rang and it was Susie, my new nanny, so I left the boys in the bathroom and went into my office to take the call. Big mistake. By the time I returned to the bathroom, the floor, the rug and the boys were soaking wet. They were both splashing each other with the water in the toilet. So, after another quick wash up, we went into the bedroom to get ready for bed. Nicki wouldn't stop taking off his diaper, so I went into the kitchen and returned with some duct tape. Yes, I duct taped his diaper so he couldn't take it off. I knew it was a versatile product but never did I ever imagine I would be using it in this fashion.

I must have said no 5000 times today. I used to list lack of patience as one of my weaknesses. I now try very hard not to lose my patience. They really are good boys at heart who give me so much love every day, and most of the time they play very well together. Rupert still likes to give Nicki hugs and pats on the back. Of course afterwards, he shoves him back on the floor, but I can tell they are bonding together more and more each day.

I have exactly four more weeks with the boys before I return to work. I will try to make every day special and treasure the time we have together.

Monday, April 5

Dear Journal: The play date that I had scheduled with a friend was cancelled for this morning. Instead we had an impromptu jam session in the kitchen. Nicki's favorite instrument is the triangle, while Rupert prefers the harmonica. I am glad the music teacher recommended I buy these for the boys, but I'll be really glad when they learn that instruments are used only for making music and not pounding on the furniture.

I went outside to bring in the mail and, as usual, there were several bills to pay. Between my insurance statements, medical bills, utilities and credit cards I seem to be averaging one or two bills every day. In the past, I have always paid my bills in full and on time. Now, for the first time, I am asking if payment plans are available so I can hold on to my cash as long as possible. Even though I return to work in May, I won't get my first paycheck until the beginning of July—and that's a long time with no cash input.

Tuesday, April 6

Dear Journal: I went to my first meeting with the Mom's Club this morning. The group is very well organized, with a monthly calendar that includes play dates, social activities and special events. One of the best things about the meeting is they hire a baby-sitter for the children so we can talk amongst ourselves. Several of the women are pregnant with their second or third child, and I was easily the oldest woman in the room.

After the meeting ended, I drove home, fed the boys and then put them to bed for their afternoon nap around 2 p.m. By 3:30 p.m., they were still making noises, so I went in to check up on them. Rupert had taken out one of the chest drawers and spilled all the clothes on the floor. I yelled at him and put him back into bed. He promptly started to cry and I felt so guilty. He is such a good boy, and I could have handled the situation much better. The amazing thing about children is their implicit trust in you. You can yell at them, and they will still smile at you the next minute.

Wednesday, April 7

Dear Journal: The boys were out of sync with their normal schedule all day. It started with Nicki sleeping until almost 8:30 am. Then, Olivia and Abby came over to play with the boys from 10 a.m. to 11:30 a.m. Nicki had been whining all morning. I decided that he might just be tired, so I laid him down for a late morning nap. After 45 minutes, I could tell he hadn't gone to sleep, so I went in to get him up for lunch. Wouldn't you know it; he has figured out how to climb out of his crib. He had opened up all the drawers, and clothes were strewn about the room.

I received the boys' certificates from the "Tales and Tunes" class at the Community Center this afternoon. I should put them in a scrapbook for each of the boys, but right now that consists of a loose file in one of the cabinet drawers in my office. Perhaps this journal will be the only baby book that the boys will ever have, and, in that case, I should include what their certificates say, just in case I never get around to pasting them into a book:

Rupert Schwartz: Loves to listen to stories and music. He knows how to take turns and returns his instruments very nicely. He likes to walk on and off the big step. He helps the teacher put equipment away.

Nickolas Schwartz: Really enjoys looking at the books and is learning to sit while we read our stories! He loves listening to music, and he often rocks from side to side when he's listening. He is learning how to take turns and how to put the instruments back.

Friday, April 9

Dear Journal: It was a nice, sunny day today, and we spent most of it outdoors. The flowers are blooming and there is a freshness in the air that tells me spring is here to stay. I took advantage of the nice weather to do some raking in the yard. It felt great to be doing some vigorous, physical exercise.

I was having lunch in the dining room while the boys were napping. I looked out the window and saw the contrails of a jet sailing across the blue sky. As the plane disappeared into a cloud, I started to ponder what exotic destination it was heading toward. Ah, I thought, it used to be me on those planes, crisscrossing the oceans in search of an adventure. Well, I don't have to travel far to find excitement these days, although I must admit part of me still longs for faraway places.

I made the mistake of wearing one of my straw hats into the boys' room to get them up from their nap. Nicki immediately wanted to wear it, and I knew if I gave it to him, I would need a hat for Rupert and another one for me. These days it doesn't matter what I'm wearing or using—the boys seem to want to wear my shoes, my sweater, use the rake or shovel, anything that I might have on or use around the house. I guess it's like eating off your parent's plate—the food always tastes better than your own.

The rest of the afternoon was delightful. The only problem was the diaper rash that has reappeared on Rupert's skin, along with small hives on his leg. I gave them a bath and put his diaper on extra loose for the night. Around 9:15 p.m., I heard Rupert crying in the bedroom. After waiting a few minutes to make sure he wasn't going to drift back off to sleep, I went in and got him up. I immediately went into the bathroom to check his diaper, and he had a really loose stool. He was crying as I tried to clean him up and apply the medicated cream. I held him for another five or ten minutes until he was almost back asleep and then took him back to bed. Poor baby. I did give him half an apple today, but I don't know if that was the cause of the rash. The apples are organic, and he ate them with no problem for six weeks. Whatever the cause, I have decided to put him back on a strict diet of bananas, rice, and waffles until the diarrhea clears up.

Saturday, April 10

Dear Journal: Today marks the four month anniversary of my court adoption hearing. When I re-read my journal entry this morning it made the details come alive once again. There was so much drama going on in Ukraine. The feeling of isolation and helplessness was so real for me during those two long weeks as Donna and I waited to take the boys out of the orphanage. I still can't believe how well the boys have adapted to their new life.

When I went in to the boys' room this morning, Rupert had taken off his diaper and had stuffed his pajamas under Nicki's crib. I never know anymore what I will find when I go into their room. Both of them may be in Nicki's crib or on the floor playing with toys. Either one of them may have his night clothes and diaper off, which means it's a good morning to change the bedding and do a load of laundry. It's amazing what I have learned in four months about the boys—their moods, what they want when they start to whine or cry, which of the boy's cry I hear in the bedroom, and how to recognize when they need to take a nap.

Nicki was so tired this morning that I put him back in his crib around 8:30 a.m. to see if he needed more sleep. I have to admit it was so nice with just Rupert around. He lay on the kitchen floor and played with this one little toy for half an hour. I could clean up in the kitchen with no distractions. His personality is very laid back, and the fact that he is ten months older than Nicki makes a big difference.

My friend Liz came over this morning, and we went to the local park to participate in an Easter egg hunt. It was more like a feeding frenzy as hundreds of children of all ages converged on the brightly colored plastic eggs with bits of candy inside. Neither of the boys had any clue as to the significance of this holiday. Afterwards, we headed back to the house, and Liz and I chatted away the morning. She had come over for dinner shortly after I moved into the house in January and now remarked upon how both boys have changed. She also said it was very obvious that they see me as their mother.

The girls came over this evening so Jack and I could go out for dinner. It was a perfect evening. We parked in Old Town Alexandria and headed to the Chart House, overlooking the Potomac, for cocktails. It was exciting to be near the water again. I spotted a small boat sailing wing on wing to take advantage of a southerly wind as it headed north up the river. Watching the boat sail up the river was enough to make my day. We decided to go ethnic for dinner and found a delightful Indian restaurant. It was far enough away from all the tourists to afford us a quiet evening with delicious food and excellent service. How nice it felt to have someone wait on me for a change.

Sunday, April 11

Dear Journal: Happy Easter. There was a 6:30 a.m. sunrise service for Mass this morning, but I just couldn't deal with getting the boys up that early. It was just as well as the clouds edged out the sun with just enough rain to stymie any thought of going outside. Instead of a walk this morning, the three of us hung out in the living room reading books, playing with toys cars and just relaxing.

I am really beginning to feel that we are now a family—my boys and me. We have all bonded so closely in the past four months that it is hard to remember what my days were like without them. Even mealtime is becoming more relaxing and enjoyable. I am working on getting them to say their names, and I am trying to make this into a little game when we eat. I haven't yet succeeded past Mama, but I know it will happen soon. The boys have learned to put their hands together to say prayers, and both can utter a fairly acceptable version of Amen.

One of the wonders of having children is watching them discover things for the first time. This past week both boys thought it was a revelation that they had pockets in their pants. Now, of course, they want to put everything in them. Rocks and food are a no no, but I'm sure there will be a few surprises for me as they become more adventurous. I got a call from my brother, John, this morning, and our conversation never got off the subject of our children. John told me how he has ruined quite a few clothes when putting pants that have crayons in the pockets in the dryer. That's one of the challenges of showing children how to do things. For example, zippers, which go down as easily as they go up, hence the number of times I now find Nicki without his pajamas on in the morning. I know it's important for them to learn new skills although I do stop and think now before showing them something new to make sure I'm ready to handle the consequences.

We went to Pat Mary's for dinner tonight and had a wonderful time. The boys were charming and behaved very well. My sister Susan and her husband Lenny had come for dinner as well. They have a daughter, Sarah, who was adopted from Korea as an infant. She couldn't be more their daughter if she had come out of Susan's womb. I asked Susan this evening if she had been given the choice of adopting a boy or a girl. She told me Lenny had wanted a girl, and when Sarah was presented to them, they chose her as their daughter.

One the way home, I started to think about whether I would love Rupert and Nicki more if I had borne them instead of adopting them. I used to think that having your own children was important. As I carried them into the house and put them to bed, I knew that it wasn't a matter of maintaining the physical chain of genetics with your offspring, it's purely a matter of love. That's all that counts in this world—one human being loving another. The boys may not be able to say "I love you" or even know what the words mean yet, but I know it exists deep inside of them, and it thrills me to the core to know that I am the recipient of such innocent and genuine affection.

Monday, April 12

Dear Journal: I made the mistake of waiting until 8 a.m. to get the boys up this morning. Not only was Rupert in

Nicki's crib again, but this time he was stark naked. The contents of his diaper were smeared all over Nicki's pajamas, the bedding, and several of the blankets. Ugh. What am I to do? Needless to say that delayed breakfast for about 30 minutes while I cleaned up.

We headed over to Kate's house this morning for a play date and lunch. Her son, Gabriel, is almost three, and he is so much bigger than Rupert. It's truly amazing the role that nutrition plays in a child's growth the first few years of his life. I wonder if there is any country in this world other than America where most children wear a full size larger than the age for which they were made.

Tuesday, April 13

Dear Journal: Rain, rain, go away, come again another day. I've been singing that little song over and over again for the past three days. Everything outside is wet and cold. I wake up each morning, and the first thing I do is look outside to see if the pavement is wet. It's amazing how your life is affected by the weather when you have two small children, and you're a stay-at-home mom.

I got a call from Rupert's pediatrician this afternoon, and I mentioned the problem with his bowel movements. He suggested that I keep Rupert off soy milk for a few days to see if that is the problem. I had actually thought about doing that yesterday but hadn't taken any action. I hope it makes a difference.

I sent an e-mail to the adoption newsgroup asking if anyone else had a child with chronic loose bowels. I am desperate for answers as to why Rupert is having such problems. I heard back from a woman today who told me that her son had the same problem. He tested positive for giardia and took Flagyl. She said he still has loose stools from time to time, but mostly his stools are normal. She said certain foods and liquids set him off, and it has been a trial and error—mostly error—routine. His biggest problem is with milk. She said he can drink it on occasion but if he has it every day, he will get foul-smelling gas and then even worse smelling loose bowel movements. She asked his pediatrician if there was anything she needed to do medically, but he said as long as her son is healthy and is gaining weight, she shouldn't worry.

Another woman wrote to tell me that her son had very runny stools for a year. She finally started giving him a teaspoon of acidolophis each day, and, within a week, it was completely cleared up. She said the doctor said her son did not have the proper flora in his stomach lining and this was the problem.

A third woman wrote that her daughter, adopted from Ukraine last August, had the same problem. She went to a pediatric gastroenterologist and, after having her re-tested for giarda and celiac, the diagnosis was a dietary problem. Milk seemed to be the main problem as well as juice. They now have her eating soy yogurt and drinking soy milk, and they put a splash of juice or Gatorade in her water for flavor.

At this point I don't think I care what the source of the problem is, as long as someone could figure out how to fix it. I can't imagine what other disease or bacteria might be causing the problem as Rupert seems to have been tested for everything under the sun.

Wednesday, April 14

Dear Journal: It rained on and off again all day. When I looked out the window this morning, the sky was gray, but no rain was in sight, so the boys and I walked to their class at the Community Center. They have made amazing progress. I spoke with their teacher afterwards, and she told me they were doing great. It's hard to describe how proud I am of my children. They are so loving and happy. I sometimes can't believe God chose me to be their mother.

It's interesting to chat with other parents who have children in this class. Last week I was talking with one of the fathers, and he said he thought the teacher in this class was too strict. I disagreed with him. The basic issue was whether a two-year-old is ready to start taking instruction about when to sit down, take turns and return things. I guess child-rearing is like politics, sex and religion. You have to be careful what you say around other parents as you're sure to find someone who will disagree with you.

I spent a lot of time with the boys this afternoon. We sat on the couch and read books and played silly games with each other. It seems much easier to interact with them now. Perhaps I'm more accepting of their needs, but, whatever it is, I'm amazed that we made it through the third straight day of rain with no major meltdowns from anyone—including me.

Tonight it was time to check my e-mails, and I came across one from a couple who has just returned from Ukraine. They brought home three children this time, making their total number of kids nine (four biological and five adopted from Ukraine). They went to one of the regions that never waives the 30-day waiting period, so they had to travel to Ukraine twice to bring these children home. It humbles me to read about these people who seem to have unlimited love in their hearts for these orphans.

Thursday, April 15

Dear Journal: Hello sunshine. The sky was bright blue this morning, and the weather has continued to improve throughout the day. I had several errands to run in the morning, including an appointment with Dr. Magrum to discuss Rupert's MRI results. He told me about the two cysts that were found in the fluid sacs in his brain. The good news is they don't pose any immediate threat to his health, but Dr. Magrum wants to monitor them to see if they grow throughout the year. He gave me the paperwork to have another MRI done on Rupert in January.

Every once in a while, I look at my house and think to myself that it's very obvious that children live here. I remember watching movies where the father is always tripping on a toy as he is walking out the door, and I used to think that was faked. Not any more. There are bikes and a wagon and stroller parked on the side of the house, and toys always seem to find a way onto the front lawn. I try very hard to keep the house tidy, but I am successful only part of the time. Even so, it's a nice feeling, knowing the boys have everything they need here—plenty of toys, a neighborhood with other children and a safe place to play.

I am always surprised at night when I empty my pants pockets. Aside from the usual tissues and keys, there are all sorts of objects I have either taken away from the boys or jammed into my pocket for safekeeping. Both boys love to put their hands in my jacket or pants pockets to see what I have inside. I have a little game that I play with the boys; whenever one of them puts his hand in my shirt pocket and doesn't find anything, I ask him, "Where is the magic dust?" They pretend to throw it at me and I shout with delight. Then we both laugh. There is such innocence with these children. They have total faith in me to protect them from all harm and comfort them from all injuries. I continue to ask God every day for strength and patience, both of which I always seem to need more of than I have in me.

Friday, April 16

Dear Journal: The weather seems to be getting warmer each day, and we are all rejuvenated by the freshness in the air. It was another busy day—errands in the morning and playtime in the afternoon. While the boys were napping, I noticed one of my neighbor's sons chasing a butterfly as he was walking home from school. I think he is 12 or 13 years old, still young enough to cherish the simple pleasures of life. It seems impossible that the boys will one day be that old.

Nicki's fascination with ice continued today. Forget about all the toys; just give him a small cup of chipped ice and he is happy. It's so interesting to watch the boys and see the differences in their personalities. Five minutes after I've given both boys a cup of ice, Nicki has either spilled or consumed everything in his cup. Rupert, on the other hand, is very careful about his share, and keeps it all until it has melted or chews it very slowly.

By 8:30 p.m., the only light on in the house was in my office. The house is absolutely silent, and I am worn out by the day's events. I did finally connect with Donna and gave her an update on the boys' progress. I must admit I felt a twinge of jealousy when she told me that she will be taking the summer off from her school job. I have to keep in mind that I have been very fortunate to have these four months with my boys, and I know it's more time off than many women ever have with their children.

It would be so nice to turn to my spouse right now and suggest we retire early to give each other back rubs. Ahhhh.

Instead I will spend a few more hours on the computer before retiring to bed, alone. Oh well. I know one day that man of mine is going to be worth the wait. He will be kind, gentle, funny, very loving and attentive. He will be my best friend. So my dear, sleep well tonight wherever you are. I can't wait for fate to bring us together.

Sunday, April 18

Dear Journal: The weather was so nice today that I stripped the boys down to their diapers and let them enjoy the outside in bare feet. I put a little plastic table and chairs outside, and they dined al fresco. I let them make as big a mess as they wanted to with their spaghetti. I didn't have the energy to reprimand them as long as they kept most of their food in their bowls.

I finally noticed an improvement in Rupert's stool today after having taken him off the soy milk Tuesday afternoon. Unfortunately, his painful diaper rash is back, and I still haven't been able to figure out if there is a food connection to this problem. Poor baby.

It's too warm for the boys to wear pajamas, so I put some duct tape on their diapers after their bath and put them to bed. I just went in to check on them, and they are both sound asleep in their own beds. I love to watch them as they sleep. I can almost hear their bodies growing as they absorb all the nutrients and stimulation from today. Nicki usually sleeps on his back, but sometimes he is curled up on his stomach. Rupert generally sleeps on his side and rarely makes use of his pillow. It's hard to believe these little boys have traveled all this way, just to be with me.

I continue to be amazed at their progress. Rupert is now speaking the word "no" and is making less use of his hand motions. I heard Nicki say "no" for the first time today. He is still using hand signals—such as pointing to his tongue when he wants to eat something that I have in my hand. They are now able to understand concepts such as pushing and pulling, and they definitely understand the difference between hot and cold. Rupert's favorite thing to do in the morning is to pull on the cord to raise the blinds in their bedroom. He puts one hand over the other, just as I do. I never taught him how to do it this way so he must have picked it up by watching me. Clever little boys.

Monday, April 19

Dear Journal: It's been almost a week since I stopped giving Rupert soy milk, but I've decided it has had no effect. I continue to find explosions in his diaper almost every morning. Other than the diaper rash, he doesn't seem to be affected—his appetite is fine, and his energy level is right up there with Nicki's.

It was so hot this morning that I decided to dress the boys in t-shirts, diapers and sandals. They looked like little street urchins by the end of the day, but at least they were comfortable. I know it's past time to go upstairs to the attic and bring down the boxes of summer clothes. It is pretty sad to say that most of their clean winter clothes are still on the floor in the laundry room, waiting to be put back into their drawers. Now I guess I'll just box them up for next winter.

While the boys were napping, I decided to call Susan Jones, whom we had met in Warsaw. She and her husband returned to Ukraine in January to bring home their younger daughter, Olga. We must have talked for close to an hour about everything under the sun. Their older daughter, whom we met in Warsaw, has become a happy, well-adjusted little girl. Susan told me that Larissa now loves baths, but in the beginning she was not keen on them at all (just like the boys). It turns out she was scrubbed down with rags and cold water at the orphanage every day. I can only imagine how Rupert and Nicki were treated.

The boys and I took a long walk this afternoon, and we got home with just enough time for me to cook dinner and give them a nice, long bath before tucking them in for the night. I think I am more tired now than I was when it was raining all those days last week. I looked at myself in the mirror today and tried to see if I could find something different in the way I look. Does being a mom change you? I feel like a totally different person on the inside, but I haven't been able to detect any physical changes on the outside. Perhaps a few more gray hairs, but I already had plenty of those.

Tuesday, April 20

Dear Journal: I spoke with Rupert's pediatrician again this morning about his diaper rash. He recommended I try another type of cream. I went to the drug store to buy some Aquaphor, which at $7.99 for three ounces is one of the most expensive creams available. After looking at all the different brands of diaper rash cream, I felt that I needed a baby version of *Consumer Reports* to figure out what the best solution was for this problem. Everyone seemed to have a favorite remedy, and I was totally out of my league here.

Of course, it's that much harder to try to compare products when both boys were running wild in the aisle of the drug store. Nicki was screaming at the top of his lungs because Rupert was trying to steal something from him. I finally broke down and bought them sunglasses to appease them and get some peace and quiet. I hated to spend $14 on two pair of sunglasses, but sometimes a separate trip to the Dollar Store just isn't worth the effort. Rupert picked out a pair of pink glasses that look just darling, and Nicki got a pair of dark blue sport glasses that make him look like he is going on 16.

I took Nicki to his third follow-up eye appointment with Dr. Deegan this morning. Nicki's eye is healing well, but Dr. Deegan held out little hope for a complete recovery. At least this is not an impairment that Nicki will have to adjust to, as he probably doesn't remember having vision in his left eye. I did a rough calculation in my head this afternoon as I was reviewing all the medical bills from the past four months. I guesstimate that it has cost over $20,000 between Nicki's two eye surgeries, the CAT scans, Rupert's MRI, various doctor visits, immunizations, blood tests and prescriptions. After the insurance pays the claims, my share will probably come close to $4,000. Yet another reason why my going back to work in ten days is a very good thing.

My nap dilemma continued this afternoon with Rupert climbing into Nicki's crib. I thought I had a solution when I took Nicki out of the crib and put him into Rupert's bed. Rupert was thrilled to be in Nicki's crib, but Nicki was all over the place. He took out toys and pulled on the blinds, enjoying his new-found freedom. I switched them back, and they finally settled down to sleep. I don't know why Rupert wants to be with Nicki. Ah, the mind of a two-year-old is a tough nut to crack.

Wednesday, April 21

Dear Journal: I heard Rupert banging on the bedroom door this morning around 7 a.m. As soon as I saw him, I knew I had to take him straight into the bathroom to be cleaned up. It doesn't seem to matter what I feed him— the results are the same, and I just don't know what else to do.

We walked to our new "Tales and Tunes" class today and the boys continue to improve; Nicki actually stayed with me and waited his turn to get a set of instruments, and Rupert was interacting much better with the movements of the songs and dance. I am just so proud of them. We walked to the local park after class and met some of the other moms from our class and the neighborhood. It was an idyllic two hours that I wish could be repeated every day. It was warm and sunny with a light breeze blowing in the air. The boys thoroughly enjoyed their time in the sandbox, and everyone played very nicely with each other. Even though I had brought bananas for morning snacks, both boys acted like starving beggars toward every mom who had food for her children. It was slightly embarrassing, but everyone just laughed and told me not to worry. These are the times I wish I had the option to be a full time, stay-at-home mom.

Nicki is getting another molar, this one in the bottom right side of his mouth. I'm sure it's painful for him, and perhaps that's why he has been so cranky lately. Mealtime seems to be the most difficult time of the day and there's always something he will cry about. I don't know if it's because he is teething or just having growing pains, but I fear the terrible two's are starting to make their appearance.

After the boys woke up from their nap, I made a snack and we started off on our afternoon walk. On the way back home, we met the couple who bought the house at the end of the street. Their four-year old boy is autistic and doesn't speak very much. They were extremely pleasant and took a real interest in the boys. After we said our good-byes, I thought about all the medical issues I have been dealing with these past few months. Suddenly they seemed very insignificant compared to the challenges this couple will face for the rest of their lives. It was just another reminder to me that having children of your own is no guarantee they will be healthy, nor is it a given that all adopted children will have emotional or behavioral issues.

Thursday, April 22

Dear Journal: As I was driving to one of my errands this morning, I started thinking about all the hours the boys have spent in the car with me. I really wish I didn't have to take them on every errand, but I don't have much choice right now. When I was growing up, the only time we went in a car was to visit relatives or take trips to the beach. I still remember how excited I was when we drove around the neighborhood in December to look at all the Christmas decorations. What a simple life it was back then.

There was a package in front of the door this afternoon addressed to the boys. I was pleasantly surprised to see it was from my godmother. She had sent two little stools for the boys with their names carved in removable letters. They are just perfect and I was so touched by her thoughtfulness. I still feel I have something to prove to her, and I want her to know that my desire to become a mother is genuine and not just another adventure. I have tremendous respect and love for her, and I am thrilled that she has accepted the boys as part of my life. I sent her a long thank-you note and invited her to attend the boys' baptism ceremony in July.

I had a tight schedule this afternoon with two doctors' appointments back to back. The first one was with the gastroenterologist to deal with Rupert's diarrhea. The second one was with Nicki's regular eye doctor. We left the gastroenterologist's office with a checklist of three action items—a stomach X-ray, more blood and stool testing and a lactose tolerance test. Then I have to wait until the 27th of May to return and find out the results of all the tests. We were late to the next appointment, so I had to wait over an hour before Nicki was examined. There wasn't much to be done, but I did get a prescription for protective glasses. The idea is to protect Nicki's right eye from accidents, and, goodness knows, there are plenty of sharp objects that he seems to find outside the house.

The evening ended on a bittersweet note when I found out that my favorite neighbors, Meg and Michael, were moving to Arizona. They have been the best neighbors anyone could ever ask for, and I will miss them dearly. This is a wonderful opportunity for them, and I wish them well in their new home.

Friday, April 23

Dear Journal: My first and last errand of the day was to take Rupert to a local lab to draw his blood and pick up more specimen containers for the stool samples. I can't even begin to imagine the effort one would have to make when dealing with a life-threatening disease or chronic behavioral issue. I know how much time and effort I have invested to deal with this issue, and I'm not even back at work yet. As bad as Rupert's problem is, I know that there is a cure for him, and I feel I am getting very close to discovering the cause of his diarrhea.

We had just enough time left in the morning to stop at the park on the way home. Nicki stayed on the swings for over 30 minutes. Rupert wandered back and forth, playing very nicely by himself. It was so nice to relax with the boys. I feel that so much of my time has been spent shuttling them back and forth to doctors, running errands to the grocery store or bank and preparing meals. This is the last weekday I will have with my boys alone. Where did all the time go?

Saturday, April 24

Dear Journal: The boys were introduced to live theatre this morning, and it was a rousing success. I had made reservations for a puppet performance of *Peter and the Wolf* at a local community center. Our seats were close to the stage, and the boys were entranced with the puppets. Rupert stood for most of the hour-long performance while Nicki spent most of the time on my lap. The two puppeteers were wonderful, and the music was just as memorable as the first time I listened to it. The boys laughed and clapped throughout the show and were properly awed by the presence of the menacing wolf. The story was slightly sanitized and abridged, but it had all the classical elements. I want to expose the boys to all types of cultural events: ballet, dances and musical performances. I think it is very important that they learn about the arts at a young age, as long as they are old enough to enjoy it and don't disrupt the rest of the audience.

Afterwards, we all went out to lunch at a nice restaurant at the local mall. Again, the boys behaved so well. We sat at a large table that was covered with paper that they could draw on with crayons. It's nice to find restaurants that cater to children but still offer a fine dining experience for the adults. I must admit that in the past I've done my share of eye-rolling when friends and I have gone out to eat, and we could hear a small child cry throughout our meal.

Monday, April 26

Dear Journal: Well, today was my first day with Susie, the boys' new nanny. I must admit I was apprehensive about the day but everything went smoothly. Susie is a nice woman, and I can tell she enjoys being around children. It's a good thing, as it rained incessantly, and we had to amuse the boys inside. Susie is from Sri Lanka and has lived in the States for 15 years.

Both boys seemed to enjoy her company although Nicki clung to my neck most of the day. I'm sure they could sense something was different, and I tried to make sure I was available to hold and hug them throughout the day. After the boys woke from their nap, we went to the local optometrist to order Nicki's protective eyeglasses. The final tab was just under $300. I'm going to have to figure out a way to glue these glasses to his clothes so he doesn't lose them or throw them away.

Once Susie left for the day, everything went back to the way it has been for the past four months. The boys were running around, playing with each other as I prepared dinner. I broiled some catfish and added some cooked carrots and rice to their dinner. It tasted delicious, even though my dinner had to be re-heated and wasn't eaten until after 8 p.m. I went to check on them a short time ago and had to take Rupert out of Nicki's crib. He's not doing it as much during nap time, but I still find him there every morning. Oh well. As long as they both keep their diapers on, I guess I'll be able to deal with it.

Tuesday, April 27

Dear Journal: Susie came around 8:30 a.m., and as soon as the boys were dressed and had brushed their teeth, we loaded them into the car to run some errands. I dropped off Rupert's stool samples and then drove to the hospital where his stomach was x-rayed.

Nicki has been eating a lot lately and always seems tired, even after a nice, long nap. I think his body is growing so much that he needs all the sleep and food he can consume. His eye is looking much better, and his teething seems to have abated. He still won't interact with Susie as much as Rupert does, demanding I pick him up every ten minutes. He likes to pretend he is a baby during mealtime and wants to sit on my lap and have me feed him. His verbal skills are rapidly improving, and he is getter better at listening to me when I tell him something. Rupert continues to be the king of toy pick-up time, and his favorite words continue to be no and mine. He is such a loving little boy with a wonderful sense of humor. I feel so close to the boys now. Tonight when I tucked Rupert in bed and said "I love you," he repeated it back to me. I was so startled I asked him to repeat it, but of course he wouldn't. But I know what I heard, and I left their bedroom with a big smile on my face.

I know now that whatever fears I had about being replaced by a nanny are groundless. It's just so hard for me to grasp how loving these children are—after having known me for only four months. I guess my problem is that I am used to dealing with adult emotions. Everything we do or say is closely judged, analyzed and accepted or rejected by those closest to us. Children don't think as we do. All they know is that I feed them when they are hungry, hold them when they are hurt, and discipline them when they are naughty. God bless all the innocent children of the world who are routinely abused by the adults in whom they have placed their trust. I can't imagine a greater gift in life than being loved by a child. I am a better person because of it, and I pray every night I remain worthy of that love.

Wednesday, April 28

Dear Journal: We are slowly settling into a rhythm with Susie as she learns the boys' daily routine. We walked to the community center for the "Tales and Tunes" class and arrived just after the class had begun. We quickly took off our shoes and joined in the singing. During the class, I introduced Susie to Lizzie, Kate's nanny. She also met another nanny from Sri Lanka who takes care of a little boy. After the class, we went to the park with some of the other moms and children. I hope Susie will make friends with the other nannies so the boys will have other children to play with during the day.

I had decided that I needed to start disappearing for a few hours each day to let the boys get used to being with Susie. I left the three of them at the house and drove to Jack's house where I spent a full hour doing yoga stretches, had a very quiet lunch, and then took a long, hot shower. It was pure bliss. By the time I arrived home, the boys were napping and life was good.

I took the boys for a short walk after Susie left for the day. It was nice to be with them—just the three of us. I kept telling the boys "Be nice to your brother," and "Let's stay together." I want them to know that they are part of something that will last through their entire life. We give each other hugs and kisses all the time, and I wouldn't trade that for anything. It has ceased to matter that we are not biologically related. The love I feel for these boys has become so deeply ingrained that I can honestly say I would be willing to give up my life for either of them.

Thursday, April 29

Dear Journal: This morning Susie took the boys to the park while I stayed home. I had made plans with my friend Virginia to come over and help me sort and pack the boys' winter clothes and organize their summer clothes. It took us almost three hours, but, by the time we were finished, I felt that a heavy weight had been lifted off my shoulders. It sounds like a simple task, but with only a short period of time each day to work on such projects, I know it would have taken me all summer to get this done without some help.

Nicki would not let me out of his sight when they returned from the park. He clung to me as if he were about to drown, and I couldn't find anything that would keep him entertained. It's hard to know whether it's better to announce my departure or simply to sneak out the side door. My usual approach is the latter, although I do feel guilty leaving without saying good-bye.

I had to leave right after lunch to make my facial appointment. This sounds like such an indulgence, but I have decided that taking care of myself is the best thing I can do for the boys. I fell asleep during the 90 minute facial and felt very refreshed as I left the building. My next appointment was with my dentist for my annual teeth cleaning. Dr. Lee was kind enough to donate a supply of toothbrushes and toothpaste for the orphanage in Ukraine, and I enjoyed giving him an update on my trip. I recalled the conversation I had with Susan Jones last week when she told me about the extensive dental work Larissa needed upon their return from Ukraine. It boggles my mind that something as simple as brushing your teeth could be lacking from the children's routine at the orphanages. I can only hope that the supplies we delivered are being used by the children instead of being sold on the black market for cash, or worse yet, stuck in a supply cabinet and never used.

I got a phone call from Suzie this evening. She asked me for a raise. I was in the middle of getting the boys ready for bed and wasn't really in the mood to talk with her about this after just four days of her working for me. I told her I would give her a raise in three months, but that we had agreed to a salary, and I wasn't ready to make any changes right now. I hope I didn't make a mistake.

Friday, April 30

Dear Journal: I was expecting Susie to arrive around 8 a.m. this morning. By 8:40 a.m., there was no sign of her, and all kinds of thoughts ran through my head. Had she decided to quit because I wouldn't give her a raise? Had she been in an accident? What would I do about work on Monday? I started to check off mentally all the friends and neighbors I could contact to help me out. I even called her house but there was no answer.

I needed to leave at 9 a.m. to take Rupert to the doctor's for a lactose intolerance test, and I didn't want to bring Nicki with me. By 8:45 a.m., I started getting Nicki dressed so I could take him with me if she didn't show up in the next 15 minutes. It was 8:55 a.m. when I heard the front door open. I rushed into the living room and there was Susie. She had overslept. She must have seen the frantic look on my face because she asked me if I thought that she wasn't going to show up. I didn't tell her what I was thinking—I told myself to just be glad she showed up.

When I walked out of the house with Rupert and tried to put him into the car seat, he started to scream bloody murder. I couldn't remember seeing him like this before. He desperately wanted to go back into the house. Neither reasoning nor threats made any difference, and I finally just put him into the car seat and drove off. It took almost

15 minutes for him to calm down, and, by then, we were almost at the doctor's office.

After we arrived, Rupert behaved so well one of the nurses said he was the best little boy she had ever dealt with for this test. It's hard to understand the thought process behind Rupert's outburst, but perhaps something scared him—maybe the fact that I was taking him somewhere and leaving Nicki behind—who knows? I did not believe for one moment that he had a problem digesting lactose. The mere chronology of his problem should have been enough to rule this out, but I just didn't have the energy to challenge the doctor. The nurse told me the doctor would call me if any of the tests come back positive. I guess that means if they're negative I have to wait three more weeks to talk with her about other possible causes of Rupert's diarrhea. I am so frustrated I could just scream.

I had to stop by the grocery store on the way back from the doctor's office. Today I was not only shopping for the boys and myself, but also for Suzie and the baby-sitters. I feel as if I'm in charge of a commissary at home. I'm constantly checking on my diaper, milk, bread and banana supply. I don't know how I'm going to handle it when I run out of food in the middle of the week. I guess I'll just have to take the boys shopping with me after work. I'm sure there will be many adjustments to be made by all of us once I return to work. These past four months have been a blessing to me, and I will always be grateful that I was able to be with the boys for so long.

Sunday, May 2

Dear Journal: Tomorrow is my first day back at work after being off for over five months. I have such mixed emotions about my return to the work force. I truly am looking forward to the mental challenges and the adult contact, but I will miss my little boys and their daily antics, along with the meltdowns, hugs, tears, and joys of discovery. No more morning trips to the park or packing in a series of errands before nap time. I will be on a strict, eight-hour schedule, and I know there will be times when I look out the window at the bright blue sky and wonder what my little fellows are doing at that moment.

Monday, May 3

Dear Journal: It was cool and rainy this morning. I thought to myself, well, at least I won't have to worry about entertaining the boys today. Susie showed up right on time as I was dressing the boys in their bedroom. We took them into the bathroom to brush their teeth at which time I made my exit. I left knowing that the boys were in good hands.

Once I arrived at the office, I met Sandra, who had been handling my responsibilities during my absence. As we started to talk about all the pending projects and new people in our group, I felt as if I had been gone only a few weeks. The issues were the same, but the projects were different. The job I have entails spending a lot of time on conference calls and responding to e-mails—very different from negotiating with a two-year-old to give you the foreign object he has just put into his mouth or project managing dinner while keeping two little boys out of trouble.

My cube still had all my notes and photos, along with the calendar I had used to count down the days before I left for my trip to Ukraine. I looked up November and my departure date was still circled in red. I can't believe it was only five-and-a-half months ago that Donna and I got on the evening flight bound for London. I felt as if I were returning to work as a totally different person. I put a photo of the boys on the wall next to my phone and I kept staring at it all day as if to remember what they looked like. I missed them and wondered what antics they were up to on this rainy Monday.

Susie had the boys waiting for me on the front porch when I returned home from work. There were no screams or crying when they saw me, so I have to assume they fared well today under Susie's care. She had fed the boys dinner and all the dishes were washed. It was so nice to spend time with the boys and not worry about cooking or cleaning up. Nicki has a slight cold, but, otherwise, they seemed in fine spirits. It was 8 p.m. on the dot when I closed their door after tucking them into their beds. I am feeling very tired, but it's probably a combination of a poor night's sleep and the late hour at which I went to bed last night.

It's quite cool out tonight, but I hope it will warm up again tomorrow. I will miss being outside during the day and taking walks to the park and working in the yard during nap time. However, right now it is important for me to return to work to earn money and focus on my career. It's funny how one's perspective changes when you have children, especially when you are an older parent. All the professional successes I have earned don't seem quite as important anymore. I have two little boys at home who count on me for everything, and I don't ever want to disappoint them. I am so grateful that I have the resources to have someone like Susie come to my home every day.

I got a letter from my Dad in the mail today. He sent me a check for the boys' new wagon and a letter with a newspaper clipping. In his letter he wrote, "As far as the enclosed is concerned—count your blessings—it could be a lot worse!" When I opened up the newspaper article I smiled. It was the obituary of a woman, aged 81, who had 11 children, including three sets of twins. Okay, I said to myself, don't forget that there are women out there whose life is much more difficult than yours. The note from Dad was a classic. He has such a wry sense of humor, and the older I get, the more I realize how fortunate I am to have him as a father. I pray to God that I will be half as good a parent to my boys as my parents were to me.

Tuesday, May 4

Dear Journal: The boys have been on a new kick for the past few days. They want to pretend they are babies and have me feed them as I cradle them in my arms. Maybe it's a reaction to Susie's presence. Perhaps they miss me taking care of them, and this is their way of showing it. It was really hard to leave this morning. Nicki caught me going out the door, and Susie had to peel him off me so I could go to work. I know I'm not the first mother to have to leave her children to go to work, but that doesn't make it any easier to walk out the door with your child screaming for you.

I'm starting to dig deeper into the projects I'll be handling at the office. It was nice to reconnect with some of the folks I had worked with last year as well as to meet the new people on our team. I miss the boys during the day and often catch myself staring at their picture. I thought if I stared hard enough at their faces, they could somehow connect with me, and I would see what they were doing at that moment.

I baked Rupert's birthday cake tonight—chocolate on chocolate. It would have been easier to just buy a cake at the bakery, but, to me, this is a labor of love. I remember when I was growing up, we always got to pick the type of cake we wanted, and it always had plenty of candies on the top. My favorite was spice cake with vanilla frosting. I wonder what Rupert's favorite cake will be in five years time?

Wednesday, May 5

Dear Journal: Happy third birthday to Rupert! Of course, he doesn't have a clue what that means yet, but I'm sure by next year it will be different. This morning was very chaotic. I got a phone call from Susie at 8:45 a.m. telling me her husband's car had broken down and could I please come pick her up. Five minutes later she called back and asked if I could pay her today for the week so they could get the car fixed. At first I was hesitant to give her a week's wages early, but then I decided there really was no reason not to help her out. I loaded the boys into the car and picked up Susie. I hope this isn't going to be a recurring problem.

I kept thinking about Rupert's birth mother today. I wondered if she was thinking of him on his birthday, curious about where he was and if he was happy with his life. I can't imagine how it would feel to give up a child who had grown inside of you for nine months because he had a medical condition that you couldn't handle. I can only be grateful that she wanted her son to have the best life possible, and, for her, that meant never seeing or hearing from him again. That is true love.

Tonight was a comedy of errors as I worked to get things ready for Rupert's party. Susie had frosted the cake and had blown up some balloons to decorate the outside of the house, but I couldn't find the candles. Fortunately, Denise, who was coming over with her three children, had some candles I could use. Then Nicki managed to cover himself from head to toe with mud and Rupert lost a shoe. I keep telling myself there is a reason God made us so that it took two people to make a baby. I wanted to take pictures of Rupert's cake and the children, but I couldn't do it and bring the cake in to the dining room, so again, Denise stepped right in and helped me out.

In the end, we all had lots of fun. Rupert was delighted with his cake and blew out all three candles by himself. Then he devoured his first helping of cake and vanilla ice cream, so I gave him a second helping. The kids had a great time, and after they finished eating, we all went outside. I brought out a little push bike for Nicki as well as Rupert's new tricycle. Rupert got on it right away and stayed there. He couldn't quite master the pedals, so he used foot action to go up and down the driveway. I know that little bike will give him years of pleasure.

Rupert and Nicki were still playing with the balloons after Denise and her children went home. You'd think they were the best toys they had ever had. They even took them into the bathtub. Nicki managed to pop his balloon, and he desperately wanted to blow up one by himself. It was comical to watch him try. He stared at me with such intensity as I blew up a new red balloon for him. I guess these are the moments you remember as a parent. Your child's first birthday party, the first bike they ever got, and their first day of school. I can't imagine my life without the boys anymore. I feel I have been repaid a thousand times over for all the effort I went through to bring them home.

I went into their room a little while ago to check on them. They are both sound asleep, curled up with the blankets; Nicki is lying on his stomach while Rupert is on lying on his back with his feet on his pillow. My little boys. So innocent. So loving.

Thursday, May 6

Dear Journal: It was a real treat to come home from work and see the boys' smiling faces. Nicki was especially happy to see me and wrapped his little arms around my neck. We spent the rest of the evening outside—the boys were on their bikes, and several neighbors stopped by to say hello. I don't know what it was, but when I looked at Nicki this evening, he suddenly seemed taller. I know he has been eating and sleeping a lot lately, and one of my friends told me that when children sleep a lot, it's a sure sign that they are growing. Before the boys went to bed I measured them against the door frame and Nicki has grown a full two inches. Rupert has grown about 1 ¾ inches, but Nicki was so small when we brought him home that I guess I just noticed it more with him.

Nicki has matured in many ways since I brought him home although he still has an "I want it now" mentality. His eye has healed nicely from the last operation, but it still causes people to ask if he has a lazy eye. There is a cosmetic procedure that can straighten out his eye, but I'm in no hurry to get it done until I know that it's affecting him socially.

Aside from Nicki's growth spurt, I can see the muscle forming in his legs, and there is a slight hint of chubbiness around his thighs. Shoes are one of the few things that I don't swap between the boys, even though their feet are the same size. I think it's important for the boys to establish a sense of identity with some things in their lives, but, for the most part, sharing is still the name of the game.

Rupert is learning new skills every day. His vocabulary continues to increase although it's still monosyllabic. I'm trying to force both boys to speak more instead of grunting and encouraging them to say multiple words. I've also introduced the common courtesy words such as please and thank you. Please ends up sounding like peas but that's to be expected. Rupert continues to vacillate between wanting to do everything himself and being a little baby and wanting to be held in my arms. I try to tease him out of sucking his thumb, but I know that will be a hard habit to break. I pray that we find a cure soon for his loose bowels problem. In addition to being a primary health problem, it has also delayed any attempt at potty training. I remember how adamant I was when I first brought him home about getting him back on the potty right away. I can't believe how much I have learned in these few short months about child care, but I know I'm still light years away from knowing it all.

Friday, May 7

Dear Journal: The boys and I have survived my first week back to work. I asked Susie to give the boys a bath but told her I would feed them dinner. I thought it was important for us to have a meal together, but I must admit by the time I put the food on the table at 6:45 p.m., I was questioning my decision.

I chatted with Shelly, one of my co-workers, at work today. She is also a single parent. Shelly has had to become an advocate for her young son who suffers from several debilitating conditions. She encouraged me to go on-line and learn more about what might be causing Rupert's problem. Shelly has not gotten much support from her son's doctors, and I must admit I have been too complacent in this matter. I've always had good doctors, but when the patient can't tell you what he's feeling, it's not as easy to diagnose the problem. I know that people come into your life for a reason, and I have to believe that my conversation with Shelly is just the boost I need to be more aggressive when discussing why Rupert is having this problem. I have a follow-up appointment with the gastroenterologist on Monday morning, and my goal is to leave her office with a firm plan in place. None of the blood or stool tests have indicated any reasons why this problem is occurring.

Saturday, May 8

Dear Journal: The three of us had a very relaxing morning. Rupert, bless his heart, slept in until 7:30 a.m., and Nicki didn't wake up until after 8 a.m. It was nice not to have to worry about timetables or hear Nicki screaming for me as I try to hurry out of the house to work.

Jack came over this morning, and we drove to the optician to pick up Nicki's new protective eye glasses. The frames are very lightweight and made out of an almost indestructible plastic. It will be a challenge to get him to wear them each day as well as to keep track of the glasses when they aren't being used. It's hard to explain to a two-year-old boy how important it is to protect the vision in his eye. All he knows is I am trying to get him to do something he doesn't want to do. This topic was definitely not in any of the baby books I have read so far. I hate to resort to bribes or threats, though that may be the only way to get him to keep the glasses on his face.

After we finished at the optician's, we drove to the marina where I keep my boat. I didn't intend to take the boys sailing but simply to get them used to the rocking motion of the boat and the closeness to the water. While Jack and the boys spent most of their time on one of our friend's large motorboat, I went on-board my boat to make a few repairs. As I was hopping off the boat, I was told that I was wanted back at the motorboat for diaper changing duty. I wondered to myself, did the legendary Amazonian warrior women have to change diapers as they returned from fighting a fierce battle? I have to admit I am tired of trying to do it all. I don't want to have to mow the lawn and grill the food and change the diapers and manage the finances and fix the squeaks and assemble the tricycles and bake the birthday cakes and host the parties and go to work and snake the toilet and run to the grocery store and, well, I guess this list would go on if I had any energy left.

My life has been one major dose of reality since the day my sister and I took the boys with us from the orphanage. I never in a million years dreamed that it would be this much work. I guess nature has a way of setting you up for this because, if women knew how hard it is to be a good mother, there may not be as many of them. But then I look at Rupert and Nicki, and I know that I would do anything in the world for them. I want to give them the best life possible with every opportunity and every scrap of knowledge I can muster. I have no regrets about my decision to adopt, but I am glad I waited until I had done everything else on my list because I know my life will never, ever be the same again.

There are times when I feel that the weight of the world is on my shoulders. I know many people have faced far greater challenges than I have, but I have really had to work hard at letting things go in my life. I can't worry that I still don't have one of the bedrooms painted or that I haven't transplanted all the spring flowers from the back of the house where the driveway will be built. Five years ago I would have whipped this property into shape within six months. Now as I survey the remaining debris in the attic and the mess in the basement, I wonder if I will finish all my projects before the time comes when I leave this place for good. But I have to remember that my priorities have changed, and I now have two little boys for whom a five minute wait seems like an eternity.

Sunday, May 9

Dear Journal: Happy first Mother's Day to me. The boys and I made it to church this morning just as Mass was starting. I spent the first 15 minutes in the play area because, every time I tried to leave, Nicki would start screaming, and I didn't have the heart to leave him. I finally took him into the hall with me, and we found an area to the side where other children were drawing with paper and crayons. Nicki stayed with me and behaved very well. Rupert, in the meantime, was quite content in the play area with the other children. What a contrast, I thought to myself, between the first time I brought the boys to church and today. Back then Rupert would not leave my side, but Nicki wandered all around with nary a care as to my whereabouts. Rupert now has the confidence to know that he can be without me and not worry. Nicki, on the other hand, was never so closely attached to one person before, and I think he craves the security and comfort of my presence. What a pair these two are—I never know what to expect from them.

There is a portion of the Mass where one can offer special intentions for prayer. There were the usual requests one would expect on Mother's Day. I suddenly felt compelled to offer up my own intention—to pray that all the children in the world who were without parents would soon find their family. There are so many children still living in a world where no one is there to kiss their bruises or tickle them when they are being difficult. It's amazing the lessons I have learned from my sons. I know every year I will grow in different ways and that their presence will bless me in ways I cannot even imagine.

Lunch was a hectic affair. Nicki had finished his lunch and Rupert was still eating, so I took Nicki into the bedroom to change his diaper. I soon heard Rupert in the other room calling out to me. He had a nasty bowel movement, and his diaper was leaking. My poor baby. It was a big mess to clean up, especially considering Nicki was screaming bloody murder because I wouldn't pick him up. The next hour was just more of the same. I finally got everyone cleaned up (and no, I didn't have time to eat any lunch) and I loaded the boys into the new wagon my folks had bought for the boys. We went for a stroll to visit a neighbor who was having an open house. It was a delightful break for all of us, and I had to drag the boys home for their afternoon nap.

I had received phone calls from several friends and relatives throughout the day and felt compelled to call them back. What I really wanted to do was ask them to come over and watch the boys for the rest of the day so I could relax. It was very sweet to know that my friends remembered me on this special day, but I just felt so alone I didn't really want to talk to anyone. I did manage to read some of the paper while lounging on the front porch while the boys napped, but that was the extent of my relaxation for the day.

The rest of the day was uneventful. The boys enjoyed a nice bubble bath this evening, and they were tucked into bed by 8:30 p.m. As I sit here this evening contemplating my future, I know this great adventure of mine has just begun. However, I feel the time has come for me to bring my adoption journal to a close. It has been a great source of comfort to me, and I'd like to think that one day I will start writing again.

I will be forever grateful to the many people who have helped me find my children. I know Rupert and Nicki are part of my destiny and that my life with them will be full of love, fun, adventure and happiness. I continue to thank God every night for the strength and love I need to give my children the best possible life.

Epilogue

⚜

Saturday, October 23

It has been ten months since I brought my boys home from Ukraine and almost five months since my last journal entry. I can barely remember what my life was like before I brought Rupert and Nicki into my life, nor can I now imagine how I could live without them.

Our trip to Buffalo in July for my sister's wedding was in many ways anticlimactic. It was a whirlwind visit and the boys behaved beautifully. My family welcomed them with open arms, and their baptismal service was conducted without a hitch, except for me crying during the service. I had no time to spend with Donna to relax and revisit our adventure, but I know the memories we created on that trip will remain with us forever.

Both boys have changed dramatically. Nicki is now as tall as Rupert was when I measured him on the door frame of their bedroom in January. His overall height has increased almost five inches. His face has lengthened, and he looks more like a little boy than a baby. He is still skinny but has very defined muscles in his legs and arms. He is quite agile and can run like the wind. Nicki has three new teeth coming in—his first new teeth in six months. I was about to make an appointment to take him to a pediatric dentist to make sure everything was all right, but I guess his body has been growing so much it didn't have any nourishment left for his new teeth.

Nicki's left eye has healed from the two surgeries, but nothing has changed as far as his lack of vision. That hasn't slowed him down one bit. He is as bold a creature as I have ever met—he has no qualms about approaching people at the park or on the beach, if they have toys to play with or food to eat. I've become a quick study of body language to understand whether his intrusion is welcomed or considered a territorial invasion.

He has a strong sense of curiosity and adventure and still tends to wander away in public places. Nicki continues to cry "No work" every morning when I depart for the office, and I still have to sneak out whenever I leave him with a baby-sitter. He knows I am his mama, the giver of his favorite treats of yogurt, cookies and bananas. He has an infectious giggle and is a real comic.

Rupert is also developing at a very rapid rate. His verbal skills are improving every day. He can count to two and can repeat the letters of his name when I point them out on a piece of paper. He is still under the care of the gastroenterologist, but the good news is I now understand what the problem is and how to treat it. When we took the boys from the orphanage, we put them in diapers, even though they had been wearing underwear. For the first few days in Kiev Rupert was noticeably uncomfortable using a diaper, but neither Donna nor I thought much of it. But according to the gastroenterologist, he started to hold his bowel movements because he didn't want to go in his diaper. This caused a backup in his body, hence the explosions. It also caused his skin to become irritated, causing the awful diaper rash. After we figured this out, the doctor put him on a daily dosage of Senna, a natural laxative, to ensure he had a bowel movement each morning. We have had a few setbacks, but for the most part, he has improved to the point where he will now tell me when he needs to go, and I'll put him on the potty.

He has grown over three inches and has added about six pounds to his weight. Rupert is still small for his age, but he is built very solidly. He is a very sweet-natured child and very loving. The only time he misbehaves is when I am tending to Nicki, especially in the morning. I'm sure there is some sibling jealousy, but, for the most part, the boys play together very well. Rupert likes to make funny faces and is going to be a real charmer although in a different way from his brother. He can be shy around people and will generally stay right by my side or sit on my lap. I keep telling myself to enjoy this time while he is still small enough for me to hold.

I did take the boys back this summer to be evaluated by Child Find. The Early Childhood Specialists performed a comprehensive series of evaluations, including a hearing test. I was thrilled beyond belief when I was told by the experts that the boys ranked average in their results and didn't qualify for any therapy.

As for me, I hardly know where to begin. I am still working full time, struggling to find a balance between my time with the boys and my own life. This past summer was very busy between housework, trips to visit friends and the park, and an attempted vacation that left me more exhausted than before I left. There were many days on the weekend I would tilt my head, catch the breeze in the trees, see the sun in the sky and think "Oh, wouldn't this be a great day to go sailing!"

But nothing I have experienced has caused me to regret, even for one second, my decision to adopt the boys. I can honestly say that this experience has changed me in more ways than I could have ever imagined. As a daughter, I loved my mother with all my heart, but until I became a mother myself, I never really understood how much love, patience, devotion and sacrifice it took to raise a child. I will do everything that is humanly possible to ensure my children know only love, kindness and goodness in their lives. I will give to them what my parents gave to me, and I pray that one day, they will feel the same way when they gaze upon their own children. I can think of no greater gift in this life than to receive the chance to make a difference in someone's life. Thank you, God, for giving me this gift.

FAMILY ALBUM

A typical Ukranian house

Playing tourist in the town

Ukraine is a very picturesque country

My first picture of the boys at the orphanage

This is where the boys lived

The playground outside the orphanage

Nicki and his big spoon

Playing with their new toys

Nicki and me

Potty time

Rupert playing with a new toy

Donna with the boys at the orphanage

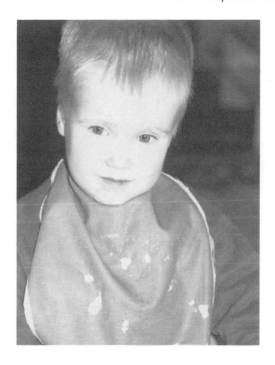

Rupert getting ready for lunch

Our first picture as a family

On the train to Kiev

Showing off Rupert at our flat in Kiev

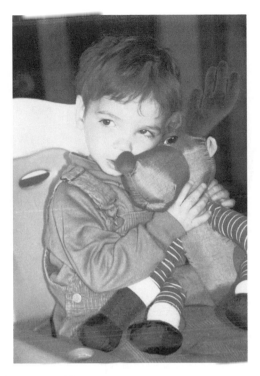

Nicki hugging one of his many new toys

Lunch time in their new home

Bathtime was never this much fun

Two American cowboys

Rupert on his new trike

Posing with Grandpa Don

Donna and me with the boys at their baptism

About The Author

♣

Margaret Schwartz was born and raised in Buffalo, New York. She moved to the Washington, D.C., area after completing college and has spent the past 25 years building a thriving sales and marketing career.

Today, Margaret is a successful marketing consultant and single mother of two adopted children. Through her book, *The Pumpkin Patch: A Single Woman's International Adoption Journey*, she discusses how her life was transformed after traveling to Ukraine to adopt two young children. She has enhanced her life through a renewed spiritual faith with the belief that one can accomplish anything in life. She has become an adoption advocate and is working with several charities to improve the well-being of orphaned and abandoned children in Ukraine. Margaret is a public speaker who regularly addresses groups of all sizes. For more information on Margaret's book and her public appearances, visit *www.pumpkin-patch.net*.